PENGUIN BOOKS
THE NEW YORK PARENTS' BOOK

Lois Gilman has spent most of her life in metropolitan New York: first as a city kid in the Bronx, then in suburban Ossining, and most recently as a Manhattan parent. She graduated from Barnard College and then did doctoral work at Columbia University, specializing in urban history. She is a Reporter-Researcher at *Time* magazine and the author of *The Adoption Resource Book*. She lives with her husband and two children in the city.

the new york parents' book
your guide to raising children in the city
lois gilman

penguin books

PENGUIN BOOKS
Viking Penguin Inc., 40 West 23rd Street,
New York, New York 10010, U.S.A.
Penguin Books Ltd, 27 Wrights Lane, London W8 5TZ
(Publishing & Editorial) and Harmondsworth, Middlesex,
England (Distribution & Warehouse)
Penguin Books Australia Ltd, Ringwood,
Victoria, Australia
Penguin Books Canada Limited, 2801 John Street,
Markham, Ontario, Canada L3R 1B4
Penguin Books (N.Z.) Ltd, 182-190 Wairau Road,
Auckland 10, New Zealand

First Published in Penguin Books 1987
Published simultaneously in Canada

Copyright © Lois Gilman, 1987
All rights reserved

The map of the New York City Community School Districts is
reproduced by permission of the New York City Board of Education.

LIBRARY OF CONGRESS CATALOGING-IN-PUBLICATION DATA
Gilman, Lois.
The New York parents' book.
Includes index.
1. Parents—Services for—New York (N.Y.)
2. Parents—Services for—New York (N.Y.)—Directories.
3. Children—Services for—New York (N.Y.)
4. Children—Services for—New York (N.Y.)—Directories.
I. Title.
HQ755.8.G52   1987   362.8'2'097471   87-69
ISBN 0-14-007992-0

Printed in the United States of America
by R. R. Donnelley & Company, Harrisonburg, Virginia
Set in Weideman Book
Designed by Liney Li

Except in the United States of America,
this book is sold subject to the condition
that it shall not, by way of trade or otherwise,
be lent, resold, hired out, or otherwise circulated
without the publisher's prior consent in any form of
binding or cover other than that in which it is
published and without a similar condition
including this condition being imposed
on the subsequent purchaser

To Ernest, Eve, and Seth

preface

"They did ordinary things that day, went to the playground, brought back a pizza, watched 'The Muppets,' Billy went to bed, and Ted Kramer got to keep his son." So ends *Kramer vs. Kramer,* Avery Corman's poignant account of a custody battle. While the reader's attention is riveted to the parents' struggle, the novel also vividly portrays their daily lives in Manhattan. First we sit with Joanna: "For a while, every child Billy's age in the playground was pushing the same giraffe, then they were all riding the same motorcycle, and now at three, they were all going off to nursery school." Later we join Ted at a playground, which had "climbing equipment Billy enjoyed, a sprinkler pond, a view of boats along the East River and a truck waiting outside, ready to serve every canned soda, ice cream and Italian ices need."

Ted's search for a baby-sitter for Billy sounds familiar to anyone who's looked for in-home care. He begins with an employment agency because "Mrs. Colby advertised in *The New York Times* and the Yellow Pages, 'Household help for discriminating people' " and Ted "wanted an agency in the business of supplying reliable people." We share his interviews with an assortment of women—the immense Puerto Rican who informs him that she has worked with many Spanish diplomats and the "Irish lady with a heavy brogue who terminated the interview on her own by severely criticizing Ted for permitting his wife to leave." Dissatisfied with the people he interviews, Ted tapes "a sign on what was the community bulletin board, a wall in the supermarket across the street. 'Housekeeper wanted, 9 to 6. Nice family.' " He finally hires Mrs. Etta Willewska, who lives in the neighborhood. Corman's sketch of city life is one every New York parent will recognize because it so beautifully captures the ordinary: the rituals of the sandbox, the playdates, the walks to school, the sprinklers, the restaurant meals.

From fiction to fact is not a great leap. As a parent you've probably shared some of Ted Kramer's minor annoyances ("The weather turned raw in the city. Weekend outdoor activity was going to be limited, and city parents would be relying on their inner resources and museums"), as well as his deeper concerns ("His Billy was going to be leaving the city in a bus, taken by strangers to a place outside somewhere, more than a cab ride away. And in the fall, Billy would start school, real school, with Board of Education door knobs. . . . Billy was going off to camp and then to school, and Ted was having separation anxieties"). Whether you've read about the Kramers or sat on a park bench yourself, you're aware that parents are worrying about child care, schools, and safety.

Indeed, the very richness and diversity of New York seems to complicate the problems and make people scramble all the harder for reliable information. They've got to pull it in, sift through it, and somehow make tough choices. There are more than twenty preschool programs in Greenwich Village alone. When it comes time for kindergarten, a parent may well be faced with an equally daunting list of public, private, and parochial schools. And so it goes. How does a parent decide?

If you're considering an afternoon's outing in New York City, you can glance at newspapers and guidebooks listing attractions for kids. But if you're thinking seriously about the basic issues of parenting—preparing for the new arrival, arranging quality child care, planning your child's education, getting needed medical services, as well as meeting the special challenges of living in New York (transportation, play, safety, shopping)—where do you turn?

If you've subscribed to *New York* magazine over the years, you've probably gotten a start. Its service articles have covered everything from "The Child-Care Perplex" to "The Smart Set" to "The Middle-Class Parents' Guide to the Public Schools." You've also probably been alarmed by pieces such as Linda Wolfe's 1984 article "The New York Mother, Bringing up Baby on the Run, Run, Run." Wolfe claims that New York motherhood is "becoming a technocratic specialty" and that "whether or not she works, the New York mother leads a life filled with unique complications and concerns." If you were wondering about expenses, perhaps you studied "The High Cost of Baby Booming," which estimated the total "price tag" of the New York child's first year of life as $27,677.52 in upwardly mobile families with an income of about $85,000)—and $71,543.21 in "privileged families" earning about $200,000! And perhaps you saw "The Baby Formula" in *Manhattan, inc.,* which presented the story of infant Jonathan Willard Emery, Jr., against the background of the expanding baby industry. There you'd have learned that "Jonathan Willard Emery, Jr.'s parents can expect to spend as much as $425,000 in the next twenty-one years."

In the last few years, an increasing number of parenting articles have appeared to keep pace with the baby boom generation's own late-blooming booming. Joining the trend, *The New York Times* has reported on the pressures parents feel when they consider private schools and chronicled the growth of upscale baby designing, while the Sunday *Daily News Magazine* featured a piece called "Deliverance: Where to Have a Baby in New York."

By now you've probably realized something else, however. *New York* and the *Times* have a decidedly Manhattan-oriented editorial slant. Their New York is often a rather selective view of reality. After all, New York has five boroughs—Brooklyn, Staten Island, the Bronx, and Queens, as well as Manhattan. In four of the boroughs, people own cars and use them all the time to get around. They may live in one- and two-family houses or small apartment buildings, not high-rises or renovated brownstones. Their lives revolve around their own neighborhood, around Toys "R" Us and McDonald's. Even if you are a Manhattanite, you may sometimes feel that the media is talking about other people's concerns—not yours.

Yet the questions that parents ask, whether they live in Manhattan, Queens, or the suburbs, are similar. If you eavesdrop on a conversation, you'd probably hear the following:

- We're expecting our first child. What should I know about the hospitals of New York? What are the alternatives? If my baby is born in a hospital, can the baby room-in?
- How do I go about finding child care for my infant? What are the options? What *are* the costs?
- There are numerous private schools in New York City. How do you ever choose?

- I'd like to send my child to a public school, but I've heard horror stories about my neighborhood school. What can I do? Whom do I talk to about putting him into another school?
- What do kids whose parents don't have country homes do in New York City during the summer?

The New York Parents' Book starts with the basic assumption that you are interested in learning more. You may live in one of the five boroughs or you may be considering moving into the city. Perhaps you are a suburbanite who uses the city's services or even a social worker or a teacher who needs some of this information for your job. You have some basic questions about child care, education, health care, and city life. The central chapters of the book survey these topics. Like other parenting books, this one sketches out alternatives and tries to help you evaluate them. Its perspective is unique, however, for all the information is focused through a New York City lens.

The New York Parents' Book, however, is not the parents' Yellow Pages. Nor is it a trendy ratings book, telling you about the "ten best," the "ten worst," the "up-and-coming," or the "undiscovered." *The New York Parents' Book*, written by one parent for others, is primarily a guide to the particular resources of New York City. All the chapters derive from a belief that parents must be informed consumers, prepared to evaluate and to synthesize information and to make their own decisions in their children's best interests.

Yet *The New York Parents' Book* would not be doing its job if it did not capture the distinctive sights and sounds that make the city so rich. The final chapter, "Utilizing Cultural Resources," like its more traditional New York counterparts, lists where to take your child if you want to visit a library, a museum, an environmental education center, or a theater.

The New York Parents' Book is intended to give you an overview of parenting issues that come up predominantly in the pre-teenage years. It is intended to be dipped into periodically—rather than read cover to cover and permanently set aside—when the need for information on a particular subject arises. Although the book is organized around a few basic topics, such as child care, health care, and education, you will want to consult the Contents and the Index to use the book most effectively. Some subjects cut across chapters. If you are interested in summer activities, for example, you will need to look at "Summer Care" and "The Y's and Community Centers of the City" in the chapter on child care,

"Sports," "Getting a Handle on the Parks Department," and "The Public Pools of New York City" in the chapter about living in New York, and "Some Special Summer Programs" in the chapter on cultural resources. While birthday parties are highlighted in chapter five, you'll also want to peruse the chapter on cultural resources.

The New York Parents' Book is just the beginning, not the end, of your learning about raising children in New York. It highlights key questions and points you in the direction that you need to go to get information. You'll still have to make some phone calls. Be prepared, however, that in some instances the addresses and phone numbers of organizations or stores listed in this book may have changed since the book went to press. Some prices, no doubt, have gone up and programs changed. Nor should you expect to find every parenting program included in these pages, since that was not my intention. *The New York Parents' Book* will have fulfilled its purpose if it makes your negotiating around the sidewalks of New York just a little bit easier.

The research for this book stretched over many years. One might say that it began when I was a graduate student at Columbia University, specializing in urban and social history and concentrating on New York City history. Later, working as an environmental historian for the High Rock Park Conservation Center on Staten Island, I had a chance to learn about Stapleton—a community far different from the one I was living in—and uncover its special personality. But the best background for writing this book has been that of a parent. You see the city anew when you push a stroller containing two children, attend a community school board meeting, or exchange news with neighbors on a park bench.

The impetus for writing this book came from our experience of moving back to New York City after living for several years in Virginia. My husband and I were familiar with Manhattan, since we'd attended both college and graduate school here. Yet, faced with the prospect of moving back with two toddlers, we hungered for information about what it was like to bring up children in New York. The seed for *The New York Parents' Book* had been planted.

Yet the book could not have grown without the help of many people. Many parents shared their special experiences with me. To protect their families' identities, their names have been changed. I have benefited from the expertise of childbirth educators Sandy Jamrog and Judith Lothian, Sandy Socolar of Child Care, Inc., Professor Lisa Fleisher of New

York University, and Dr. Marji Gold of Montefiore, who read selected sections of the manuscript. I would also like to thank Stephanie Sporn, David Hertz, Dr. Louis Cooper, Jill Blair, Doreen DeMartini, Eileen Hansen, Dr. Mary Ann Howland, the Youth Coordinators of the New York City Youth Bureau, the United Parents Associations, Janice Parker, Howard Johnson, Patsy Wainwright, James Dubbs, Margaret T. Corey, Anne Miller, Beth Styer, Susan Ginsberg, Charlene Stokamer, Blanche and Sam Gelber, Diana Cassidy, Crystal Harris, Dr. Doris Wethers, Gloria Rubin, Dr. Ivan R. Koota, Betsy Swerzy, Sarah Brezavar, Vicki Breitbart, Dr. Grant Higginson, Barbara Genco, and Dr. Elihu Sussman.

Where would this book be without friends and relatives? When I needed them, I knew that I could turn to David Heim, Katherine Foran, Eleanor Prescott, Nicholas Garaufis, Danise Hoover, Harriet Elsky, Rona Silverman, Kathy Heller, Dan Carlinsky, Jeanne Heymann, Susan Stone Wong, Amy Teplin-Post, Susan and Brian McCarthy, and the "honorary Gilman" Deirdre Laughton. My New York mother, Lotte S. Prager, moved me to suburbia as a child but gave me the freedom to come back as a teenager.

This book is dedicated to three very special people: Eve, Seth, and Ernest Gilman. To see New York through Seth's and Eve's eyes has meant to delight in fire engines parked in front of Grand Union, frozen candy bars at the Staten Island Zoo, a flock of pigeons on a city street, and the nearest playground. Nineteen years ago Eleanor Prescott suggested to Ernest Gilman that he recruit Lois Prager for his newspaper staff. Eleanor's had many brilliant ideas, but no doubt that was her best. He has remained my one temptation to idolatry.

contents

Preface vii

Chapter One Becoming a Family 1
Getting Advice About Giving Birth . . . Finding a Birth Attendant and a Hospital . . . The Key Questions You'll Want to Ask a Birth Attendant and Hospital . . . Required by New York State . . . Childbirth Education Classes . . . Giving Birth in a New York City Hospital . . . Genetic Counseling . . . Adopting a Child . . . What You'll Want to Ask Yourself—and Others—About Adoption . . . Talking About Being a Parent . . . Help with Special Concerns

Chapter Two Choosing Child Care 39
What's Available: Information and Referral . . . The Basics: In-home Care . . . When You Turn to an Agency . . . In-home Care: Some Tips on Hiring . . . The Finances of Child Care . . . New York's Public Day Care . . . Private Family Day Care . . . Day Care in Licensed Centers . . . After-school Care . . . The Y's and Community Centers of the City . . . Summer Care . . . Holiday Care . . . Baby-sitting . . . Where to Look for a Student . . . Be Prepared

Chapter Three Choosing Schools   71
Schools for Under-fives . . . Beyond Nursery School: Considering What's Best for Your Child . . . Beyond Nursery: Taking the Measure of a School . . . The Public Schools of New York City . . . Gifted and Talented Programs . . . Nonpublic Schools . . . Have You Wondered About Private Schools? . . . Special Education . . . Rights . . . Schooling at Home . . . Homework Help

Chapter Four Meeting Your Child's Health Care Needs   99
Choosing a Physician for Your Child . . . Find Out About . . . Children in Hospitals . . . Using a Hospital's Emergency Room . . . Summoning an Ambulance . . . Pediatric Care in the Hospitals of New York City . . . Poisoning . . . Learning About First Aid . . . For Your Information . . . Special Needs, Special Concerns . . . Prescription Drugs . . . Dental Care . . . Mental Health

Chapter Five Meeting the Challenges of Living in New York City   131
Making Space . . . Bunk Beds . . . Playgrounds and Playrooms . . . Getting Around . . . Buckle Up . . . Street Smarts . . . Sports: Indoors and Outdoors . . . Getting a Handle on the Parks Department . . . Finding an Ice Skating Rink . . . The Public Pools of New York City . . . Recreation for the Tiniest Tots . . . Celebrating a Birthday . . . Is Your Child Welcome Here? . . . Shopping . . . Clothing and Furniture . . . Books . . . Toys

Chapter Six Utilizing Cultural Resources   171
Libraries . . . Museums . . . Some Special Summer Programs . . . Environmental Education . . . Zoos and Aquariums . . . Not for Tourists Only . . . Performing Arts . . . Puppetry . . . Performing Arts Especially for Groups . . . Annual Spectacles

Index   213

the new york parents' book

chapter 1
becoming a family

Seven years ago Abigail Smith gave birth to her first child, Christine, in a prominent Manhattan teaching hospital. The obstetrician was a man who came well recommended by a friend. It was a fairly routine, "traditional" birth from a medical standpoint. Yet, from Abigail's point of view, the experience was—and still is—profoundly upsetting. "My doctor assured me: 'If you want to have a healthy baby, leave it to me,'" she recalls ruefully. "So I did."

When Abigail arrived at the hospital to give birth, she was attached to an I.V. and a fetal monitor and told not to get out of bed. "While I labored, my doctor sat outside. I was examined, however, by six different house doctors." When Abigail finally started pushing, her doctor decided to use forceps. "At that point," she remembers, "my husband was told that he was not permitted in the delivery room because of a hospital rule prohibiting husbands when forceps were used. William waited outside although the delivery room was packed with people. Nobody talked to me. The doctor supervised the birth, while the chief resident acted." Abigail was further upset at her postpartum checkup. She recalls: "My doctor said to me, 'Well, that was a pretty good birth.' I said, 'Whose birth were you at?' He said, 'You're lucky you had such a good doctor.'"

Three years later, ready for a second child, Abigail was determined to do things differently. She made a detailed list of what she wanted in the birth experience, and she went looking for it. She switched obstetricians and decided to use a labor coach in addition to her husband. She went on tours of hospitals in Manhattan and looked at their birthing rooms—"Most were just potted plants and wallpaper." Then she found a hospital, less than a mile from where she'd previously given birth, which permitted her, the labor coach, her husband, her doctor, her daughter, and an adult friend who served as Christine's companion to attend the birth. Her pediatrician even agreed to release her baby from the hospital three hours after his birth ("I signed a hospital form saying that it was against medical advice"). This time the birth experience went as she'd hoped.

Elaine Genessee made a different choice—a freestanding birth center and a midwife. She chose the Childbearing Center, staffed by nurse-midwives. Her husband, her mother, and her brother were with her while she labored. Yet, in the end, she gave birth in a hospital. When her contractions suddenly stopped, her midwife, fearing a possible complication, summoned the backup obstetrician and an ambulance. Despite this change in plans, she recalls, "My delivery was exactly as I had planned it. I gave birth on a labor room bed. I didn't have any anesthetic or an episiotomy. I went home fourteen hours later. I would have gone home earlier, but I had difficulty getting a pediatrician's OK."

Thirty-eight-year-old Linda Carlton had a very different idea of what the optimum birth would be. After two miscarriages and a long history of infertility, she was looking forward to having her baby at a high-tech Manhattan teaching hospital: "I wanted every available monitor, every available precaution. I was not going to take any chances." In this case, Linda's prudence was warranted. When her daughter was born with a low birth weight, the infant was immediately put into the hospital's neonatal intensive care nursery.

Three women and three different experiences. In 1985, 118,542 women gave birth in New York City hospitals: 31,722 gave birth in municipal hospitals, 85,965 in nonprofit voluntary hospitals, and 429 in proprietary hospitals. At the Childbearing Center, the only freestanding birth center in New York City, 266 women gave birth, and 146 women even gave birth at home.

The range of choices available to you may be few or many. Your pregnancy risk, financial circumstances, health insurance, and access to medical care all affect your options—as does the amount of time you can devote to gathering information. Recognizing the limitations that your own situation may impose, it's still advisable to explore alternatives. You may be surprised at what the possibilities are.

Getting Advice About Giving Birth

Johanna Hopkins, like Abigail Smith, had some ideas about the kind of birth experience she wanted. She'd listened to the advice of her friends, but she had one requirement of her own. Her first child had been delivered by cesarean, yet she'd read that some women had given birth to second babies vaginally. She'd heard that some doctors and hospitals did not encourage this. So she talked with people familiar with childbirth policies at various hospitals in New York. Whatever your needs, there are people around who will gladly talk with you and outline some of the basic issues.

You might begin by talking with childbirth educators. The educators, who sometimes are nurses, teach classes in preparation for childbirth (see page 11), but they're ready to help you at any time—even before you're pregnant. Some educators are on a hospital staff; others are independent. The educator is used to fielding the question: "I want *this* kind of birth. Can you tell me who's going to help give it to me?" She's usually pretty candid about doctors and, depending upon her affiliation, about hospitals. Says Judy Lothian, who has served as president of ASPO/Lamaze: "Our whole philosophy is that the consumer makes her own choice." If you have questions, contact:

- **American Society for Psychoprophylaxis in Obstetrics** ASPO/ Lamaze (Box 725, Midtown Station, New York, N.Y. 10018: 212-831-9327): The giant in the field of childbirth education, with more than two hundred local members, ASPO has affiliated instructors at most area hospitals. You can get a list of childbirth educators in your neighborhood from them.

- **Metropolitan New York/Childbirth Education Association** (P.O. Box 2036, New York, N.Y. 10185: 212-866-6373 and 6 Tuxedo Avenue, New Hyde Park, N.Y. 10040: 516-741-0375): Has educators teaching in the five boroughs and holds seminars and workshops for parents and educators.

Several information and referral services can also help:

- **Women's Counseling Project** (Reid Hall, 3001 Broadway, New York, N.Y. 10025: 212-280-3063): This independent collective gives free advice on topics ranging from health and abortion to legal and social services for women in the New York metropolitan area. The obstetric advisory service can tell you about obstetricians and midwives (information about fees included) around the city. The physicians and midwives surveyed are primarily in Brooklyn and Manhattan, since the referral list got its start from reports by satisfied patients. The Project's staff interviews the health care professionals and makes site visits. Says one counselor: "We pick out people who are sensitive to women's desires to control their own childbirth experience. We've tried to pick doctors whom we feel comfortable with."

◆ **New York City Pregnancy Healthline** (230-1111; no area code is needed): You've probably seen the advertisements on subways and buses for New York City's free pregnancy advisory service. The Department of Health's hotline seeks to promote healthy pregnancy outcomes. If you need a referral for medical care (no referrals to private physicians), the telephone counselor will ask you for basic biographical information. She'll want to know where you live and work, your health insurance status, your eligibility for Medicaid, and your previous pregnancy history. She'll then offer to set up an appointment for you at a hospital, clinic, or health care center and later will follow up to see that you kept it. The Pregnancy Healthline has surveyed all area hospitals, so it can give you borough-by-borough information about childbirth. You can also get some fact sheets by mail on health-related issues (e.g., nutrition, amniocentesis).

◆ **Planned Parenthood of New York City** (380 Second Avenue, New York, N.Y. 10010: 212-777-2002).

If you're thinking about a midwife-attended birth, start by calling the **Maternity Center Association** (48 East 92 Street, New York, N.Y. 10128: 212-369-7300), which operates the Childbearing Center. Since the Maternity Center is concerned about alternatives in childbirth, it's also an excellent resource for steering you to specific obstetricians and midwives, not necessarily affiliated with their organization, with similar attitudes. You may also want to contact the **American College of Nurse-Midwives** (1522 K Street N.W., Washington, D.C. 20005: 202-347-5445), which certifies nurse-midwives. Although nurse-midwives often function as part of hospital staffs, some in New York City have private practices.

The county chapters of the **Medical Society of the State of New York** (Bronx: 212-548-4401; Brooklyn: 718-467-9000; Manhattan: 212-399-

9040; Queens: 718-268-7300; Staten Island: 718-987-3377) will refer you to member physicians. Each Medical Society has a "referral panel" of members who are, for example, pediatricians, obstetricians, or family practitioners. Tell the Medical Society where you live (or where you want to give birth) and they'll give you the names of several doctors. You'll also be told some details about the physicians' credentials: medical education, specialization, hospital affiliations, and board certification. You can also get in touch with the **American College of Obstetricians and Gynecologists** (600 Maryland Avenue S.W., Washington, D.C. 20024: 202-638-5577) and the **American Academy of Family Physicians** (1740 West 92 Street, Kansas City, Mo. 64114: 816-333-9700). Both will send you a list of members (names and addresses) in New York City.

If you've identified a particular hospital where you would like to give birth, you can always call its obstetric floor and ask the nursing supervisor or the physician who's head of obstetrics and gynecology for the names of physicians on staff. Indicate any special preferences you have.

Finding a Birth Attendant and a Hospital

Who will attend your child's birth and where it will take place are interconnected. Doctors and midwives are all affiliated with hospitals, typically just one or two. If you already have a physician you like, then you are going to have your child in the hospital where he or she is affiliated. When you select a doctor, you are therefore choosing a hospital. Knowing this, Johanna Hopkins began by selecting a hospital. She settled on the hospital and her obstetrician long before she became pregnant.

You may have more, or less, opportunity to choose. If you belong to an H.M.O. (Health Maintenance Organization), such as the Health Insurance Plan (H.I.P.), you will be limited to the doctors and hospitals affiliated with it. Your financial situation will also influence your decisions. If you decide to look around, keep the following in mind:

◆ You can choose an obstetrician, a family physician, a nurse-midwife, or a lay midwife to attend the birth. You might have your baby in a hospital delivery room, a hospital birthing room, a birthing center, or your home. The hospitals of New York City range from small community hospitals to teaching hospitals with all the latest obstetrical technology.

♦ When you ask relatives or friends about their pregnancy and birth experience, question them closely. Find out what they liked about the doctor (and the hospital) and what they didn't like. Ask what they'd do next time *and* what they'd do differently. Be sure you talk to several women, not just one or two, who've given birth recently.

♦ If you ask your internist or pediatrician to recommend another medical practitioner, recognize that referral patterns by medical practitioners usually develop from admitting patterns. The odds are very high that you'll be sent to someone affiliated with the hospital where your doctor has admitting privileges. "Unless the doctor has multiple admitting privileges," says Elizabeth Sommers of the Greater New York Hospital Association, "you are likely to get another physician at the primary physician's hospital." Observes one health care professional: "They are a single medical community."

♦ Rules in hospitals differ. Fathers are encouraged at most hospitals to spend as much time as they wish with Mom and the new baby. At a few area hospitals, including Manhattan's Lenox Hill, Dad can even spend the night. LaGuardia Hospital in Queens is at the opposite end of this spectrum, restricting father visitation to four hours daily. While father attendance at delivery is routine, some hospitals banish fathers if a cesarean is required. Others will let them in except if the cesarean is performed under general anesthetic or in an emergency.

Policies concerning siblings also vary. Most permit brothers and sisters to visit their mother and the newborn during designated hours but restrict the youngsters to seeing the baby through the nursery window. Some set up tours for children and hold special childbirth preparation classes. St. Vincent's Hospital in Manhattan goes one step further, letting children visit or stay in the mother's room from 10 A.M. to 10 P.M., and allowing them to attend the birth if their parents request it. Says Anne Miller of St. Vincent's: "Our hospital policy is for you to make the choice."

When you ask about hospital policies, be sure that you find out what's currently in place and, since you're looking nine months ahead, whether there are plans afoot to change it. You may be able to enlist your doctor's support in getting what you want, since doctors are powerful people in hospitals. Reports one childbirth educator: "Doctors can do pretty much what they want in a hospital."

◆ Feel free to visit more than one hospital for a tour of its labor and delivery facilities and to do so even before you're pregnant. The tour, usually arranged by the parent educator or an obstetric nurse, gives you a chance to find out about the hospital's regulations. Says Parent Educator Charlene Stokamer of Presbyterian Hospital: "We often get people on tours who are shopping around." Don't hesitate to take a hospital tour more than once. The questions that you ask at the beginning of your pregnancy, when you've begun to do some reading and thinking and want to inquire about the hospital's overall philosophy, will be different from those that come up toward the end of your pregnancy, when you're focused on exactly what will be happening to you during labor and delivery.

◆ If you have a vision of solitude, then find out how crowded the obstetrical services are on a "typical" day. Because some hospitals are in vogue, you may encounter occasional—or frequent—overcrowding. In June 1984, *The New York Times* reported that "some of the city's best-known hospitals are facing periodic overcrowding in their obstetric units, ranging from a shortage of labor rooms to a lack of beds for women who have already delivered." The *Times* noted that "on some days, the obstetric units at such hospitals as New York Hospital, New York University Hospital, Presbyterian Hospital and Mount Sinai Medical Center have become so crowded that women have been asked to go through labor in the recovery room—spaces usually reserved for women who have already given birth. A number of these hospitals have sometimes run out of beds on the obstetric floor and have had to place women elsewhere, separated from their infants, until beds near the nursery are clear. In still other hospitals, women are temporarily lodged in the hall." In 1985 a childbirth educator in Queens remarked that Long Island Jewish "doesn't have the beds for people. They're in the halls the first night. I kid about it and say that after you deliver, you can't be guaranteed a room. Yet people go there." The hospital chart in this chapter indicates that the problem persists.

◆ Maternity services can be profitable for hospitals and many now woo prospective patients. In April 1986, *The New York Times* reported that metropolitan hospitals were actively competing for maternity patients. According to the *Times,* St. Luke's–Roosevelt Hospital Center in Manhattan was offering free T-shirts, baby blankets, and dinners of shrimp cocktail and filet mignon to parents whose babies were born there. That was not the only pitch around. In its 1986 survey of hospital deliveries, *PARENTGUIDE NEWS* noted that Mount Sinai Hospital in Manhattan was offering a "Stork Club" dinner, Booth Memorial Hospital in Queens provided a bottle of nonalcoholic wine and flowers to each mother after delivery, and Methodist Hospital in Brooklyn served up dinner, a free "Life Begins at Methodist Hospital" T-shirt and baby photos. Dennis Crimi of St. Luke's told the *Times*: "Big hospitals don't talk about open hearts or transplants, it's market shares and babies."

♦ Know what your expenses will be and what your insurance will cover. The costs of giving birth can vary widely. If you use a public clinic or belong to an H.M.O., your expenses for medical care could be minimal. They could, however, be substantial. Darcie Bundy in *The Affordable Baby* (New York: Harper & Row, 1985) noted that "in Manhattan where obstetrician fees commonly ranged from $1,200 to $2,500 in 1984, while insurers were quoting $1,800 as 'reasonable and customary,' I know many women who had to pay $1,000 out of pocket on obstetrician bills *alone*—and these were people with comprehensive health insurance plans!" Within one twenty-block radius in New York City in mid-1984, Bundy reports, women were paying between $1,500 and $3,000. Among the expenses that you may have to cover, in full or in part, are doctor/midwife, hospital (mother/baby), prenatal lab work, vitamins, childbirth preparation, and, if you're over thirty-five, genetic counseling.

▽ ▽ ▽ ▽ ▽ ▽ ▽ ▽ ▽ ▽ ▽

THE KEY QUESTIONS YOU'LL WANT TO ASK A BIRTH ATTENDANT AND HOSPITAL

There are no right and wrong answers to these questions. Dip into the childbirth literature beforehand. When you decide on a birth attendant, make an appointment, bring your spouse (or another companion), and try to have the appointment without a physical. Think through what's most important for you to ask.

Don't be embarrassed to ask your prospective birth attendant:

♦ What are the common situations in which you decide that the mother should have a cesarean?
♦ Under what circumstances would you not attend the birth? If you are not there, who will be there? How will I get to know your backup?
♦ At what point in labor do you arrive?

- How long do your patients routinely stay in the hospital after delivery?
- How do you feel about fathers at delivery? How do you feel about fathers attending a cesarean birth? How do you feel about children at birth?

If you are considering someone who is in a group practice, find out how the doctors cover for each other. How do the doctors' attitudes in the practice differ? Observed one Queens childbirth educator: "There's one practice in the area that's notorious. One doctor will tell you everything is one way; the other men in the practice say that's not so." Be sure that you meet the others in the practice, since you have a good chance of getting one of them. If you are considering a midwife, find out about her backup physician and the arrangements in case of a medical emergency. Nurse-midwives are by law required to work under the administrative direction and consultation of a licensed physician.

Listen to what the doctor says, but no less to how he says it. Observes Judith Lothian: "You learn something if a doctor tells you, 'It's the most ridiculous thing in the world.'" In hindsight, Abigail Smith realized that her doctor's comment, "If you want to have a healthy baby, leave it to me," stated baldly at her first meeting, summed up his vision of childbirth.

The chart in this chapter gives a brief overview of hospitals. You might also inquire about the number of labor beds in the hospital, the number of labor rooms, and the number of delivery rooms. You should also be aware that the neonate nurseries in all hospitals with maternity service have been classified by the New York City Department of Health: Level One, Level Two, or Level Three. A Level One nursery is for low-risk pregnancies and offers basic maternity and newborn care. Level Two facilities vary, but all have "special care" nurseries. Level Two nurseries should be able to handle the majority of high-risk pregnancies and most premature or sick neonates. Level Three nurseries can take care of *all* high-risk pregnancies, deliveries, and critically ill neonates. Level Three nurseries will have a complete array of consultants, including pediatric cardiologists, pediatric neurologists, pediatric surgeons, and specialized anesthesiologists. Level One and Level Two institutions transfer their sick infants to Level Three nurseries. While Level Two nurseries can generally care for many of their sick infants, Level One should not and are expected to send their sick infants to Level Three facilities. If you know that you are an "at-risk" patient, be sure that you consider the hospital's nursery level. You'll want to discuss with your doctor how you can ensure giving birth at a hospital equipped to deal with high-risk maternity and newborn patients. Ask also about the house staff. What's the size? If there are students, interns, and residents, can the mother refuse to have observers?

You'll also want to explore with the hospital:

- What does rooming-in really mean? At most hospitals, you are permitted to keep your baby with you some of the time, but most hospitals send babies back to the nursery during general visiting hours and at night. What are the rules for private and semiprivate rooms? St. Vincent's in Manhattan has twenty-four-hour rooming-in and the baby stays even when visitors appear. Says Miller: "We presume your baby's going to room-in twenty-four hours. We've told the mothers they can tell us when they want the baby out."
- Who can be present in the delivery or birthing room? Can you give birth in the labor room? Where does recovery take place? Many hospitals tout their birthing rooms. Find out how many there are, who can use them, and how frequently they are used. One medical administrator commented about a birthing room: "We dust it regularly. Nobody has ever wanted to use it. There has not been a great demand for it."
- Cesareans: Who's permitted to be present and under what circumstances? If you've had a cesarean previously, will the hospital let you try to give birth vaginally?
- Photo- or video-taking in the labor, delivery, or recovery room?
- Discharge: How long do patients routinely stay in the hospital after giving birth? Is early discharge possible?
- When is the baby routinely separated from the parents?
- What are the policies for parents if the infant is in intensive care? How much time can you spend with the baby? What type of care can you provide? Is there a parent support group? If the baby were to die, will you be allowed a quiet time when you can hold the baby by yourself?

△ △ △ △ △ △ △ △ △ △ △

Required by New York State

Did you know that New York State requires hospitals to give you information about breast-feeding? In 1984, New York State mandated that hospitals, "with the advice of the maternity staff, shall formulate a program of instruction *and provide assistance* for *each* maternity patient in the fundamentals of (normal) infant care *including infant feeding choices and techniques,* postpregnancy care and family planning." At the minimum a hospital must have on staff one person trained in breast-feeding physiology and its policies must encourage, not discourage, women. Hospitals are expected to place the baby for breast-feeding "immediately following delivery, unless contraindicated," restrict the infant's supplemental feedings, and provide for feeding newborns on demand. Standing orders for antilactation drugs are prohibited. If you have any questions, or want further information, contact the New York State Department of Health, Breast Feeding Steering Committee (212-340-3300). For a breast-feeding support group, contact **La Leche League** (9616 Minneapolis Avenue, Franklin Park, Ill. 60131-8209: 312-455-7730). For details about local chapters, contact the Brooklyn office (718-833-3971).

Pregnant women in New York State are entitled to leaves of absence. A maternity leave is treated as a disability leave. Your leave should be the same as that of any employee who takes a disability leave. New York State also prohibits an employer from forcing a pregnant employee to take a maternity leave while she is capable of performing her job. If you want to take a paternity leave or adoption leave, however, it must be granted at the discretion of the individual employer. If you have any questions, or want further information, check with the Office of the Attorney General (120 Broadway, New York, N.Y. 10271: 212-341-2000) or with Catalyst (250 Park Avenue South, New York, N.Y. 10003: 212-777-8900).

Under federal and state law, employers are required to treat pregnancy-related disabilities on an equal basis with any other medical disability. You are entitled to the same disability coverage, including health insurance, as any other employee.

Childbirth Education Classes

Before you give birth you'll probably want to enroll in a preparation for childbirth class. These courses help you get ready for the birth itself, including training in breathing and relaxation techniques. You'll find the courses offered at hospitals, Y's and settlement houses, parenting centers, doctor's offices, or the homes of childbirth educators. The instructors are usually accredited by one of several professional organizations. Although the majority of classes start toward the end of a woman's pregnancy, you'll find several programs that begin when you're still in your first trimester.

The size, cost, and content of classes vary. In-hospital classes often have ten to twenty couples enrolled, while out-of-hospital classes usually have five to ten couples. Hospital classes may be free or have a charge of perhaps $50 to $75. An instructor who offers private classes in Manhattan might

(continued on page 22)

GIVING BIRTH IN A NEW YORK CITY HOSPITAL

The information in these charts comes primarily from a survey sent to area hospitals with obstetrical beds. The survey, done in summer 1986, was mailed initially to the chairman of the Department of Obstetrics. It was later sent in the fall of 1986 to selected childbirth educators. I followed up by telephone repeatedly in the fall of 1986 in an attempt to reach all hospitals. If a section is blank, it is because I did not receive an answer. Where I was unable to obtain a hospital's co-operation, I have relied on public sources to fill in selected details.

A few basic points for clarification:

◆ The medical school with which a department is affiliated is put in parentheses.
◆ Res. Prog. means "Residency Program" in Obstetrics except where indicated that it is in Family Medicine.

Hospital (Medical School)	Type	Res. Prog.	Mid-wives	Nursery Level	Overcrowding Problems?	Cesarean Birthrate	No. of Labor Coaches Permitted	Father at Caesarean Birth?
BRONX								
Bronx Municipal Hospital Center–Jacobi (Albert Einstein College of Medicine)	M	Yes		III				Yes
Jack D. Weiler Hospital (Albert Einstein)	V	Yes	Yes	III	Occasionally; Summer busy. Occup. Rate: 96%	19%	One	Yes
North Central Bronx (Albert Einstein)	M	Family Med.	Yes	II	Yes		One or Two	Yes
Bronx–Lebanon Hospital Cntr.	V			II				
Lincoln Medical and Mental Health Center (N.Y. Medical College)	M	Yes	Yes	II	Yes. "Every month."	18.4%	One	No

12 | THE NEW YORK PARENTS' BOOK

- "Visiting hours" means general visiting hours, rather than the times that fathers can visit.
- "View baby thru glass" means that the baby is in the nursery; the visiting child sees the sibling through the nursery window.
- Any material in quotation marks comes directly from the survey and was said or written by hospital personnel.
- M stands for "municipal," V stands for "voluntary."
- Occup. Rate stands for "Occupancy Rate."
- The designations Level One (I), Level Two (II), and Level Three (III) for nurseries are based on information provided by the New York City Department of Health, Bureau of Maternity Services and Family Planning. In some instances, the hospitals provided me with different designations for their nurseries.

Father Visiting Postpartum	Young Sibling Visits	Rooming-in	Childbirth Classes	Languages Routinely Spoken	Other information: This material comes from information provided by hospital personnel.
8 A.M.–8 P.M.	No	Rare		English Spanish	
Anytime. Overnight stay OK if mother in private room.	Noon–8 P.M. Can see baby in mother's room.	Yes. In nursery during visiting hrs.	Yes. 212-904-2951	English Spanish	"Family-centered care for all patients regardless of risk status. Special program for bereaved parents; early discharge postpartum available; home care follow-up arranged as needed."
8 A.M.–8 P.M.	Yes	Full or part		English Spanish	
10 A.M.–10 P.M. if mother has rooming-in.	No	Yes	Yes. 212-579-5923	English Spanish	"This hospital is community-oriented and family-centered approach."

BECOMING A FAMILY | 13

Hospital (Medical School)	Type	Res. Prog.	Mid-wives	Nursery Level	Overcrowding Problems?	Cesarean Birthrate	No. of Labor Coaches Permitted	Father at Caesarean Birth?
BRONX								
Our Lady of Mercy Medical Cntr. (N.Y. Medical College)	V	No	No	II	"We are quite frequently overcrowded, but we do accommodate." Occup. Rate: 75–80%	ca. 25%	One	Yes, if Dr. permits.
BROOKLYN								
Brookdale Hospital Medical Cntr. (SUNY Health Science Cntr.–Brooklyn)	V	Yes	Yes	III	"Often."		One	If pre-arranged.
Brooklyn Hospital Cntr. (SUNY)	V	Yes	No	III	Occup. Rate: 95%		One	Arrange with Dr.
Coney Island Hospital (SUNY)	M	Yes	Yes	I	"Infrequent." Occup. Rate: 85%	18%	One	Individual Dr.'s decision.
Interfaith Medical Cntr. (SUNY)	V	Yes	Yes	III	No. Occup. Rate: 85–90%		One	No
Kings County Hospital Cntr. (SUNY)	M	Yes	Yes	III	"Intermittent." Occup. Rate: 90%		One	Yes
Long Island College Hospital (SUNY)	V	Yes	Yes	II	No	23%		Depends upon Dr.
Lutheran Medical Cntr. (SUNY)	V	Yes	No	II	Occup. Rate: 80%	18%		Yes

Father Visiting Postpartum	Young Sibling Visits	Rooming-in	Childbirth Classes	Languages Routinely Spoken	Other information: This material comes from information provided by hospital personnel.
10 A.M.–10 P.M.	Yes. One hr. daily. See baby thru nursery window.	If mother wishes. In nursery for visiting hrs.	Yes. 914-472-6945	English	
	No	Baby in nursery. "Scheduled times for all mothers."	Open to anyone. 718-240-5443	English Spanish Hebrew Yiddish Russian Haitian	Parent support group for premature infants.
9 A.M.–9 P.M.	Yes. Must be two years old. View baby thru glass.	In nursery. Out for feedings. Two single rooms for rooming-in.	Yes. 718-376-5667	English Spanish French	"We give compassionate nursing care." Parent support group in neonatal I.C.U. (N.I.C.U.).
Extended evening hrs.	By appointment. View baby thru glass.	Yes. Baby in nursery in late evening.	Yes. 718-615-4644	English	"Full-time anesthesia coverage, full-time neonatologist."
Until 8 P.M.	Upon request. View baby thru glass.	Can stay in crib in mother's room. In nursery for visiting hrs.	Yes. 718-240-4601	English Spanish	"Women can receive their entire prenatal care through our clinics."
All times. Not overnight.	Upon request.	Can stay at mother's side. In nursery for visiting hrs.	Open to anyone. 718-735-3468	English Spanish Patois	"This hospital is known to the inner city people of Brooklyn. They vote with their feet. Kings County has remarkably good outcomes. We just wish people would come early."
"Anytime."	Must be over two. Daily. View baby thru glass.	Encouraged. Baby must be in nursery during evening visiting hrs.	Yes. 718-780-1972	English Spanish French	"Relatively new facility offering the latest in obstetrical care. Wonderful view from the rooms overlooking the harbor."
Until 9:30 P.M.	Daily. View baby thru glass.	Modified. In nursery during visiting hrs. and at night.	Open to anyone. 718-630-7535	English Spanish Greek Arabic Chinese	"Family-centered nursing provided. Mother and baby cared for by the same nurse. Baby is with Mother."

BECOMING A FAMILY

Hospital (Medical School)	Type	Res. Prog.	Mid-wives	Nursery Level	Overcrowding Problems?	Cesarean Birthrate	No. of Labor Coaches Permitted	Father at Caesarean Birth?
BROOKLYN								
Maimonides Medical Cntr. (SUNY)	V	Yes	No	II	Yes. About one week a month. Occup. Rate: Fluctuates from "85 to 110%"	22.5%	One	No
Methodist Hospital (SUNY)	V	No	Yes	II	Rarely. Occup. Rate: 90–100%	20–23%	Two	Yes
St. Mary's Hospital (Cornell Medical School)	V	Yes	Yes	I	Occup. Rate: ca. 100%	ca. 20%	One	No
SUNY Health Science Center— University Hospital: also known as Downstate SUNY	State	Yes	Yes	III	Rarely. Occup. Rate: 90%		One	If he's been to cesarean prep. class.
Victory Memorial	V	No	No	I	"Rarely."		One	"If mother is awake."
Woodhull Medical and Mental Health Cntr. (SUNY)	M	No	Yes	I	Yes. "Occurs periodically."	20%	One	No
MANHATTAN								
Bellevue Hospital Cntr. (New York Univ.)	M	Yes	Yes	III				
Beth Israel Medical Cntr. (Mount Sinai)	V	Yes	Yes	II	Occup. Rate: 100%		One	Yes
Harlem Hospital Cntr. (Columbia Univ.)	M	Yes	Yes	II	"Absolutely." Occup. Rate: 100%	18%	One	No

16 | THE NEW YORK PARENTS' BOOK

Father Visiting Postpartum	Young Sibling Visits	Rooming-in	Childbirth Classes	Languages Routinely Spoken	Other information: This material comes from information provided by hospital personnel.
8 A.M.–10 P.M.	Twice weekly. Visit in mother's room.	Usually in nursery. "Flexible modified." In nursery during general visiting hrs.	Yes. 718-270-8219	English Spanish Hebrew Yiddish	"Family-centered concept of nursing. Initiated the mother/infant unit. The postpartum unit has been renovated to provide a 'home-like' environment."
All day	Daily. View baby thru glass.	Twenty-four hr. rooming-in OK.	Open to public.	English Spanish	Older sibling can attend birth if parents request.
Visiting hrs.	No. "Holidays" only	Baby in nursery.	Open to anyone 718-774-3600	English Spanish French	
Noon–8:30 P.M.	Daily. View baby thru glass.	Flexible setup. Cannot be with mother if visitors other than father.	Open to people giving birth at hospital. 718-270-2608	English Spanish French	
Noon–9:30 P.M.	Daily. View baby thru glass.	Overnight possible. Baby in nursery when there are visitors.	Open to people giving birth at hospital. 718-630-1430	English Italian	
	Not under thirteen yrs.	In nursery	Yes. 718-963-5894	English Spanish French Creole	"The prenatal program is comprehensive and entails, in addition to medical care, patient education from a multidisciplinary team—physician, certified nurse-midwife, nurse counselor, nutritionist, social worker, nurse."
Anytime. Father can sleep over.	Noon–7 P.M. Visit with baby in mother's room.	Twenty-four hrs. OK.	Open to anyone. 212-420-2998	English Yiddish Spanish	Older sibling may be present at the birth if parents request. Support group for parents with babies in N.I.C.U. Bereavement support group. Foster godmother program for babies in N.I.C.U.
10 A.M.–10 P.M.	No	10 A.M.–10 P.M.	Yes. 212-491-1599	English Spanish	

BECOMING A FAMILY | 17

Hospital (Medical School)	Type	Res. Prog.	Mid-wives	Nursery Level	Overcrowding Problems?	Cesarean Birthrate	No. of Labor Coaches Permitted	Father at Caesarean Birth?
MANHATTAN								
Lenox Hill Hospital (N.Y. Medical College)	V	Yes	No	II	Occasionally.	20%	One	No
Metropolitan Hospital Cntr. (N.Y. Medical College)	M	Yes	Yes	II	"Variable. Usually summer months." Occup. Rate: 80%		One	No
Mount Sinai Medical Cntr. (Mount Sinai School of Med.)	V	Yes	Yes	III	"During peak periods for births."	22.8%	One	If general anesthesia not used.
New York Hospital–Cornell Medical Cntr. (Cornell Medical School)	V	Yes	No	III	No. Occup. Rate: 70%	30% "We have high-risk population."	Two. "One at a time."	Yes
New York Infirmary–Beekman Downtown (NYU)	V	Yes	No	I	"Rarely" Occup. Rate: 85%	22%	One	Yes "within bounds of written policy."
Presbyterian Hospital (Columbia University College of Physicians and Surgeons)	V	Yes	Yes	III	Occasionally. Occup. Rate: 90%	Primary: 14% Repeat: 9% Total: 23%	Usually one	Yes. If mother awake and C-section planned and Dr.'s permission
St. Luke's–Roosevelt Hospital Cntr. (Columbia)	V	Yes	Yes	II	Yes. "Seasonal."	20–22%	One	Yes

18 | THE NEW YORK PARENTS' BOOK

Father Visiting Postpartum	Young Sibling Visits	Rooming-in	Childbirth Classes	Languages Routinely Spoken	Other information: This material comes from information provided by hospital personnel.
Anytime in private room. Sleepover OK. 9 A.M.–11 P.M. in semiprivate.	Daily. View baby thru glass.	Total in private; modified in semi.	Yes. Includes sibling and cesarean prep. 212-439-2238	English Spanish	"The facilities are beautiful. We have two birthing rooms and a birthing chair."
All day till 8 P.M.	Yes. View baby thru glass.	Twenty-four hr. possible.	212-230-6595	English Spanish	Children may be present at the birth if parents request.
Private: unlimited; sleepover OK. Semiprivate: 10 A.M.–10 P.M.	Daily. View baby thru glass.	Modified or full. During visiting hrs. baby goes to nursery.	Yes. Includes sibling and cesarean prep. 212-650-7491	English Spanish	Tours for expectant parents twice weekly.
Any time. Sleepover OK in private rooms.	Yes. View baby thru glass.	Yes. Can be with mother at any time except general visiting hrs.	Extensive; "The Childbearing Year"; sibling class 212-472-5477	English	Support group for parents with babies in N.I.C.U. "Tertiary center offering comprehensive patient service . . . Obstetric services are family-centered in philosophy with strong emphasis on patient teaching."
Anytime. Sleepover permitted in private rooms.	Daily.	Modified. Baby in room when mother awake.	Yes 212-312-5000 ext. 4422	English Chinese Spanish	"Active birthing room with a state-of-the-art Adel birthing bed . . . strive to provide personal family-oriented birthing experience."
Anytime. Father may sleep over.	Yes. View baby thru glass.	Yes. Baby in nursery during visiting hours.	Extensive; sibling and cesarean prep; post-birth reunion; open to anyone. 212-305-2040	English Spanish	Photographs may be taken in the delivery room. "The policies are flexible and, within the realm of safety, very liberal. The intensive care nursery is extremely good and there is a transitional nursery right in the labor room suite to stabilize ill or small babies immediately after birth before they are moved to the N.I.C.U."
Anytime. Overnight OK in private rooms.	Daily. View baby thru glass.	Partial in semi; full in private.	Yes	English Spanish	"Each labor room is a potential birthing room. Each delivery room is a potential operating room. Policies are flexible to accommodate all needs of patients."

Hospital (Medical School)	Type	Res. Prog.	Mid-wives	Nursery Level	Overcrowding Problems?	Cesarean Birthrate	No. of Labor Coaches Permitted	Father at Caesarean Birth?
MANHATTAN								
St. Vincent's Hospital and Medical Cntr. (N.Y. Medical College)	V	Yes	Yes	III	"Rare." Occup. Rate: 96%	16%	Two. "More if important."	Yes
NYU Medical Center, University Hospital (New York University)	V	Yes	No	III	Occup. Rate: 85%		One	"Not yet."
QUEENS								
Booth Memorial Medical Cntr. (NYU)	V	Yes	No	II	Yes. About 25% of the time. Occup. Rate: 90%		One	If cesarean prep. class and if not emergency and if regional anesthesia.
City Hospital Cntr. at Elmhurst (Mount Sinai)	M	Yes	Yes	II	Yes. "During the summer months (July–September)." Occup. Rate: 95%	15.2%	One	Yes
Flushing Hospital and Medical Cntr.	V		No	II	Occup. Rate: 90%	25%	One	If took childbirth class.
Jamaica Hospital (Cornell)	V	Yes	No	I	No. Occup. Rate: 80%	20%	One	
LaGuardia Hospital (Cornell)	V	Yes	Yes	I	"Sometimes. Probably about twice a month." Occup. Rate: about 85%	ca. 20%	One	Not usually. Up to Dr.
Long Island Jewish Medical Cntr. (SUNY Health Science Cntr.–Stonybrook)	V	Yes	No	III	Yes. 20–30% of the time. Occup. Rate: 100%		One	Yes

20 | THE NEW YORK PARENTS' BOOK

Father Visiting Postpartum	Young Sibling Visits	Rooming-in	Childbirth Classes	Languages Routinely Spoken	Other information: This material comes from information provided by hospital personnel.
10 A.M.–10 P.M. Overnight OK in private and sometimes semi.	10 A.M.–10 P.M. Visit baby in mother's room.	Twenty-four hrs.	Yes. Includes sibling class and after discharge. 212-790-7946	English Spanish Chinese	Children may attend birth if parents request.
Unlimited. Overnight OK in private rooms.	Daily. View baby thru glass.	Varies from 16–24 hrs.	Yes. 212-340-7007	English	"We do have a birthing chair. N.Y.U. is well-known for high-risk pregnancy care."
Anytime	Daily. View baby thru glass.	All day possible. Baby in nursery for visiting hrs. and at night.	Varied. Includes sibling and cesarean prep. 718-670-1156	English Spanish	
11 A.M.–8 P.M.	At discretion of head nurse.	Twenty-four hrs.	Varied. 718-830-1581	English Spanish	
Anytime	Daily. View baby thru glass.	Baby usually in nursery. Modified OK (9 A.M.–2 P.M.).	Yes. 718-670-5697	English Spanish Korean	"This staff in labor and delivery and postpartum have been part of the Flushing Hospital family for many years. They are caring individuals. There's minimal turnover of staff because they enjoy working with new mothers."
9:00 A.M.–9:30 P.M.	No	Modified (9:00 A.M.–2:30 P.M.)	Not in hospital.	English Spanish	"The largest portion of our patients are low-income, high-risk population. We also have approximately 10 percent of our patients presenting with no prenatal care."
2:30 P.M.–3:30 P.M. 6:30 P.M.–8:00 P.M. 8:30 P.M.–10:00 P.M.	No	No. In nursery. Out for feedings four times daily.	Yes. Open to anyone. 718-830-4232	English	Run by the Health Insurance Plan (H.I.P.).
Anytime. Overnight OK.	Daily. View baby thru glass.	In mother's room except during visiting hrs.	Variety. 718-470-7915	English Hebrew	"We have implemented family centered maternity care in which one nurse cares for the mother-infant dyad as a family unit."

BECOMING A FAMILY | 21

Hospital (Medical School)	Type	Res. Prog.	Mid-wives	Nursery Level	Overcrowding Problems?	Cesarean Birthrate	No. of Labor Coaches Permitted	Father at Caesarean Birth?
QUEENS								
Queens Hospital Cntr. (SUNY–Stonybrook)	M	Yes	No	II	Yes. "Three-quarters of the year." Occup. Rate: 100%	ca. 17–20%	One	If took childbirth class.
St. John's Episcopal Hospital	V	Yes	No	I	"Rarely." Occup. Rate: 65–75%	25%	One	Usually no.
St. John's Queens Hospital	V			I				
STATEN ISLAND								
St. Vincent's Medical Cntr. of Richmond	V	Yes	No	III	Occup. Rate: ca. 90%	ca. 20–22%	No restrictions	If took childbirth class.
Staten Island Hospital (SUNY–Brooklyn)	V	Yes	No	II	"Present overcrowding being relieved by soon-to-be approved maternity and nursery space." (7/86) Occup. Rate: "105–110%"	ca. 18–20%	One	Yes

(continued from page 11)

charge up to $250, while in the other boroughs you'll more likely pay between $70 and $150. Some classes focus primarily on the birth process; others branch out into extensive parent education. The instructor's training is likely to affect the class content. If the instructor has been certified by ASPO/Lamaze, for example, the course will stress those childbirth management techniques over others.

Childbirth educators feel that there are other important differences that you should consider. Stephanie Sporn, who teaches classes independently, believes that often "a hospital class teaches you how to be a good patient in the hospital. The educator will explain why you need an I.V. and teach you

Father Visiting Postpartum	Young Sibling Visits	Rooming-in	Childbirth Classes	Languages Routinely Spoken	Other information: This material comes from information provided by hospital personnel.
Anytime; no overnight	No. Over fourteen only.	In nursery except for feedings.		English Spanish	
Regular hrs. and special father's hrs. and anytime in the day if necessary.	Special hrs.	Room-in daytime; nursery at night.	Yes. 718-917-3000	English	"This is a brand-new building with magnificent views of JFK Airport and ocean; with a new birthing room, modern delivery room, backup obstetricians, and a supportive nursing staff."
Yes					
Anytime; no overnight	Special hrs. Visit baby in mother's room.	Twenty-four hrs.; in nursery for visiting hrs.	Yes. 718-390-1161	English Spanish	
Anytime; no overnight	Anytime. View baby thru glass.	Yes	Open to anyone. 718-390-9447	English Spanish Italian	"Offers comprehensive family care."

what you should do to be a good patient. You're told what to do and you accept it. You're not necessarily versed on what you can do for yourself." Yet there are also clear advantages to the hospital class. It offers continuity and familiarizes you with the hospital's routines and policies ahead of time. The hospital tour, in fact, is built right into the classes. Your childbirth educator may even be the nurse who works in the labor room.

Balance these facts about hospital classes with those about ones offered on the outside. Since classes are usually smaller, you'll probably get more personal attention and have more access to the instructor. Says Sporn: "There's a tremendous amount of information that can be passed in a small class. I offer tips—such as turn off the lights to relax." Your

BECOMING A FAMILY | 23

instructor also has a clearly defined role—to serve you, not the hospital where she's employed. The instructor may emphasize a variety of techniques, since she's not being paid to promulgate the party line. The disadvantages are also clear: less peer review and a possible unfamiliarity with what's going on inside a particular hospital.

For recommendations about childbirth education classes, ask your doctor, the hospital where you plan to give birth, or professional childbirth education organizations. You might be in touch with:

- **ASPO/Lamaze** (Box 725, Midtown Station, New York, N.Y. 10018: 212-831-9327) or the national headquarters (800-368-4404), which will refer you to instructors who teach the Lamaze technique of childbirth based on the ideas of the French obstetrician Dr. Fernand Lamaze. Among its more famous practitioners is Elisabeth Bing, who runs the Elisabeth Bing Center for Parents.

- **Bradley** (c/o American Academy of Husband-Coached Childbirth, Box 5224, Sherman Oaks, Calif. 91413: 800-423-2397), which will send you a list of local teachers who follow the precepts of Dr. Robert Bradley.

- **Metropolitan New York/Childbirth Education Association** (P.O. Box 2036, New York, N.Y. 10185: 212-866-6373 or 6 Tuxedo Avenue, New Hyde Park, N.Y. 10040: 516-741-0375), which stresses the Co-operative method of childbirth. Their classes begin early in pregnancy.

Don't hesitate to ask a childbirth educator the following:

- What method do you follow?
- What is your training and certification?
- What is the size of the class that you teach?
- What does your class cover? Can you send me an outline or a reading list? If some particular aspect of childbirth is critical to you, find out if it will be covered before the class begins.

Talk with former students. What do they say? Was the educator accessible to them to answer questions? What was the educator's attitude toward physicians or midwives?

Childbirth education classes are not for parents only. The Maternity Center Association has sibling preparation classes open to the public. Designed for siblings between the ages of two and eight, the classes use illustrations, soft sculptures, dolls with umbilical cords, and photographs of newborns to show children what happens before and after birth. Children practice holding, diapering, and dressing dolls. For details, contact the Parent Education Department (212-369-7300). You'll also find sibling education classes at several area hospitals.

▽ ▽ ▽ ▽ ▽ ▽ ▽ ▽ ▽ ▽ ▽

GENETIC COUNSELING

Chances are that if you are over thirty-five, your doctor will ask you to consider genetic counseling. The genetic counselor, affiliated with a hospital, will discuss with you the outpatient procedures that can be used today to identify possible genetic problems in the fetus. Using a procedure known as amniocentesis, a physician can extract for analysis a small amount of amniotic fluid surrounding the fetus. This diagnostic test, done during the woman's second trimester of pregnancy, can detect chromosomal abnormalities, including those resulting from Down syndrome. A second test, chorionic villi sampling (CVS), performed around the eighth week of pregnancy, is being done experimentally at several hospitals, including Presbyterian, Mount Sinai, and New York Hospital–Cornell Medical Center in Manhattan. If either of these tests reveals a genetic abnormality, you will be given information about a therapeutic abortion.

You may also be referred for prenatal diagnostic testing if you are Jewish (to assess the chances of your being a carrier of Tay-Sachs), if you are black (to determine whether you are a carrier of sickle cell anemia), if you are of Mediterranean descent (to determine whether you are a carrier of thalassemia), if you have given birth to a child with a hereditary disease, or if you are known to have a family history of birth defects.

For an interesting discussion of genetic counseling, see Barbara Katz Rothman, *The Tentative Pregnancy* (New York: Penguin, 1987).

△ △ △ △ △ △ △ △ △ △ △

Adopting a Child

Make our Easter a happy one. Couple seeks to adopt healthy, white infant. CALL...

That was the simple message that Jessica and John Wadsworth sent out. The Wadsworths, a couple in their thirties, wanted to be parents and

Jessica had been trying unsuccessfully to become pregnant for several years. They decided that their route to parenthood lay in pursuing a nonagency (known as a private or independent) adoption to find a healthy white newborn. So they placed this advertisement in the classified section of several community newspapers around the country, hoping that a pregnant woman would get in touch.

"It was horrible to sit by the telephone," recalls Jessica. But one night, a few months after the Wadsworths started running the ads, the phone rang and on the line was a young woman, far into her pregnancy, interested in talking about placing her baby. They chatted, and over the next few weeks, spoke again and again. Through the help of two attorneys (one representing them, one the birth mother), the possible adoption was discussed and some tentative arrangements were made. When their son was just three days old, Jessica and John brought him home. Recalls Jessica: "It was so exciting. It's so hard to believe that adoptions happen all the time."

They do. Carolyn and Tim O'Malley are the parents of two children—Rebecca, aged six, and Sean, aged nine months—placed with them as babies with the help of a Catholic adoption agency, not a want ad. Linda Small is a single parent whose six-year-old daughter, Lisa, came through an agency that concentrates on finding new parents for older children. Lisa began living with Linda first as a foster child. Isaac and Susan Bernstein's two children were born in South Korea and joined their family as infants through the intercountry adoption program of Spence-Chapin Services to Families and Children. Sylvia and Warren Hager also adopted from abroad, but arranged the adoption of their son in Colombia themselves. The options are several and New Yorkers do them all.

If you are considering an adoption, you probably start with some questions. Any adoption you pursue, whether agency or independent, must be finalized in a court of law. All agency adoptions follow a basic pattern. You find an agency to work with and file an application. An agency worker does a "home study" of your family. This typically involves a series of meetings, interviews, and sometimes training sessions conducted by an agency worker. The home study culminates in a written report that describes you and recommends that a child be placed in your home. You work with the agency personnel to find a child. The agency may select a child for you from among its children or you may search for a child by contacting special adoption exchanges. Or you may apply to a foreign agency. Finally, a child is placed with you. After a prescribed waiting period, the adoption is finalized in court. With an independent U.S. adoption, you may bypass an agency initially (a home study in some states is done after the baby is in your home), but you still must complete the adoption in court.

While this section can just skim the surface, the summary that follows should orient you to the logistics and red tape that are so much a part of this family-making process (for a fuller description of adoption, see Lois Gilman, *The Adoption Resource Book,* New York: Harper & Row, 1987). You should also be in touch with an adoption support group (some are connected to agencies; a few others are mentioned in this book) for guidance.

◆ **Agency Adoptions of U.S.-born Children:** Agencies place both infants and older children. The largest number of children available for adoption are Black and Hispanic. Many of the white children placed through agencies are older, often more than ten years old, part of a sibling group, or have a physical, mental, or emotional handicap. All agencies place babies, but the number of healthy white infants can be quite small in comparison to the demand. The waiting period for a child can vary from a few weeks or months to years. A couple hoping to adopt a white infant is likely be told the wait could be long.

When an agency has difficulty finding adoptive parents for a particular child, it places a photo listing (photograph and description) of a child in one of a series of volumes called *New York State's Waiting Children,* known as the "Blue Books" because of their color. These books, available at adoption agencies and at some public libraries, contain photo listings of several hundred children from New York State. You can look through them to see if there's a featured child who interests you. The listings are updated biweekly. When a child is deemed "hard to place" because of age or the need for special care, the state will offer a subsidy (a monthly payment) for the child.

There is one public agency, Special Services for Children, and some thirty private adoption agencies in New York City alone. All agencies are required by New York State to hold a monthly orientation meeting for prospective adoptive parents. For information about agencies, you might want to get the New York Junior League's *Adoption: A Guide to Adopting in the New York Area* (available from the Adoption Opportunities Committee, Junior League of the City of New York, 130 East 80 Street, New York, N.Y. 10021: 212-288-6220), which gives a detailed description of the agencies and the type of children they frequently place. You can also call New York City's Adoption and Foster Care Hotline (212-266-2273). They'll send you basic information sheets, including a list of New York State agencies. If you wish, they will refer you to a particular agency.

◆ **Adopting Independently:** This form of adoption is legal in New York State and is often pursued when people want to adopt healthy white newborns. Couples or singles find a mother (and sometimes a father) willing to place her child with them. Often they pay her medical and legal expenses. They gamble emotionally and financially, fearing that the birth parents may change their minds—before or after the birth (birth parents have a legally mandated period of time in which they are permitted to change their minds and may revoke their consent). Once the waiting period has elapsed, the birth parents have no legal claim on the child.

The first step is to find the birth mother. Many people succeed through "spreading the word," telling everyone they know—family, friends, neighbors, colleagues, doctors, even the hairdresser—about their interest in adopting. Some blanket the United States with letters; others mail out biographies with photos of themselves. Still others, like the Wadsworths, advertise. Quite often, within months or weeks of beginning their search, they become parents.

The legitimate costs, including medical and legal fees and perhaps a stipend for reasonable living expenses, can run from a few thousand dollars to as much as $10,000. Medical complications such as a cesarean can skyrocket costs if the birth mother has no health insurance. Because their son's birth mother had complete medical coverage, the Wadsworths spent less than $3,000, including $1,600 for attorneys' fees and $600 for advertising. If they'd adopted a hard-to-place child through an agency, there could have been no fee; if they'd adopted an infant, however, the agency would most likely have based the fee on a percentage of their income.

If you are tempted to pursue an independent adoption, be sure that you understand exactly what is allowable under New York State law. All expenses should be clearly documented. Examine any fee carefully to see if it is consistent with the time spent and the services provided. You should not be financing down payments on homes, vacations, or college tuitions. Beware of adoption entrepreneurs or search services who promise to find babies for you. Don't give anyone a "finder's fee."

◆ **Adopting from Abroad:** People seeking to adopt younger children often turn to foreign sources, since infants are more readily placed, usually within a few months to two years of filing an application. The majority of intercountry adoptions are arranged by U.S. agencies working with a foreign counterpart. Some people, however, prefer working directly with foreign agencies or private intermediaries. Most intercountry adoptions involve children coming from India, Latin America, the Philippines, and South Korea.

All foreign adoptions require a home study and must be approved by the U.S. Immigration and Naturalization Service (26 Federal Plaza, New York, N.Y. 10278: for forms, call 212-349-5286), as well as by New York State and the country of origin. The costs are usually $5,000 to $10,000. Adoptive parent groups can get you started.

▽ ▽ ▽ ▽ ▽ ▽ ▽ ▽ ▽ ▽ ▽ ▽

WHAT YOU'LL WANT TO ASK YOURSELF—AND OTHERS—ABOUT ADOPTION

If You Expect to Be Working with an Agency, Inquire:

- What are your requirements for people wishing to adopt?
- What are your fees?
- What type of children are in your agency's caseload (infants, older children, white, Black, Hispanic, sibling groups, handicapped?) How many children did your agency place last year? What were the characteristics of those children? How long is the wait for a particular type of child?
- How long after I apply does the home study begin?
- Could you describe your home study process and how long it is likely to take?
- What type of contact, if any, does your agency encourage between birth parents and adoptive parents?
- What type of pre- and post-placement support services do you offer adoptive families?

If You Are Thinking about an Independent Adoption, You Need to Determine:

- How do you plan on going about finding a child? Do you feel comfortable running an advertisement in a newspaper?
- If you have a particular situation in mind, are the circumstances involved legal in New York State?

- What are the projected expenses? Can you afford them?
- Are you willing to have contact with the birth parents?
- What medical problems in the child, if any, will you accept?
- Whom will you turn to for legal advice? What role does your attorney expect to play? What are the fees? Have you arranged for separate counsel for the birth parents?
- How much risk and uncertainty are you willing to live with?

If You Are Considering an Intercountry Adoption, Decide:

- What type of family history do you feel you need to have for a child? What medical problems in the child, if any, will you accept?
- Do you want to adopt through an intercountry agency adoption program or do you want to try adopting independently?
- What expenses can you afford?
- Can you take the time to travel abroad to pick up your child?

△ △ △ △ △ △ △ △ △ △ △

Talking About Being a Parent

The vision of mommies sitting day in and day out on the park bench exchanging child-rearing tips has faded as women in ever-increasing numbers have returned to work. Yet the desire to share the ups and downs of parenting remains. It begins with the need to bemoan your exhausted state with another who's been kept up all night by an incessantly demanding infant. Later the subjects are different: How do you discipline a two-year-old? Is there a right or wrong way to toilet train? Can you go back to work and not feel guilty? How does a working mother apportion her time?

Parents are still talking to each other about child rearing, but more often in organized programs at hospitals, schools, Y's, community centers, and the American Red Cross than in the park. Observes Susan Ginsberg of the Bank Street College of Education: "Women have a lack of confidence that they're an 'OK' mother. They read so much and all the advice is conflicting. Working parents have a lack of opportunity to talk about issues. The nonworking ones feel isolated and the working ones feel isolated. People have a need to talk."

Perhaps the first parenting program that you'll enroll in will be the one offered at the hospital where you give birth. Consider what you can find at some Manhattan hospitals. Classes at New York Hospital, grouped together under the rubric of "The Childbearing Year," start with the childbirth-oriented classes: early pregnancy, preparation for vaginal or cesarean birth, "refresher" courses for second-timers, and sibling tours. There's also "adapting to parenthood." After the baby's born and the mother's still in the hospital, there are lecture/demonstrations on baby care, feeding, burping, and behavioral development. After discharge, the mother is welcome to enroll in a "new mothers" discussion group. In addition, the Department of Pediatrics sponsors a "Parents' Lecture Series," which looks at children's health care issues. Topics have ranged from "Stress Between Parents and Children and Peer Pressure" to "Sex Education" to a panel in which you ask physicians about any pediatric health questions you've got. (To be put on the mailing list for these free lectures, call the Development Office: 212-472-6693.)

Presbyterian Hospital offers as many choices, including a telephone counseling service for moments of panic after the baby's at home, while the Department of Pediatrics at Mount Sinai has held an annual spring lecture series, "Children in the Eighties," covering newborns to adolescents (call 212-650-6737—the Postgraduate School—for details). At Lenox Hill Hospital you'll find the so-called Skhool for Parents (100 East 77 Street, New York, N.Y. 10021: 212-877-8700). Its basic curriculum, "Guidelines to Easier Parenting," touches on discipline, independence, sexuality, aggression, and communication, while an "advanced" curriculum tackles single parenting or raising a handicapped child.

Hospital-based programs are just one category of many that have blossomed in recent years. Says Ginsberg: "There's an enormous potpourri of programs. It's staggering. It's really amazing how much there is." Some of the programs are intended to serve solely as settings for parents to meet informally and talk. Others, drawing upon specialists in child development, have formal curricula designed to make people more effective parents. To sample what's available:

♦ **At Y's and Community Centers:** The Parenting Center at Manhattan's 92 Street Y (1395 Lexington Avenue, New York, N.Y. 10128: 212-427-6000) is known citywide and has served as the model for many community-based programs. You'll find discussion groups for new mothers and fathers (and special programs for adoptive parents), seminars on topics ranging from "Sleep" to "When Parents Disagree." Its most legendary offering is "Parkbench" for mothers, fathers, or caregivers. Substituting a playroom for a park, the Y gives people a place to talk at designated times while their children run around. So that working moms don't feel left out, there's a special evening session. In fact, all over the city, the Y's and community centers are catering to parents. At the Brooklyn YWCA, the offerings have run the gamut from a new mothers' support group to discussions about how to choose "the best book for preschoolers" and how to make the best use of attractions in downtown Brooklyn. You'll find special programs for single parents, for example, at the Samuel Field YM-YWHA in Queens. To learn what your local Y or community center offers (see Chapter Two for names and addresses), call them.

◆ **At Special Parenting and Family Centers:** The Elisabeth Bing Center for Parents (164 West 79 Street, New York, N.Y. 10024: 212-362-5304) and Family Focus (1370 Lexington Avenue, New York, N.Y. 10128: 212-410-0035) are two places in Manhattan with parenting classes. In Brooklyn, Families First (250 Baltic Street, Brooklyn, N.Y. 11201: 718-855-3131) serves parents of children up to three years old with drop-in hours, support groups, mother-infant-toddler programs, and special events, such as the annual "Nursery School Fair."

◆ **In Churches and Synagogues:** The Archdiocese of New York's Parent Education Office (203 Sand Lane, Staten Island, N.Y. 10305: 718-816-7801) runs a series of programs: "Good Beginnings" (birth to three; special group also for adoptive parents), "Growing Up Together" (four to adolescence), and "Parents and Teens Together." At Our Lady Queen of Peace on Staten Island (62 Cloister Place: 718-351-8589), there's a Parenting Center. You'll also find similar centers in other churches. The Union of American Hebrew Congregations (838 Fifth Avenue, New York, N.Y. 10021: 212-249-0100), the parent body for Reform Judaism, has initiated nationwide Jewish Parenting Centers for parents with infants and toddlers. You'll find one at Manhattan's Stephen Wise Free Synagogue (30 West 68 Street, New York, N.Y. 10023: 212-877-4050). Check with the U.A.H.C. about others.

◆ **In College Classrooms:** The Bank Street College of Education (610 West 112 Street, New York, N.Y. 10025: 212-663-7200) has developed weekend workshops for parents. Among previous offerings: "Choosing Child Care," "Think Before You Talk: How to Communicate Effectively with Your Kids," and "Getting Through the Toddler Years." The Parent

Service Center at Pace University has discussion groups for parents of children from the ages of newborn to three. Classes, combining parent talk with child play, are organized by the age of the child. Check with the Department of Psychology, School of Continuing Education, or School of Education at your local university or college. If you've got a question about child rearing, you can call the CHIPS' Warm Line, manned by New York University's Children and Infant Parenting Service (212-598-3174). This hotline, under the direction of psychologist Lawrence Balter, gives nonmedical advice to parents. You might ask about sleeping, eating, crying, discipline, or tantrums. Call, leave a message, and within forty-eight hours someone connected with the service will get in touch with you.

◆ **In Your Doctor's Office:** Parents typically look to their child's doctor for advice on child rearing. Some pediatricians have now set up structured (and usually free) educational programs in their offices. Patients who use the group practice of Queens pediatrician Dr. Ivan Koota, for example, can participate in expectant parents' evenings, mothers' discussion groups, and classes in first aid and infant care. The physicians also lecture at the local Y. On staff is a parent educator, and one room in the office is designated for use as the "Parent Room," containing a lending library and a bulletin board with community and program notices. Says Dr. Koota: "We look upon our program often as a symbol, a statement that we are interested in problems. We care to hear when you have the need to tell."

◆ **In Support Groups:** If you've got a special interest, such as raising twins or adopted children, there's a parent group just for you. The New York City **Self-Help Clearinghouse** (1012 Eighth Avenue, Brooklyn, N.Y. 11215: 718-788-8787) can also steer you to specialized groups. New moms and dads can also link up with **Parents' Resources** (Box 107, Planetarium Station, New York, N.Y. 10024: 212-866-4776), which organizes neighborhood peer support groups. This organization, whose membership comes primarily from Manhattan, also has an informative newsletter and holds periodic forums on topics such as "Feeding and Nutrition" and "Child Safety." You can also order reprints of articles from the newsletter. For a local referral, you can also check with the **Family Resource Coalition** (230 North Michigan Avenue, Chicago, Ill. 60601: 312-726-4750), which serves as a national clearinghouse.

You might also want to subscribe to one of the specialized New York

City newsletters that have made their debut in recent years. Among them: *The Big Apple Parents' Paper* (212-254-0853), *PARENTGUIDE NEWS* (800-824-5000), *The New York Parents & Kids Directory* (212-473-3348), and *New York Family* (212-744-0309). To see samples, check doctors' offices, schools and libraries for drop copies.

HELP WITH SPECIAL CONCERNS

Adoption

- **Adoptive Parents Committee** (210 Fifth Avenue, New York, N.Y. 10010: 212-683-9221): Parent support group, with chapters in the city, Long Island, and Westchester. Many members have adopted independently or from abroad. Annual adoption conference held in November.
- **Center for Adoptive Families/Brief Family Therapy Center** (430 West 14 Street, New York, N.Y. 10014: 212-645-2112): Short-term family therapy for adoptive families and individuals.
- **Council on Adoptable Children** (666 Broadway, New York, N.Y. 10012: 212-475-0222): Advocacy group for the adoption of Black, Hispanic, and special needs children.
- **Latin America Parents Association** (P.O. Box 72, Seaford, N.Y. 11783: 516-795-7427): Parent support group whose members have adopted—or plan to adopt—from Central and South America. Fact sheets provide an overview of adoption, current "sources," immigration and naturalization information, travel help, local attorneys, social workers, and translators. Frequent how-to workshops.

Child Abuse

- **New York State Child Abuse and Maltreatment Center** (800-342-3720): To report a case of suspected child abuse anytime. To report cases involving the sexual abuse of children to the New York City Police Department, dial 911 if there is an emergency in progress or call the Sex Crimes Report Line at 212-732-7706 or your local police precinct.
- **Emergency Children's Service** (241 Church Street, New York, N.Y. 10013: 212-334-7676): Emergency assistance for the abused, assaulted, maltreated, or neglected child.
- **New York Foundling Hospital Crisis Intervention Nursery** (1175 Third Avenue, New York, N.Y. 10021: 212-472-8555 or 212-472-2233, extension 604): For emergency placement of a preschool child of a parent

under stress. This nursery is a seven-day-a-week *free* service that accommodates up to ten preschool children for at least two days and provides a "cooling off" period for their parents.

Death and Grief

- **Bereavement and Loss Center of New York** (170 East 83 Street, New York, N.Y. 10028: 212-879-5655): Counseling available.
- **Early Childhood Bereavement Project** (Columbia–Presbyterian Medical Center, New York, N.Y. 10032: 212-960-2344): Free counseling and evaluation service for children ages three to six who have lost a parent within the preceding four months.
- **Helping Children in Crisis** (New York Center for Crisis Services, 305 West End Avenue, New York, N.Y. 10023: 212-570-7035): This program helps respond to children's needs in dealing with a loss, including the death of a classmate or a parent, or divorce. Counseling for families is also available.
- **New York City Information and Counseling Program for Sudden Infant Death** (520 First Avenue, New York, N.Y. 10016: 212-866-8854): Crisis intervention and bereavement counseling for families to whom SIDS has happened. Monthly parent group meetings, networking, and individual counseling available.

Fathering

- **Bank Street College of Education's Fatherhood Project** (610 West 112 Street, New York, N.Y. 10025: 212-663-7200): This nationwide research effort looked at male involvement in child rearing and culminated with the publication of the comprehensive resource book *Fatherhood USA* (New York: Garland, 1984). The Fatherhood Project still serves as an information clearinghouse. They'll tell you where special workshops for fathers take place and can direct you to groups such as Gay Fathers Forum of New York and Equal Rights for Fathers (chapters throughout the state).

Hospitalized Child

- **Parents for Parents** (125 Northmore Drive, Yorktown Heights, N.Y. 10598: 914-962-3326): A self-help group that uses a telephone network to provide support for parents of hospitalized children. Meetings at Presbyterian and other metropolitan-area hospitals.
- **Parent Care** (University of Utah Medical Center, 50 North Medical Drive, Salt Lake City, Utah 84132: 801-581-5323): Links parents of critically ill newborns with support groups. They'll direct you to local groups.

Interracial Families

- **Biracial Family Resource Center** (800 Riverside Drive, New York, N.Y. 10032: 212-928-7601): Organizes support groups, events for children, and seminars.
- **Council on Interracial Books for Children** (1841 Broadway, New York, N.Y. 10023: 212-757-5339): Although this group's main function is to analyze books for children, they held a landmark conference on "Children of Interracial Families" in 1984. They can direct you to resource materials for parents and children.
- **INTERace** (P.O. Box 7143, Flushing, N.Y. 11352): For couples and people of mixed racial heritage to discuss problems and participate in lectures, entertainment, and counseling.

Missing Children

- **National Center for Missing and Exploited Children** (800-843-5678) and **Missing Children Search** (800-222-1464): Two nationwide hotlines. Locally, call 911. If you think your child is a runaway, contact the twenty-four-hour Runaway Hotline operated by the Victim Services Agency (212-61-YOUTH) and the National Runaway Switchboard (800-621-4000).

Sex Education

- **Planned Parenthood's Parent Education Program** (161-10 Jamaica Avenue, Jamaica, N.Y. 11432: 718-526-5990 and 349 East 149 Street, Bronx, N.Y. 10451: 212-292-8000): Help with how to talk to your kids about sex. PEP organizes workshops and seminars (also special programs just for teenagers) and will take their program to your group.

Single Parents

- **Kindred Spirits** (c/o Manhattan's 92 Street Y: 212-427-6000): Brings together single parents and children with extensive programming and workshops in the boroughs and surrounding suburbs.
- **Parents without Partners** (8807 Colesville Road, Silver Spring, Md. 20910: 301-588-9354 or 800-638-8078): Self-help group that provides support and information about single parenting issues. There are chapters around the city and the national organization can direct you to them.
- **Single Mothers by Choice** (P.O. Box 7788, F.D.R. Station, New York, N.Y. 10150: 212-988-0993): Support group for women who have decided to have a baby outside of wedlock.
- **Single Parent Resource Center** (1165 Broadway, New York, N.Y. 10001: 212-213-0047): Clearinghouse of information on single parent

programs in the United States and abroad. Educational and recreational activities for parents and children are offered.
- **Sisterhood of Black Single Mothers** (1360 Fulton Street, Brooklyn, N.Y. 11216: 718-638-0413): Self-help organization of Black women who are either separated, divorced, never married, widowed, or whose men are incarcerated.

Stepfamilies

- **Stepfamily Association, New York Chapter** (c/o Jewish Board of Family and Children's Services, 120 West 57 Street, New York, N.Y. 10019: 212-582-9100): Support groups, workshops, networking for parents and children.

Twins and Triplets:

- **National Organization of Mothers of Twins Clubs, Inc.** (12404 Princess Jeanne, N.E., Albuquerque, N.M. 87112-4640: 505-275-0955): For parents of twins, triplets, quadruplets, and quintuplets, parents of adopted children born at approximately the same time, and grandparents. Local clubs (call the national office for help in finding the borough chapters) meet to discuss care and other topics. The local clubs are also a great resource for parents of children close in age who need to buy used twin baby furniture and paraphernalia such as strollers or carriages, since the clubs maintain a list of used equipment for sale.

△   △   △   △   △   △   △   △   △   △   △

chapter 2
choosing child care

Five years ago the Golden family faced the challenge of relocating to Manhattan from out of state when Edward got a teaching job at a local university. Housing and even a job transfer for Louise fell into place with surprising ease, but then came the hitch. Recalls Louise: "We had to start work right away, and where would we find good and affordable child care for our one-year-old and two-year-old on short notice? In the beginning I thought I'd put the two children in a day-care center. However, when I started to call, I learned that the few centers near our home did not take children under three." Louise's next step was to call a few women she'd heard about who provided family day care for children in their homes. "One woman boasted to me that each year one of her day-care charges had been accepted to Hunter's nursery school. She was sure that would interest me."

But Louise was concerned with arranging child care now, not with getting her children into Harvard at the turn of the century, and the charge of $200 per week seemed very steep for out-of-home care. Finally, Louise talked with a colleague's wife who said she'd check at the local sandbox: "Alice called me up excitedly, said, 'Get Danielle,' and hung up." Danielle, an energetic twenty-two-year-old, was the prized sitter of Alice's friend, and the family had just announced that they were moving. "It was crazy. I checked out her references and then I called her up. We talked. I said, 'We have to meet first, but will you consider working for us?' Alice was right. We didn't need enrichment programs. We needed Danielle, and we got her, and we've had her ever since."

What are the arrangements that New York's working parents make? Child Care, Inc., New York City's child care information and resource service, hears from over four thousand parents each year who are looking for child care and educational programs for their children. Sandy Socolar, director of their Child Care Information Service, notes: "With families so scattered these days, it's surprising how many new parents are able to work out their child care arrangements within their immediate family, either with the help of a grandparent or an aunt, or by alternating their working hours so they can divide their child care between themselves." Socolar reports, however, that "this tends not to last, and after the first nine months to a year, they too are looking for some kind of child care outside their family." At this point, some opt for in-home care by a nanny; many take their children to the home of a friend or neighbor. A few are able to find space in one of the limited number of infant-toddler centers in New York City.

Based on parent calls to Child Care, Inc., Socolar reports that "most children under two are in the care of an individual, either in their home or in the caregiver's home." By the time that a child is two years old, however, Child Care, Inc., has found that most parents would like their children to be in a good educational setting with a good teacher and other children. Says Socolar: "Most of the parents are looking for an all-day center to fit their working hours. However, some prefer a part-day program—a nursery school in the mornings, for example—and continue to have their nanny or a neighbor care for their child the rest of the time." A family's child care plan generally differs from year to year as the child grows and the family's needs change. This chapter will explore all these possibilities.

All working parents follow similar steps in arranging child care. First you ask: What's available? There are three basic alternatives: (1) a caregiver in your home; (2) family day care provided by an individual in her home for your child and usually several others, including perhaps the caregiver's children; and (3) group care offered in a day-care center or school. Then you need to determine if the situation is within reach, geographically and financially. Observes Anne Mitchell, a child care expert at the Bank Street College of Education: "Thinking about cost is critical. The younger the child, the harder it is to find child care and the more it is going to cost. If your child is three, you have more options." Parents who may fondly recall their own service as occasional dollar-an-hour baby-sitters often have no idea of the expense of child care in New York today and are shocked to find out.

Finally, you've got to evaluate how you feel about the various child care options. If you believe that babies belong at home in their own cribs, you probably won't be excited to learn that a model infant-toddler center is located down the street. But if you feel that young children thrive on stimulation from others, you're more likely to consider the center as a possibility. If this is the first time you are looking for child care, you may not yet have a clear sense of your own feelings. Start by asking relatives, friends, and neighbors about their child care arrangements. Ask them: What do they like about it? What do they dislike? Had they tried something else? If so, why did they make the switch? The following questions may also prove helpful:

- How important do you feel it is for your child to be in his own home? How much time each day do you feel that he should spend at home?
- How important do you feel it is for your child to spend time with other children? For what period of time?
- How much stimulation do you want your child to have? What kind? From whom? At what age?
- How important is continuity of care to you? In which situation are you likely to get continuity of care? How will you feel if you have to hire several people over the course of a year to care for your child in your home?
- If you are thinking about taking your child outside your home, how much time do you want to spend making him commute? How far away from home—or office—do you want to go?
- What attracts you most about in-home care? What worries you?
- What attracts you most about center care? What worries you?
- What attracts you most about care outside your home? What worries you?
- How much of a concern is it to you that your child may pick up colds, diarrhea, or other common childhood illnesses in an out-of-home setting? Will your own work schedule be flexible enough, or will you have the backup, to accommodate his inevitable sick days?
- What will fit best into your family and work life?
- What can you really afford to pay for child care? How much of your paycheck would you like to allocate for child care?

What's Available: Information and Referral

While recommendations from relatives, friends, and neighbors are often the keys to finding child care, there are more systematic ways to help you collect information. **Child Care, Inc.** (275 Seventh Avenue, New York, N.Y. 10001: 212-929-4999; hrs.: Mon.–Thurs. 11–4) serves parents in the five boroughs through its free telephone consultation *Child Care Information Service.* Its files contain data about all licensed centers and services in the city (arranged by ZIP code). Its counselors can advise you on topics ranging from infant-toddler programs, family day-care agencies, day-care centers, nursery schools, and kindergartens to school-age programs for after-school, vacations, and holidays. Says Socolar: "We keep detailed information on each program's service options, including the ages of children the program enrolls, the hours of service they offer each age group—part-day, school-day, or all-day—and for school children, which schools are served by each after-school program. The child care information is maintained in five borough resource books, and we provide parents with printed lists of the programs in their neighborhood or on their way to work." Child Care, Inc., has also produced a number of booklets and fact sheets (available free or at a nominal fee) covering everything from basic financial data to things to look for if you are considering hiring an in-home caregiver, finding a family day-care home, or deciding on a school or center for child care.

Child Care, Inc., advises on strategies for finding child care and identifies places for you to check. It does not, however, tell you about specific openings. You will need to phone to find out the exact hours a center or school is open, their fees for the length of day you need, and whether they have openings in your child's age group. Child Care, Inc., does not list individual job applicants.

Manhattan residents can also turn to two more specialized referral centers. The **Family Resource Center** (137 East 2 Street, New York, N.Y. 10009: 212-677-6602) maintains a family day-care provider registry for Lower Manhattan, as well as a baby-sitter registry for the five boroughs. You can obtain the names of individuals screened by the Center—which interviews and checks the references of its applicants, and inspects the homes of family day-care providers. The Center also maintains an emergency referral service listing people willing to provide backup child care on days that your child or caregiver is ill, as well as a co-operative child care registry for baby-sitting exchanges and playgroups. The **West Side Y's Family Center** (5 West 63 Street, New York, N.Y. 10023: 212-787-4400) has a similar registry (available to you after an interview) of people looking for full- and part-time work.

If you live or work in Westchester, the **Child Care Council of Westchester** (470 Mamaroneck Avenue, White Plains, N.Y. 10605: 914-761-3456) gives advice on day-care centers, in-home care, family day care, after-school programs, and summer camps. The Child Care Council will also direct you to specific family day-care providers (whom they have investigated). Family day care is a large part of the referral service of the **Day Care Council of Nassau County** (54 Washington Street, Hempstead, N.Y. 11550: 516-538-1362). Their Child Care Switchboard keeps track of registered family day-care homes. These caregivers are trained by the Day Care Council. Observes one counselor: "We know what the person is like, as well as geographic and other details. We do outreach and find the people who do family day care. We actively recruit day-care providers." You can also ask the Day Care Council of Nassau County about day-care centers and schools.

No matter how good an information service is, there are many kinds of child care you will probably have to locate on your own. Reports Anne Mitchell: "The research on how people find child care shows that it is through word of mouth or driving around or seeing signs for things. It's a real folksy way of getting information." Fortified with what you learn from others, you're ready to begin your own search.

The Basics: In-home Care

Shortly after Bonita Brewer, who lives on the Upper West Side, gave birth to her daughter four years ago, she found her home caregiver. "Fenula had come to our building to interview for a job as a companion," Bonita recalls. "As she was leaving, she told the doorman that she was looking for a baby-sitting job. Our doorman knew that I had just had a baby and that I worked. He suspected that I might be looking for a sitter. So he told me." The match was made.

Hiring someone to work in their home is the preference of many families, but it is usually the most expensive form of child care available. Sandy Socolar estimates that the cost of in-home care ranges between $160 and $400 weekly ($8,300 and $20,000 a year), with most parents paying between $180 and $250 a week ($9,400 and $13,000 a year) for forty to fifty hours of care. Ilana Knapp of the Working Mother's Committee of the Financial Women's Association of New York (many of whose members live in Manhattan, Brooklyn Heights, or Park Slope) estimates that colleagues pay between $225 and $375 a week plus carfare, with the average being $260. The real costs of in-home care are higher than the base pay, however. Your expenses are likely to include carfare (as much as four rides per day if your employee is commuting from an outer borough), taxes, and benefits: two weeks' or more paid vacation, and compensation for sick days and holidays. You may decide to pay for health insurance coverage, and you will probably want to give her a bonus at Christmas. Nor will you necessarily save money if you hire someone to live in. According to one mother who's tried both: "It's no cheaper for live-in. People don't seem to consider room and board as part of their salary." Live-in caregivers tend to work longer hours, and many of them need to meet the cost of maintaining a permanent residence elsewhere to which they can go on days off.

Many people succeed in finding an in-home caregiver by telling friends, neighbors, or perhaps the wife of their building's superintendent. Or they may tack up notices (with little pull-off flaps listing their phone number) at the obstetrician's or pediatrician's office, in a playroom, a supermarket, or innumerable other places where parents and children get together. In Manhattan, some overeager mothers have even approached caregivers in the park and asked them if they are happy in their present job. More often, they inquire around the park bench if anyone "knows someone who's leaving." It's also common to advertise in the "Help Wanted" section of *The New York Times*, in the local *Pennysaver*, or newspapers such as *The Village Voice, Our Town, France Amérique,* or the *Bayside Times*. The *Irish Echo* has become a key place to advertise for applicants of all nationalities and ethnic backgrounds.

You can also check with the Household Employment Office of the New York State Employment Service, which has offices in the five boroughs. Employment agencies in the metropolitan area also advertise home care placements, including baby nurse services, full-time permanent child care, part-time child care, and one-time-only baby-sitters. They can save you time by doing an initial screening of applicants for a fee.

There are many sources for finding people from abroad to work for you. Some agencies will suggest that they can help. You can also consider looking for someone abroad through your personal connections or by checking the "Situations Wanted" section of *The New York Times'* Sunday classified ads. This procedure also involves considerable paperwork.

You must certify that you have had no success in filling the job with a U.S. worker. Your first step is to apply for "labor certification," filing forms with the New York State Labor Department's Alien Certification Office (718-797-7224). Once the job has been certified, you must file Form I-140, along with the certification and supporting documents, with the United States Immigration and Naturalization Service. There are still further steps after that. For advice on this very complicated procedure, contact an experienced immigration attorney. The legal referral service of the Association of the Bar of the City of New York (212-382-6625) or that of the American Immigration Lawyers Association (202-331-0046) can help.

Chances are that you also have known families with a foreign *au pair* residing with them. What you may not have realized is that this is typically an illegal arrangement, since the young people have usually entered on tourist or student visas. In 1986, two experimental programs, sanctioned by the federal government, got under way to permit Western Europeans between the ages of eighteen and twenty-five to come to the United States legally on a cultural exchange (J-1) visa to live with American host families to do paid child care *for one year*. After that the young people are expected to return to their countries of residence. To learn about these programs, both of which are currently placing *au pairs* in New York City, contact the Au Pair in America Program (AIFS Scholarship Foundation, 100 Greenwich Avenue, Greenwich, Conn. 06830: 800-243-4567 or 203-869-9090) and AuPair/Homestay USA (c/o Experiment in International Living, 1522 K Street N.W., Washington, D.C. 20005: 202-371-9410).

Whether you want a live-in caregiver or someone who works days, and whether you use an agency or search on your own, you'll still need to determine:

- What the days and hours are that your employee will work.
- What the pay will be (how much you are paying and what you will pay for overtime; when you will pay your employee and if you are paying by cash or check; what holidays and vacation your employee is entitled to; how you will handle sick days; how much Social Security you are paying; whether you will provide health insurance coverage).
- What you expect in the care of your child.
- What other tasks your caregiver is expected to perform—for example, cleaning, cooking, or laundry.

- What your policy is on visitors, phone calls, and television watching.
- What the terms are for you—or your employee—to give notice of termination of the job and what pay your employee will be entitled to.
- What personal rules of conduct are acceptable to both you and a live-in caregiver to assure that you can both comfortably occupy the same space.

Before you start your search, sort these matters out. Compile a worksheet for your use that outlines the job and your requirements. When you describe your job to an agency or to a prospective employee, have it handy so that you can go over the key points.

When You Turn to an Agency

Audrey Valentine has used several agencies, starting when she was pregnant and searching for a baby nurse. She recalls: "I wanted someone to take care of our new baby, but also someone to take care of us. I wanted someone to cook and clean." On the advice of friends, Audrey contacted one of the well-known baby nurse/nanny agencies, but was told that their women usually took care of the baby only, and "might, in fact, expect to be cooked for." She ended up using a less specialized employment agency, hiring a woman who would cook and shop and get up in the middle of the night. Several years later, Audrey went to another agency to find a live-in caregiver. She insisted on visiting the agency because "If you do the whole thing over the telephone, you are just another name to the agency. I got a look at the type of applicants waiting in the office, and the agency got a sense of my son Walter and me." Afterward she interviewed seven people and selected a young woman who works for her during the day and attends college at night.

What happens when you contact an agency? Typically, you call the agency, give your job order, and describe your family's needs. You may never set foot in the agency's office. Once you've outlined your situation, the agency takes your request and calls you back to tell you about possible applicants. If you're interested, they then send them out to meet you. You usually negotiate the salary and pay a fee for the agency's service. Some agencies divide the fee between the employer and the employee, but with caregivers in short supply, this is not the usual practice.

Be sure that you understand:

- Exactly how the agency works: What, if any, guarantees does the agency offer and for how long a period? What happens if the person you hire doesn't work out? Will they send a replacement?
- Whether the agency frequently serves your neighborhood: Some send job applicants only to Manhattan and sometimes selected neighborhoods in Queens and Brooklyn.
- Whom you want to employ: "A baby nurse," reports one employment counselor, "is there for mommy and baby. She is not a domestic. A nanny is more like a governess. A nanny and someone who does child care are different people."
- The type of people the agency places: What category of jobs does the agency fill most regularly? Some agencies specialize in nannies. Others seem to have a lot of prospective employees who are undocumented and who need to be sponsored.
- What you can expect to pay one of their applicants for child care: There may be a broad range of rates based, for example, on the applicant's experience. One employment counselor reported that "All sponsorship girls start at $200 a week, while anyone else with a checkable reference starts at about $250. I have girls who are making $400 a week." Find out why the differences exist and what the reasons are for the variation in pay.
- What the financial arrangements are: What do you pay? What, if anything, does the prospective employee pay? What is the fee schedule? What are the charges for a replacement referral? Under what circumstances, if any, will the agency refund your money? (If the agency is licensed by New York City, there are rules about deposits, fee ceilings, and return of fees that the agency should follow.)
- What the agency requires from you: What forms must you fill out? What does the agency want to know about you?
- How fast the agency thinks it can help you: How many people will you be seeing and when?
- How you can reach the agency if there's a problem.
- What the buzzwords are: One common one is "what type of person don't you want?" (You might think it's about smokers or neatness, but chances are that it's a thinly veiled ethnic question.) "How do you feel about sponsorship?" is another.

In 1986, there were nearly seven hundred employment agencies (not all of course place household help) licensed by New York City's Department of Consumer Affairs. Licensed agencies post a bond and are expected to conform to city regulations concerning fees. If you've got questions, check with Consumer Affairs (call 212-566-5599 to find out whether an agency is licensed or 212-577-0111 to find out if there have been any complaints against it). One look in the Yellow Pages of your telephone book (under "Employment Agencies" and "Sitting Services") will tell you that there are plenty of agencies to approach. For a boiled-down list, however, contact Child Care, Inc. They surveyed more than fifty agencies in the five boroughs, Long Island, Connecticut, Westchester, and New Jersey and created the packet—"In-Home Care: A Guide to Finding and Working with an In-Home Caregiver." Their list specifies whether the agency places live-ins, live-outs, baby nurses, part-timers, and temporary caregivers. The packet is available by mail for $4.00.

Don't take any agency at its word about its applicants. The staff is always quick to assure you that "With all our people, their references have been checked and they must have recent experience in the job." They may also promise that "If the client has a two-year-old child, the baby-sitter will have had similar experiences." Reports one mother: "The agency had assured me that the woman had worked with children, but when I asked her about her previous jobs, I learned she'd never taken care of a child younger than sixteen." This same mother was sent a prospective employee who brought along her own interpreter; so much for the claim that she was English-speaking. Nor should you expect agencies to be particularly attuned to your individual needs. Whom they send often depends upon their particular applicant pool at the time you make your request. The basic advice for using any agency: Do so, but proceed with caution and list your job with more than one.

In-home Care: Some Tips on Hiring

The telephone interview is usually your first step in weeding out candidates. Have at hand the worksheet that you devised outlining the job. Be sure that you give the ages of your children, the days and hours you need covered, the salary, and the expected duties. In addition, you might also want to create a questionnaire that you can fill out while you talk on the telephone:

- What is your name, address, and current telephone number?
- What are you currently doing?

- Why are you looking for a job now?
- What are your long-range plans?
- What is your past experience in child care? How many children did you care for? For how long? Why did you stop?
- What do you like about children?
- What else are you doing now?
- Whom can you give me for references? (Be sure to get current names and telephone numbers.)
- When would you be available to start work?
- How can I reach you if I'm interested in meeting you?
- Are you available for overtime? Under what circumstances?

Look for gaps in the job history and find out why they exist. Has she had a stable employment record in positions such as the one you're offering, or have there been too many short stints or jobs that will not have given her the kind of background you'd like to count on? Do you have any reason to suspect that the applicant has health problems or other difficulties in her personal life that could complicate yours? Consider how far she lives from your home. Will mornings cause you additional anxiety because she takes three subways and is constantly late because of delays on the A train? Find out a little about her own family. If she has young children, who's minding them while she's minding yours? If she tells you that her family's still abroad, will she be taking trips home to visit them? How would you feel about hiring someone who's clearly using this as an interim job? Use some of the information that you gather from preliminary telephone interviews to think of possible issues that might crop up and how you'd react to them.

You'll probably want to check references *before* you meet with the prospective employee. Be sure that you learn from a former employer the basic details of her previous job, including pay and hours, dependability, and the reason she left. Don't hesitate to ask: What was her relationship with your children? What did you like about her? What problems did you have? Would you use her again? Why? Why not? If you use an employment agency, do your own reference check, even though you're told the employee has been screened. Don't just settle for written references. Cautions Socolar: "A parent has to check the references very thoroughly—in depth and in detail. I don't think you can trust any agency to assure you that you're getting the right person."

You'll probably end up with a handful of people whom you choose to interview at your home. Be sure that you have your child there, so that you can observe her interactions with him. Says one mother: "I watched the people carefully. Ninety-five percent of the people who came to my home did not look at the children." Discuss child-rearing issues that are important to you. To do this, you might come up with examples of some situations that concern you. Perhaps you'd like to know: What would you do if Jonathan grabbed a toy from another child in the playground? How would you respond if Sarah insisted that she's not hungry and threw her lunch on the floor? What would you do if Eli had trouble falling asleep at naptime? The interview is for you—and your child—to get a sense of the person. Finally, you'll need to review money matters and any rules of the household. After you've met with the prospective employee, feel free to check back with a reference if you have questions.

Should you hire someone sight unseen? To find a mother's helper for the summer, Audrey Valentine went to a local employment agency that advertised on U.S. college campuses for students interested in summer work. The girls submitted to the agency a five-page application, accompanied by references, a small autobiography, and a photo of themselves. Audrey went to the office, looked at the applications, and selected several that interested her. She then hired one of the girls—Lizzy—"cold." That summer Audrey learned just what a mistake she'd made. "If I had met Lizzy for five minutes," she says, "I would have known she was not the right person for the job. She was not good with children and didn't want to play with my Walter. She was very reclusive." Lizzy left four weeks early. "It was really kind of crummy," remembers Audrey. Unless you meet the person you're considering, how are you going to know that the person you get will be good with children?

Ideally, the person you hire will be with your family for the next few years. Realistically, however, families may have two or three home caregivers over a period of months or years. The experiences of Carol Conley could happen to you. She found Katherine to live in through her advertisement in the "Situations Wanted" section of *The New York Times*. One Friday evening several weeks later, Katherine went out after being paid. She didn't come home that night—nothing unusual. The next day, says Carol, "I happened to go into her room to water the plants and found it stripped of her possessions with a note on her bed. She'd left for good." Observes Anne Mitchell: "The biggest problem with hiring someone in-house is that you don't know exactly what you want. It's hard to judge the longevity of a person."

For reasons such as these, many families choose to look for child care outside their home. Their options—like yours—are many.

▽ ▽ ▽ ▽ ▽ ▽ ▽ ▽ ▽ ▽ ▽

THE FINANCES OF CHILD CARE

If you are the employer of a home caregiver, you have several financial responsibilities. They are:

- *Payment of Federal and State Minimum Wage:* Your employee must be paid at least the federal minimum wage rate specified. You are also obligated to pay the state minimum wage.
- *Payment of Social Security Tax for Your Employee:* If you pay a household employee cash wages of $50 or more in a calendar quarter, those wages are subject to the Social Security tax. Both you and your employee pay a share of the tax. You may deduct the employee's share out of each paycheck, or you may elect to pay the total tax yourself. Your Social Security payments must be filed quarterly on Internal Revenue Service Form 942. Once a year, you must also file a W-2 Form with the Social Security Administration, showing the wages and Social Security tax paid. If you fail to pay the Social Security tax, you may find at a later point that your employee has applied for Social Security benefits. You will then have to pay back taxes in full plus penalties.
- *Unemployment Tax:* You must pay a federal unemployment tax if you have paid employees $1,000 or more in any one calendar quarter. This is filed with the Internal Revenue Service annually. In New York State, if you pay your employees $500 or more per quarter, then you must also pay state unemployment tax. Contact the New York State Department of Labor's Employer's Service (718-797-7032) for details. On the federal tax you receive a credit for the state unemployment tax that you pay.
- *Worker's Compensation:* In New York State if you employ a worker forty or more hours per week, you are required to purchase both Worker's Compensation and Disability Benefits Insurance. If you have a part-time employee, you can purchase Worker's Compensation, but not disability benefits. For full details contact the State Insurance Fund (212-962-8900). If you don't have Worker's Compensation for your part-time employee, then she may be protected by your homeowner's or renter's insurance policy.
- *Compensation to Your Employee:* Be clear on exactly what the pay is and how you will handle overtime and carfare. Your employee should know

how much sick time, holiday time, and vacation pay she is entitled to. You should also conduct a periodic (often an annual) salary review.

Benefits That You Can Get:

◆ If you are using child care in order to work, you can claim the *Child Care Tax Credit* on your federal income tax. There is, however, a dollar limit on the child care expenses you can count. New York State residents are also entitled to a state tax credit.

△ △ △ △ △ △ △ △ △ △ △

New York's Public Day Care

New York City has an extensive publicly funded child care program, although it only reaches a fraction of the families who are eligible. In 1984, for example, the New York City Commission on the Status of Women reported that there were some 2,100 licensed family day-care homes serving approximately 80,000 children. The Commission estimated that there were 123,000 preschool children who met the criteria for publicly subsidized centers, but there was room for only 28,000.

The Agency for Child Development (A.C.D.) administers publicly funded day care in New York City for more than 42,000 children. That includes day-care centers for preschool children, family day-care homes for children from eight weeks to twelve years of age, and some afterschool programs. Day-care centers are open weekdays year-round from 8 to 6. A licensed family day-care provider may care for up to five children under fourteen (including her own) in her home, with no more than two of them under the age of two.

Many middle-income families don't realize that they qualify for subsidized day care. Income eligibility for A.C.D.'s subsidized day care is tied to New York State's median income, not to the federal poverty guidelines. In 1986, a family could apply for publicly funded day care if their gross annual income was below 115 percent of the state median income. Under these terms, a family of two (a single parent and child) could have a gross income of up to $24,757, while a family of three's income could be $27,332, and a family of four's $29,935. To get full details about eligibility requirements and to make an appointment to apply for child care, phone the Agency for Child Development (212-FOR KIDS or 212-

553-6423). Be aware that there are almost always long waiting lists for every available space in A.C.D. centers and day-care homes.

There are also several voluntary child-care agencies to which you can apply directly for publicly funded family day care. They include: Catholic Home Bureau, Graham-Windham Services, New York Foundling Hospital, Sheltering Arms, and St. Joseph's Children's Services. For a list of those agencies with day-care homes in your neighborhood, contact the Agency for Child Development or Child Care, Inc.

Private Family Day Care

Family day care is the most varied of the child care arrangements in New York City. While a licensed family day-care provider is restricted to caring for no more than five children at any one time with no more than two children under two years of age, over ninety percent of the family day-care providers in New York City are unlicensed and adhere to no uniform standards. They care for as few, or as many, children as they choose. Some providers elect to care for only one or two children and charge accordingly. Others will take on the care of some children full-time, some part-time, and a few who arrive after school lets out. The charge for child care from 8 to 6, set by the caregiver, also fluctuates dramatically by neighborhood. According to Child Care, Inc., families may pay "anywhere from $40 to upward of $110 weekly and it depends mainly on supply and demand." In Flatbush, a family might pay as little as $40 a week, while in Forest Hills or the Upper West Side of Manhattan you might pay as much as $180 a week to take your child to the home of a neighbor. Families in Nassau County can expect to pay $50–80 a week, while in Westchester they're likely to pay around $100.

Most families find a day-care mother by asking around among friends and neighbors or at local schools, churches, and other community centers. One-year-old Nathaniel Stewart of Bayside is cared for by a former nurse who chose to stay home with her children (who are now school-aged) rather than work shifts at a hospital. She decided to care for some friends' children, three-year-old Gregory and Nathaniel. In some neighborhoods, parents can also turn to "day-care networks," which make referrals without income considerations to "licensed" or "certified" providers that they monitor. The Brooklyn agency Brookwood Child Care created its CUDDLE program, for example, after the agency received

CHOOSING CHILD CARE | 53

inquiries about its publicly funded family day care from two-paycheck families over A.C.D.'s income ceilings. Recalls one social worker: "We kept getting calls from women who said they liked the idea of a family setting and licensed homes. They asked: 'Could we use your existing programs and pay for it?' We'd have to turn them away." Now Brookwood's program is one of several in New York City:

- **Brookwood Child Care CUDDLE** (363 Adelphi Street, Brooklyn, N.Y. 11238: 718-783-2610): Serves families who live or work close to, or in, Brooklyn Heights, Boerum Hill, Clinton Hill, Cobble Hill, Fort Greene, and downtown Brooklyn by referring parents to full-time and part-time providers. After an agency interview, you are given the name of caregivers who are convenient to your home. No charge for the referral. The agency, rather than you, pays the caregivers. Expect to pay the agency $80 to $100 for full-time care and $40 to $60 for part-time care. They also operate a program of publicly subsidized family day care in these same neighborhoods.

- **Church of the Living Hope Family Day Care Network** (161 East 104 Street, New York, N.Y. 10029: 212-427-2431): All the family day-care providers live above 96 Street, so that the network serves people who live or work on the Upper East Side or in East Harlem. The fees for care are set by the caregivers and you pay them directly.

- **Church of the Open Door FDC Network** (1374 Bedford Avenue, Brooklyn, N.Y. 11216: 718-498-0256): Serves Brooklyn, particularly East New York and Brownsville. The fees for care are set by the caregivers and you pay them directly.

- **Jewish Child Care Association** (575 Lexington Avenue, New York, N.Y. 10022: 212-371-1313): Primarily serves Brooklyn, Queens, Staten Island, and Co-Op City in the Bronx. Phone for an intake appointment. If they have openings, they will refer you to a family day-care home. They provide ongoing monitoring of the home and consultation with the parents. You pay the agency and the agency pays the caregivers. In 1985, fees ranged between $80 and $100. They also operate a program of publicly subsidized family day care in these same areas.

- **Jewish Family Child Care Network of the 92 Street YM-YWHA** (1395 Lexington Avenue, New York, N.Y. 10128: 212-427-6000): Serves mainly the Upper East and West Sides of Manhattan between

79 and 96 streets. The fees for child care are set by the caregivers and you pay them directly.

- **Kingsbridge Child Care Network** (2805 University Avenue, Bronx, N.Y. 10468: 212-796-7950): Serves the Kingsbridge Heights neighborhood. Phone for an intake interview and you're directed to a possible caregiver. You pay the caregiver directly.

- **Talbot Perkins Children's Services** (116 West 32 Street, New York, N.Y. 10001: 212-736-2510): Serves several neighborhoods in Brooklyn, including Carroll Gardens, Cobble Hill, Park Slope, and Windsor Terrace. After your initial telephone call, they will send you an application and will arrange for an interview with you if they can match you with a home ($25 fee if you go for an interview). Talbot Perkins pays the day-care providers and does the bookkeeping. The approximate charge: for full-time (fifty hours), $100; part-time, variable. They also operate a program of publicly subsidized family day care in Brooklyn.

Most of these programs are small, representing anywhere from twenty to fifty family day-care providers, so they don't serve large numbers of children. You can also check with New York City's Department of Health (212-334-7741), which awards "Certificates of Approval" to some nonagency providers. The number of certificate holders was tiny in 1985, but according to Co-ordinator of Family Day Care Harriet Yarmolinski: "We have every expectation that it will increase." Residents of Lower Manhattan can consult the Family Resource Center's family day-care provider registry (137 East 2 Street, New York, N.Y. 10009: 212-677-6602). These day-care providers are not licensed, but the Center screens them and makes home visits.

A few other publicly funded family day-care agencies occasionally have space for children whose families are over A.C.D.'s ceilings, particularly if the children are over two. Check with the Children's Health Service (690 Amsterdam Avenue, New York, N.Y. 10025: 212-865-3741), Cardinal McCloskey Family Day Care (349 East 149 Street, Bronx, N.Y. 10451: 212-993-7700), and the Society for Seamen's Children (26 Bay Street, Staten Island, N.Y. 10301: 718-447-7740).

If you explore the possibility of using family day care, you'll need to decide what is acceptable to you and your child. If the caregiver speaks your language haltingly or not at all, how are you going to communicate about shared care—or make yourself understood in an emergency? Find out from the provider just how many children under the age of three she would be willing to care for, and consider how much individual attention your child will get. If there are two infants or toddlers close in age, your child essentially will be treated as a twin. Do you want that? What would you consider a good age combination for one caregiver to take on: Two infants together? A three-year-old and a one-year-old? As one child care expert observed: "Family day care needs to be very carefully thought out. Should you put your child in a situation that you would not create for yourself at home?"

Finally, you'll have to work out the basics of the child care arrangement. Negotiate the hours of care, payment policies, what you and the caregiver will provide (e.g., lunch, clothing), arrangements for a substitute caregiver, and the amount of termination notice required. It will make for a more stable working relationship if the two of you write out these points in a parent/provider agreement. Be sure that your caregiver has adequate health information about your child and knows whom to contact in an emergency. Child Care, Inc., has a packet on "Family Day Care" (available by mail for $3) that provides pointers on choosing a good caregiver and includes a model agreement and an emergency form that you can leave with your caregiver.

Day Care in Licensed Centers

While care by an individual in the family's home or the caregiver's home is the child care choice of most families, some gravitate toward center-based care. "From the time that my son Ned was six months old, I had a full-time sitter," says Dorothy Layton. "I couldn't imagine taking him out. I don't see how I could have handled the details, and I couldn't imagine having an infant in a group situation." Yet the arrangement she had was also very stressful. "Yolanda would tend to be late in the morning. That was bad enough because I'd be late. Since my husband and I split all the child care, one of us was always panting at the gate to get out. To top it off, I would come home and give her almost all of my paycheck. The expense was really quite crushing." By the time that Ned was two, the Laytons had decided it was time for a change and enrolled him in a neighborhood day-care center. Ned stayed there year-round from 9 to 6 for the next three years, and Dorothy feels that for him, an only child, "having playmates was in some ways like having an extended family. He thrived."

New York's day-care centers have a wide variety of sponsorships: publicly funded A.C.D. centers, nonprofit centers, church-based centers, university-based centers that accept some families from the community, parent co-op boards, owner-operated centers, and for-profit franchise chains. In 1985, the Department of Health estimated that there were 1,100 early childhood programs in New York City. (There were 325 A.C.D. day-care centers and 147 part-day Head Start programs. The rest were made up of independent part-day nursery schools and all-day centers.)

Any center or school in New York City that cares for more than five children under the age of six must meet the minimum standards set by the Department of Health, the Fire Department, and the Department of Buildings. They must have a license issued by the Department of Health's Bureau of Day Care. Child Care, Inc., estimates that parents will pay between $65 and $125 per week for all-day care for a preschooler and $90 and $185 weekly for an infant or toddler. Fees vary by the type of program and by neighborhood, with programs in Manhattan generally more expensive than in the other boroughs. Centers for infants and toddlers are particularly costly. At one Manhattan center, for example, parents were charged $185 per week ($37 per day) for a full week of care from 8:00 to 5:45 and $41 per day for part-time care.

While infant and toddler care is expensive, the bigger problem is finding it. In 1984, the New York City Commission on the Status of Women reported that "the situation is acute for infant care services . . . and the publicly subsidized programs can, at present, serve less than 5 percent of the infants whose parents qualify." In 1986, there were only thirty-two all-day licensed centers for infants and toddlers. Most day-care centers don't enroll children under three. Finding center care for a child under six months of age is close to impossible. The situation at one Manhattan center (which takes children six months through three years) is typical: Parents are advised to "wait until the baby is a month or two old before applying," but also that "most of our openings come available in September."

Child Care, Inc., can refer you to centers and schools throughout the city. For children under two, it puts out a *Directory of Child Care for Infants and Toddlers* ($2), listing all of the licensed day-care centers and part-day programs, borough by borough. Some of the programs in this booklet require that an adult be with the child, so that this is as much a guide to activity programs for infants and toddlers as it is a guide to child care. If you are looking for a day-care center, or a nursery school, for your two- to five-year-old (see also Chapter Three), Child Care, Inc. can make up an individualized packet for you, including the booklet *Choosing an Early Childhood Program,* along with printouts of the licensed all-day, school-day, and part-day programs for young children in your neighborhood or on your way to work. This early childhood packet costs $4 (free for parents who are income-eligible for publicly funded day care). You'll need to phone the Child Care Information Service for an order form on which you can list the child care packets you want and the ZIP codes for which you want printouts. To find out if a particular center or nursery school is licensed, or to report any instance of substandard care, you can call the borough office of the Health Department's Bureau of Day Care (Bronx: 212-583-5500, ext. 55 and 56; Brooklyn and Staten Island: 718-574-2101; Manhattan: 212-334-7744; Queens: 718-658-6600, ext. 842).

Your key task, however, is figuring out if a particular program suits your needs. Says Socolar: "Having a license just means that the program met the most basic requirements at the time they got the license. You should still try to visit several programs so you can compare them for quality." In evaluating a program, be it center care or family day care, the National Association for the Education of Young Children (1834 Connecticut Avenue N.W., Washington, D.C. 20009: 800-424-2460 or 202-232-8777) and other child care experts, such as the Child Care Action Campaign (99 Hudson Street, New York, N.Y. 10013: 212-334-9595) recommend that you:

- Look at the size and scale of a program: How many children are cared for by one person? How much individual attention does each child receive?
- Evaluate the space where the program takes place: How does the group fit into the rooms provided? Does it seem cramped? Look at cleanliness, safety, and emergency plans. Are there smoke detectors and fire extinguishers? Is there grass or a padded surface under climbing equipment?
- Analyze the play equipment: Is there a variety? What types of toys, books, and art materials are there? Are they readily available and geared to the children's level?
- Observe the staff: What is their relationship to the children? How do they interact with the children? How do they interact with each

other? How accessible are they to the children—to you? How long have they been there? How much turnover is there?
- Look at the overall program offered and how the staff handles the daily activities: If you can spend a part of the day there, try to observe arrivals and departures, the structured eating times, indoor activities (what they are; how the group is broken up; what choices the children have), active group play both indoors and outdoors, and transitions.
- How does the staff deal with problem behavior? If a child needs consoling, what happens?
- Examine the attitude of the staff toward visitors: Are you welcome? Can you drop in without an appointment? What is their reaction if you drop by unannounced?
- Get references: Have you seen their license? Will they refer you to parents currently using the center?

Always ask yourself: Would I like to spend my day here? Says Mitchell: "If it feels OK to you, then it's probably OK." Take the time to look and to interview. "You get the information when you ask questions," reports Mitchell. "It's not just a question of what you want as an adult, but also what you know about your child."

After-school Care

As children get older, the child care arrangements change. By the time a child enters kindergarten or first grade, the pressing need for full-time care is replaced by that of filling in the few hours until Mom or Dad get home. Some families enroll their children in five-day-a-week after-school care (often center-based programs), while others choose enrichment activities (e.g., ballet, pottery, music, sports). The child's weekly schedule is often stitched together, with a program at a local Y or community center one day, visiting at a friend's on another, and on still a third, being cared for by a baby-sitter or fending for himself.

After-school care is usually less costly for parents than the full-time arrangements that may have been necessary for the preschool child. But it's often much more nerve-wracking. There's the problem of logistics: If the program's not at the school, how do you get the child there and how do you get him home? Then there are the hours: Often the program ends before parents can get out of work. Beyond that there's the frequent complication of school half-days, holidays, and vacations. Observes Dorothy Layton, who's now dependent on an after-school program: "It's inconsistent. It hasn't really occurred to them that both parents work. They don't realize that if it's a holiday, the children still need to be taken care of. It's always meant having to find some alternative. The whole philosophy of day care is: 'We are here to serve the family.' Once the child gets a little older, there's no such philosophy." When after-school care is stitched together, there is always the chance of a missed connection. Observes Susan Ginsberg, of the Bank Street College of Education, "People make two or three arrangements in one day and they break down. And then *they* break down."

School-based programs are attractive since they provide continuous care, but they're not as widespread as families would like. Walden, Dalton, Friends Seminary, Calhoun, and Nightingale-Bamford are among the few independent schools that offer extensive after-school care. Free after-school care is not the rule within the New York City public school system; your community school district (see Chapter Three) can tell you what—if anything—is done locally.

Throughout the five boroughs, local Y's and community centers provide a wide range of activities, as well as formal after-school programs. You may also want to check with the Police Athletic League (212-477-9450), the Girl Scout Council of Greater New York (212-645-4000), and the Boy Scouts of America, Greater New York Council (212-242-1100) about their offerings. For an overview, check also with the Youth Coordinator of your local Community Board, as well as Child Care, Inc. You can also call the New York City Department of Health, Bureau for Day Camps and Recreation (93 Worth Street, Room 1003, New York, N.Y. 10013: 212-566-7763 or 212-566-7764), which licenses school-age programs to ensure that they meet certain minimum standards for safety and staff. Many of these centers operate after-school programs during the school year. Each spring the Bureau issues free updated borough directories, arranged by ZIP codes, that give the name of the program, its address, and the age group it serves. The Parents League of New York, Inc. (212-737-7385) can advise you about programs at independent schools.

If you live in Manhattan (or your child attends school there), you may want to purchase a copy of *Afterschool* (cost: $7.95, postage and handling $1.50, available by mail) created by The Resourceful Family (490 Riverside Drive, New York, N.Y. 10027: 212-222-5900). The book details both public and private after-school resources in Manhattan for children between the ages of six and fourteen. The directory, organized alphabetically by program, gives hours, enrollment, eligibility and fees, and whether transportation arrangements are possible. It also notes evening, school holiday, and summer alternatives. Peter Lawrence's *A Kid's New York* (New York: Avon Books, 1982) has a cursory rundown of a variety of enrichment activities in the five boroughs, including acting, cooking, dance, music, woodworking, and athletics.

Determining the best after-school plan for your child requires that you shop around. These questions, suggested by The Resourceful Family in *Afterschool,* may help:

- Is the location convenient for your child—and you?
- Does this program provide "care" for your child every weekday after school lets out, or does it provide activities only some days of the week?
- What activities does the after-school program offer?
- What is the size of the program?
- Is your child eligible for the program? Is it open to all? Is it limited to members? Is it restricted to children in the school or the neighborhood?
- How much does the program cost? According to The Resourceful Family, care programs generally cost less than "activity" programs.
- How will your child get there after school? Is transportation provided?
- What about activities during school holidays?

THE Y'S AND COMMUNITY CENTERS OF THE CITY

New York's Y's and community centers are a fundamental resource. Whether you're looking for enrichment and after-school activities, a day-care center, nursery school, summer day or overnight camp, or even a school holiday program, these centers are likely to have it. Although some of the Jewish Y's have religious-oriented curricula, all strive to serve the entire community, with special attention to the neighborhoods in which they are located.

The **YMCA of Greater New York** (422 Ninth Avenue, New York, N.Y. 10001: 212-564-1300) will mail you its free comprehensive program guide for all member Y's. This booklet lists the activities offered, but does not give specific days and times for any of the Y's. The **Associated YM-YWHAs of**

Greater New York (130 East 59 Street, New York, N.Y. 10022: 212-751-8880) can tell you about their affiliated Jewish Y's, or you can call the Jewish Information and Referral Service (212-753-2288). **United Neighborhood Houses of New York** (101 East 15 Street, New York, N.Y. 10003: 212-677-0300) will tell you about the offerings at their centers. You'll also find community centers in New York City Housing Authority buildings. To find out about these centers, check with the **New York City Housing Authority,** Department of Social and Community Services (250 Broadway, Room 1500, New York, N.Y. 10007: 212-306-3000). The Housing Authority operates more than one hundred centers. The best way to learn about any Y or community center, however, is to contact their membership or program offices individually. Among the possibilities are:

Bronx

Bronx House (990 Pelham Parkway: 212-792-1800)
Bronx River Neighborhood Centers (1619 East 174 Street: 212-991-1100)
Bronx YMCA of Greater New York (2244 Westchester Avenue: 212-931-2500)
Bronx YMCA: Castle Hill Day Camp and Family Center (2 Castle Hill Avenue: 212-792-9736)
Bronx YMCA: Jacobi Sports Center (Pelham Parkway/Eastchester Road: 212-792-9717)
Bronx YMCA: Bailey Avenue Center (2660 Bailey Avenue: 212-796-2559)
Claremont Neighborhood Centers (489 East 169 Street: 212-588-1000)
East Side House Settlement (337 Alexander Avenue: 212-665-5250)
Mosholu-Montefiore Community Center (3450 Dekalb Avenue: 212-882-4000)
Riverdale Neighborhood House (5521 Mosholu Avenue: 212-549-8100)
Riverdale YM&YWHA (5625 Arlington Avenue: 212-548-8200)
Seneca Center (871 Hunts Point Avenue: 212-542-7740)
Southeast Bronx Neighborhood Centers (955 Tinton Avenue: 212-542-2727)
Tip Neighborhood House (1028 East 179 Street: 212-893-1224)

Brooklyn

Bedford Technical School YMCA (1121 Bedford Avenue: 718-789-1497)
Brooklyn Central Branch YMCA (157 Montague Street: 718-522-6000)
Brooklyn YWCA (30 Third Avenue: 718-875-1190)
Colony–South Brooklyn Houses (297 Dean Street: 718-625-3810)
Eastern District Branch YMCA (125 Humboldt Street: 718-782-8300)
Greenpoint Branch YMCA (99 Meserole Avenue: 718-389-3700)

Hebrew Educational Society of Brooklyn (9502 Seaview Avenue: 718-241-3000)
Jewish Community House of Bensonhurst (7802 Bay Parkway: 718-331-6800)
Kings Bay YM-YWHA (3495 Nostrand Avenue: 718-648-7703)
Prospect Park—Bay Ridge Branch YMCA (357 9 Street: 718-768-7100)
Recreation Rooms and Settlement (715 East 105 Street: 718-649-1461)
School Settlement (120 Jackson Street: 718-389-1810)
Shorefront YM-YWHA of Brighton—Manhattan Beach (3300 Coney Island: 718-646-1444)
Twelve Towns YMCA (570 Jamaica Avenue: 718-277-1600)
Willoughby House Settlement (285 Myrtle Avenue: 718-875-4372)
YM&YWHA of Boro Park (4912 Fourteenth Avenue: 718-438-5921)

Manhattan

Boys Harbor (1 East 104 Street: 212-427-2244)
Children's Aid Society (105 East 22 Street, New York 10010: 212-949-4800)
Chinatown Center YMCA (100 Hester Street: 212-219-8393)
Chinatown Planning Council (13 Elizabeth Street: 212-431-7800)
Educational Alliance (197 East Broadway: 212-475-6200)
Educational Alliance West (51 East 10 Street: 212-420-1150)
Emanu-El Midtown YM-YWHA (344 East 14 Street: 212-674-7200)
Goddard—Riverside Community Center (593 Columbus Avenue: 212-873-6600)
Grand Street Settlement (80 Pitt Street: 212-674-1740)
Greenwich House (27 Barrow Street: 212-242-4140)
Grosvenor Neighborhood House (176 West 105 Street: 212-749-8500)
Hamilton—Madison House (50 Madison Street: 212-349-3724)
Harlem Branch YMCA (180 West 135 Street: 212-281-4100)
Harlem YWCA (2 West 115 Street: 212-831-9039)
Hartley House (413 West 46 Street: 212-246-9885)
Henry Street Settlement (265 Henry Street: 212-766-9200)
Hudson Guild (441 West 26 Street: 212-760-9800)
Stanley M. Isaacs Neighborhood Center (415 East 93 Street: 212-427-1100)
James Weldon Johnson Community Center (2205 First Avenue: 212-860-7250)
LaGuardia Memorial House (307 East 116 Street: 212-534-7800)
Lenox Hill Neighborhood Association (331 East 70 Street: 212-744-5022)
McBurney Branch YMCA (215 West 23 Street: 212-741-9216)
92 Street YM-YWHA (1395 Lexington Avenue: 212-427-6000)

Recreation Rooms and Settlement (12 Avenue D: 212-777-6963)
Rena Coa Multi-Service Center (1920 Amsterdam Avenue: 212-368-3295)
St. Matthew's and St. Timothy's Neighborhood Center (26 West 84 Street: 212-362-6750)
Third Street Music School Settlement (235 East 11 Street: 212-777-3240)
Union Street Settlement (237 East 104 Street: 212-360-8823)
University Settlement (184 Eldridge Street: 212-674-9120)
Vanderbilt Branch YMCA (224 East 47 Street: 212-755-2410)
West Side YMCA (5 West 63 Street: 212-787-4400)
William Sloane House Branch YMCA (356 West 34 Street: 212-760-5850)
YM&YWHA of Washington Heights and Inwood (54 Nagle Avenue: 212-569-6200)
YWCA of the City of New York (610 Lexington Avenue: 212-755-4500)

Queens

Central Queens Branch YMCA (89-25 Parsons Boulevard: 718-739-6600)
Central Queens YM-YWHA (67-09 108 Street: 718-268-5011)
Eastern Queens Branch YMCA (238-10 Hillside Avenue: 718-479-0505)
Flushing Branch YMCA (138-46 Northern Boulevard: 718-961-6880; also Bayside Center, 214-13 35 Avenue: 718-229-5972)
Forest Hills Community House (106-25 62 Drive: 718-592-5757)
Gustave Hartman YM-YWHA (710 Hartman Lane: 718-471-0200)
Jacob A. Riis Neighborhood House (10-25 41 Avenue: 718-784-3271)
Long Island City Branch YMCA (27-04 41 Avenue: 718-729-6363)
Martin de Porres Community Center (4-25 Astoria Boulevard: 718-726-2626)
Samuel Field YM-YWHA (58-20 Little Neck: 718-225-6750)
YM-YWHA of Greater Flushing (45-35 Kissena Boulevard: 718-461-3030)

Staten Island

Jewish Community Center of Staten Island (475 Victory Boulevard: 718-981-1500)
Staten Island Branch YMCA (651 Broadway: 718-981-4933)

△ △ △ △ △ △ △ △ △ △ △

Summer Care

For the working parent of a school-aged child, summer is not a welcome vacation break but rather a stretch of two or three months in which child care must be patched together. Summer camp is one solution. Parents discover, however, that camp programs run for four to eight weeks—not the full length of the vacation period. The assumption: Someone's got time off. Summer child care can also be costly, since some summer camps have price tags of close to $1,000 a month, with transportation extra. Five-year-olds may be expected to take bus rides of up to an hour to get them out to that wooded campus in Westchester, Long Island, Rockland, or New Jersey.

Many of the programs that offer after-school care also have summer programs. Check with the Y's, settlement houses, community centers, the Police Athletic League, the Scouts, and in some neighborhoods, the churches. The Y's often have both on-site programs and camps at a more rustic setting, as well as day and sleep-away programs. The YMCA of Greater New York has a special brochure describing the camps run by its members. Several of the independent schools, including Bank Street, Cathedral, Dalton, Walden, and the United Nations International School, run summer programs, but you may discover that the summer session of a particular independent school lasts only for the month of June or from mid-June through the end of July. Several museums have summer "camp" programs designed more for enrichment than child care (see Chapter Six), while for the sports enthusiast there are also specialized basketball, gymnastics, or tennis camps (see Chapter Five).

The New York City Parks and Recreation Department operates a free urban day camp program for children ages six to fourteen at various playgrounds and recreational centers. These summer "play camps," which also feature day trips, usually operate from July 5 through the end of August (the most common hours: 9:00–4:30). For further details, including the dates for the required pre-registration in May and June, contact the borough offices of the Department's Recreation division: Bronx: 212-430-1824; Brooklyn: 718-965-8937; Manhattan: 212-408-0210; Queens: 718-520-5918; Staten Island: 718-720-6863. The Parks Department features day camps for handicapped youth through **R.E.A.C.H.** (Recreation, Education, Athletics, and Creative Arts for the Handicapped: 212-860-1842). The New York City Board of Education also provides a variety of summer programs. Check with your community school district for details. If you'd like your children to have a sleep-away experience in the country for part of the summer but can't afford to pay for this opportunity, check with the **Fresh Air Fund** (212-221-0900) in March or April. The Fund sends children on two-week sessions to overnight camp in upstate New York and also places city children as guests of volunteer host families in a "Friendly Town" in the suburban or rural northeast. Recruitment for the program takes place through social service agencies, and the Fund will refer you to the appropriate one.

Child Care, Inc., and the New York City Bureau for Day Camps and Recreation (212-566-7763 or 212-566-7764), which issues a borough-wide *New York City Day Camp Directory* (available free upon request; the directory is arranged by ZIP code), can help. The Bureau licenses every day camp in New York City by issuing a permit that certifies that it meets minimum standards for safety and staff. Their day camp directory is just a basic list, giving the name and location of the camp, whether there is a fee, and the ages and sex of the children served. The Bureau also issues a separate directory of camps for children with special needs and the booklet *Choosing a Day Camp for Your Child.* Although Assistant Director Quentin E. Fletcher says that "we try not to give opinions," they will tell you if they have complaints on record about a particular camp. The Parents League has a Summer Advisory Service (free to members), which has files containing descriptive literature from camps, summer schools, travel groups (both U.S. and abroad), and other summer activities suitable for school-aged children. You'll also find comments from members whose children have participated in these activities.

To learn about summer camp programs—both inside and outside New York City—you might also attend the National Children's Camp Show at the Walden School (1 West 88 Street, New York, N.Y. 10024: 212-877-7621; usually held in January). Private day and sleep-over camps, and programs for teens, set-up exhibits. **Resources for Children with Special Needs** (200 Park Avenue South, Suite 816, New York, N.Y. 10003: 212-677-4650) also has its own "Special Camp Fair," highlighting programs for children with various disabilities, and publishes a directory. To find out about camps that adhere to Jewish traditions or dietary laws, call the Federation of Jewish Philanthropies' Jewish Information and Referral Service (212-753-2288) or the Association of Jewish Sponsored Camps (212-751-0477), which compiles a directory of sleep-away camps, *Jewish Camps for All Ages.* The American Camping Association—New York Section (43 West 23 Street, New York, N.Y. 10010: 212-645-6620) has a free camp referral service and will tell you about member camps.

If you're thinking about a summer "mother's helper," check with local high schools, the Parents League, and employment agencies. Be sure to convey a clear idea of what the job entails. Write down what you expect the helper to do and the hours she's on and off. If your helper will be living with you at a summer house, establish some basic ground rules on such matters as socializing with, or entertaining, her friends, and the use of the family car and the telephone.

▽ ▽ ▽ ▽ ▽ ▽ ▽ ▽ ▽ ▽ ▽

HOLIDAY CARE

The holidays and vacations that punctuate the school year are equally problem-provoking, since often there's no one at home to care for the kids. To meet that need, some after-school programs, and some cultural agencies, have developed special holiday activities. The Educational Alliance West, for example, has offered "Holiday Trips for Kids," day-long junkets featuring, for example, a trip to the Museum of Natural History combined with a visit to the Big Apple Circus.

Some suggestions on where to look for these special activities:

- **After-school Programs.**
- **Y's and Community Centers.**
- **Independent Schools:** Bank Street, Caedmon, Cathedral, Dalton, Friends Seminary, the Lenox School, Rodeph Shalom, and Walden have had holiday offerings. Their programs may not be limited to children enrolled in the school or the regular after-school program.
- **Sports Clubs:** Astros (838 West End Avenue, New York, N.Y. 10025: 212-749-7202); Billdave (206 East 85 Street, New York, N.Y. 10028: 212-535-7151); Cavalier Athletic Club (19 West 96 Street, New York, N.Y. 10025: 212-580-1755); Champions (1160 Fifth Avenue, New York, N.Y. 10029: 212-427-3800). These organizations also run after-school and summer programs.
- **Museums:** Both the Bronx Zoo and the New York Aquarium have run part-day workshops (from 10–3) during the Christmas holiday.

△ △ △ △ △ △ △ △ △ △ △

Baby-sitting

Each family's way of finding an occasional or part-time baby-sitter is different. While talking with friends and neighbors will usually uncover a few baby-sitters for the occasional day or evening out, you could also check with local high schools, community centers, church offices, or senior citizens centers. Some employment agencies will send you sitters on a one-time-only basis (their typical fee: around $5.00 to $7.00 per hr., with carfare and/or cabfare additional). There's usually a minimum number of hours required and no guarantee that you'll get the same sitter the next time you call.

Colleges, universities, and nursing schools are other places to tap. The Barnard College Baby-sitting Service (212-280-2035)—probably the best-known and best-organized student service in the city—requires you to register, sign an agreement, and give your pediatrician for a reference. For $3.50 per hr. (50 cents additional for more than two children; cab fare after 9 P.M. and a minimum of two hours), you can call up and list your job. The Service, an invaluable resource for many Manhattan families, operates during the school year. Students come to check Barnard's job book for listings. Most programs, however, don't work this way. Families who have used New York University's Student Employment Services report that they can easily find students for regular part-time help, but are less successful in lining up an occasional sitter on short notice. The reason: The jobs are posted on a bulletin board along with many other kinds of work. Says a student who works there: "We can't promise too much." If you're interested in a high school student and are a member of the Parents League, you can look at their registry of independent school youngsters interested in baby-sitting. You can also contact individual public, private, and parochial schools in your neighborhood. Dorothy Layton has found a group of teenagers for baby-sitting through the after-school program her son's enrolled in.

Baby-sitting co-operatives, often formed in apartment complexes, block associations, or mothers' groups, are an inexpensive but time-consuming way for you to get occasional child care. Child Care, Inc., the Family Resource Center, or the parent support organization, Parents Resources, may be able to steer you to groups.

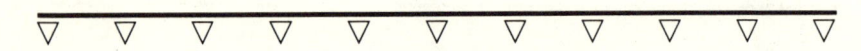

▽ ▽ ▽ ▽ ▽ ▽ ▽ ▽ ▽ ▽ ▽

WHERE TO LOOK FOR A STUDENT

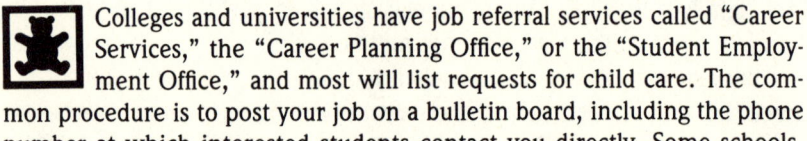

Colleges and universities have job referral services called "Career Services," the "Career Planning Office," or the "Student Employment Office," and most will list requests for child care. The common procedure is to post your job on a bulletin board, including the phone number at which interested students contact you directly. Some schools, however, put the job description on a bulletin board but do not post your name and phone number. An interested student then speaks to an employment counselor.

It's usually easier to find college students through an employment service to fill a permanent, part-time job than it is to get them for baby-sitting with little notice. If you are looking for a sitter on a regular basis, part-time and possibly only a few hours a week, then a student is an excellent possibility. You might also advertise that you want to hear from students interested in occasional baby-sitting. Be prepared for breaks in their availability, however, because of vacations, exams, or changes in their class schedules from semester to semester.

Nursing school students also baby-sit. They're usually available evenings and weekends, since they will have classes or clinical programs during the day. You'll find that the basic procedure is often to post the job request on a dormitory bulletin board. Send a written request to the Helen Fuld School of Nursing, North General Hospital (1919 Madison Avenue, New York, N.Y. 10035) or to St. Vincent's Hospital School of Nursing (written request to: Co-ordinator of Student Affairs, St. Vincent's Hospital School of Nursing, 27 Christopher St., New York, N.Y. 10014; evenings and weekends best; your note is posted in the dormitories).

You might also check with:
Bank Street College of Education (212-663-7200)
Barnard College Baby-sitting Service (212-280-2035)
Beth Israel Nursing School (212-420-2000)
City University Job Location Department (212-947-6000, ext. 333)
   (They will list your job with all the colleges; best for jobs of a more permanent nature. Queensborough Community College will not list any jobs in the home, reports an employment counselor, since the school doesn't prescreen the students.)
   Baruch College (212-725-3062)
   Borough of Manhattan Community College (212-618-1464)
   Bronx Community College (212-220-6414)
   Brooklyn College (718-780-5696)
   City College (212-690-6744)
   College of Staten Island (718-390-7790)
   Hostos Community College (212-960-1179)
   Hunter College (212-772-4849)
   Kingsborough Community College (718-934-5115)
   LaGuardia Community College (718-482-5238)
   Lehman College (212-960-8366)
   Medgar Evers College (718-735-1849)
   New York City Technical College (718-643-8848)

CHOOSING CHILD CARE | 69

Queens College (718-520-7791)
York College (718-262-2273)
College of Mount Saint Vincent (212-549-8000)
Columbia University (212-280-2391)
Fashion Institute of Technology (212-760-7654)
Julliard School (212-799-5000, ext. 313)
Long Island University (718-403-1039)
Manhattan College (212-920-0224)
Manhattan School of Music (212-749-2802, ext. 453)
Mannes College of Music (212-580-0210)
Marymount Manhattan College (212-517-0472)
  (You must fill out an application or write a letter.)
New York University (212-598-2971)
Pratt Institute (718-636-3506)
Teachers College, Columbia University (212-678-3175)
Stern College (212-340-7715)
Wagner College (718-390-3100, ext. 3181)

△ △ △ △ △ △ △ △ △ △ △

Be Prepared

Your care provider needs current information about you and your child. Leave the phone numbers where you can be reached and the name, address, and telephone number of one or several reliable adults who can make a responsible decision in your behalf in case of an emergency. Include also the name, address, and telephone number of your child's physician or medical facility and your written authorization for emergency medical care. Your authorization should specify your caregiver's name and your child's name, and bear the signatures of both parents. Update this information whenever necessary. Even if you temporarily change your schedule and the numbers where you can be reached, be sure to let the people involved know.

chapter 3
choosing schools

It is the fall of 1983 and Brooke Hampton is two years old. Her parents, Judy and Don, must make the first of many decisions about her education. They live on the Upper East Side of Manhattan. Where should Brooke go to nursery school? They visit a variety of programs (taking Brooke along for interviews) and decide on an independent nursery school that is often a "feeder" school for Manhattan private schools. Barely two years later, they face the same decision again—this time about elementary school. Judy spends months school-shopping, applying to private schools, taking Brooke to interviews, meeting with the admissions staff, and finally waiting for the acceptance notices.

Sarah Spiegal, the parent of a kindergartner in Queens, also chose to send her child to a private school. Unlike the Hamptons, she had no sense of the intense competition that often overwhelms parents in Manhattan. She recalls: "I applied to a private school in Queens in June for September. My child walked in at five and a half. I don't know anybody who's had difficulty getting their child in." A few years later, however, Sarah pulled her son out, enrolling him instead in a gifted program in a public school.

Ann and Bob Posner of Middle Village, Queens, made still another choice for their son, Joseph. When he was nursery-school-aged, Ann waited until May to act and registered him at the Lost Battalion Hall Nursery School, a neighborhood program run by the New York City Parks Department. Says Ann: "I heard from people that there was this marvelous public program." Two years later the Posners sent him to a neighborhood parochial school.

George and Joan Laughton's daughter, Carolyn, never attended preschool because the Laughtons decided not to send her. When she was three, Carolyn started reading. Says Joan: "There weren't any really great nursery schools and it became increasingly obvious to us that she was going to be bored." Instead the Laughtons decided to tutor her at home, using a correspondence course, and found that "she was in second grade before she was eligible to go into kindergarten." The search at age five became to find a school that would put her where she belonged educationally, not chronologically. "The public schools," recalls Joan, "wouldn't believe us. From most private schools we got the reaction: 'This is ridiculous. We're not going to put her in with second-graders.' " But one school did. In 1986, Carolyn was seven and in the fourth grade.

These choices are among the many open to New York City parents. For some, discussion about their child's education begins when they seek day care outside their home. You'll find children enrolled in full-time public or private day-care programs. For others, there's a seemingly natural progression from Lamaze classes to "Mommy and Me" and toddler programs. But for many parents, the decisions about education begin when their child is ready for nursery school. While they are looking at preschool programs, they are also beginning to think about the future—elementary school.

Schools for Under-fives

The shape of preschool education in New York City is likely to undergo dramatic change. In 1986 the Early Childhood Education Commission, appointed by Mayor Edward Koch, recommended that New York City should make formal instruction available to all four-year-olds. In its report, *Take a Giant Step: An Equal Step in Education for All New York City Four-Year-Olds,* the Commission urged that the city expand its existing services to accommodate the city's 100,000 four-year-olds. The Commission found that less than half of these children were enrolled in preschool programs and urged that "to be consistent with our long-standing political and social commitment to free public education and to racial and ethnic integration, this education should be universally available." In response to that report, the Board of Education expects to make programs for four-year-olds available to all children in the next few years.

Until that goal is implemented, however, if you are interested in a public program for a four-year-old, check with your local community school district to find out whether a school-based prekindergarten exists. In some districts, you'll find already in place, for example, half-day sessions, morning or afternoon, with fifteen children in a class, one teacher and one paraprofessional. Residence in the school's district, or income eligibility, is often a requirement for admission.

Project Head Start (71 Worth Street, New York, N.Y. 10013: 212-334-7815) is probably the best known of the public programs serving more than 12,000 children ages three and four. To qualify, the children should live in families with incomes below the federal poverty guidelines. Up to ten percent of the enrollment can be over the income guidelines, however. Ten percent of the space in any individual program is reserved for children with special needs. If your child is handicapped, you should inquire about the program, since eligibility is based on this consideration as well as on age and income. The **New York City Department of Parks and Recreation** also offers free recreational preschool programs held in Parks Department buildings. Children must be three and a half by September and live within a twenty-block radius of the program. There are about twenty children in each two-and-a-half-hour program, with a teacher and a parent. Registration is usually the last two weeks in May on a first-come, first-served basis. Contact the borough co-ordinators (Manhattan: 212-408-0204; Brooklyn: 718-965-8942; Bronx: 212-430-1825; Queens: 718-520-5918; Staten Island: 718-720-6864) for details.

There's a variety of private programs, both half- and full-day, ranging from intimate neighborhood schools to larger independent nursery schools to nursery classes that are the first "grade" in some private elementary schools. You'll find both toddler and nursery programs offered at churches, synagogues, Y's, settlement houses, and community centers. Be sure to check with local colleges and universities, and if there's a music school in your neighborhood, with them. Manhattan's Third Street Music School Settlement, for example, runs a special nursery program, "Learning, the Arts, and Me," which mixes music, art, dramatics, and creative movement, while the Diller–Quaile School of Music has preschool programs for two- and three-year-olds. Although there are some half-day programs for toddlers (in addition to day care programs) and even some schools just for toddlers—Manhattan's Beginnings is one—the majority of offerings for this age are short classes, once or twice a week, in music, movement, collage, and art. (For a discussion of exercise classes, see Chapter Five.) Don't be surprised when you sign your tot up for toddler classes if you, or your caregiver, are asked to stay with your child.

Some of the nonpublic nursery schools, such as Manhattan's Brick Church School, First Presbyterian Nursery School, Medical Center Nursery School, and Columbia Greenhouse Nursery School, belong to the Independent Schools Admissions Association of Greater New York (ISAAGNY). Most ISAAGNY schools are on the Upper East Side or the Upper West Side. ISAAGNY itself is composed of nursery, primary, and secondary schools. **The Parents League of New York, Inc.** (115 East 82 Street, New York, N.Y. 10028: 212-737-7385) can advise you whether a school belongs to ISAAGNY, and if you join the League (membership: $25), a member will be glad to talk with you about these schools. If you're thinking about sending your child to an independent school for the elementary years, you'll probably want to purchase the *New York Independent Schools Directory* (available from the League or the Educational Records Bureau), which has capsule portraits of ISAAGNY schools, prepared by the schools, including enrollment information and details about their curriculum. ISAAGNY nursery schools adhere to certain basic admission procedures, including notifying families of admission and requiring parent replies by specific dates. Tuitions in the nursery programs for half-day nursery in 1986 ranged from approximately $2,000 to more than $6,000.

If you are interested in a Montessori-based curriculum, with its focus on a carefully prepared environment that guarantees exposure to material and experiences, you can get a listing of schools from the **American Montessori Society** (150 Fifth Avenue, New York, N.Y. 10011: 212-924-3209). Some Montessori programs extend into the elementary grades.

If you are Jewish and want your child to participate in a religious program, the **Board of Jewish Education of Greater New York** (426 West 58 Street, New York, N.Y. 10019: 212-245-8200) has compiled a list of nursery programs. Residents of Lower Manhattan have still another resource—the *Directory of Downtown Schools* (available for $1 from the Downtown Schools Association, c/o Little Red School House, 1196 Bleecker Street, New York, N.Y. 10012: 212-477-5316). The directory lists licensed public, private and parochial schools, encompassing day care and nursery up through high schools below 34 Street. The description of each school indicates the ages of the children served, the tuition, and the nature of the program. For an overview of Manhattan's nonpublic nursery schools, you might look at Linda Faulhaber's *The Manhattan Directory of Private Nursery Schools* (New York, Soho Press, 1987).

Child Care, Inc. is the basic information and referral link for parents and serves the five boroughs (see Chapter Two). They will prepare for you a customized packet that includes printouts of the programs in your neighborhood or on your way to work.

Any program (which is not family day care) enrolling more than five children under the age of six must be licensed by the New York City Department of Health. The Department of Health requires that there be two adults for every ten children if the group is made up predominantly of two-year-olds; two adults for fifteen children for three-year-olds; two adults for twenty children for four-year-olds; and two adults for twenty-five children for five-year-olds. In addition, at least one teacher must be certified in early childhood education. There are also regulations pertaining to the facility. To find out whether a program is licensed—and whether there have been any complaints about it—call 212-334-7813 for a private program, or the Agency for Child Development (212-553-6421) for public programs.

No doubt you'll be looking at the physical plant of the school. Although you'll be examining the rooms carefully, don't let your preconceptions about how a school should look override other considerations. Since many preschools in New York City are sandwiched into churches, community centers, and other buildings not designed primarily for use by children, their physical appearance may be old and appear unattractive, even dingy. While many schools have their own outdoor play spaces, it's also possible that the children will have to trek to a rooftop or to a nearby playground—even across a street—to play outdoors. Louise Golden's children attended a nursery school in the basement of a Catholic church. "When we first visited, we were appalled. You entered through a wet corridor and the rooms in the school were tiny. At first glance, the nursery school seemed awful." Louise and her husband overcame their reservations, however, after they observed the quality of the teaching and discovered the lovely parish garden off to the side of the school. Recalls Louise: "The garden was very special. The children were out there year-round. When spring came, they planted flowers and were always capturing bugs and looking at them under the microscope. My son spent most of his days in this truly unique space." In contrast, the school with the spiffiest facilities may also offer the most unimaginative, cookie-cutter kind of program. A warm environment may be more important than a shiny one. You must also decide whether you want your child in a school of fifty or fewer students—typical of a nursery school—or in a school of two hundred fifty, five hundred, or more, characteristic of an ongoing school. Putting your child in an elementary school's prekindergarten means that he's contending with eight- and nine-year-olds, as well as four-year-olds.

If you expect to send your child on to a private elementary school, don't panic about getting your child into the "right" nursery school. Independent schools draw their kindergartens from many nursery schools, not one or two. That pattern continues as the years progress. Observes Margaret Corey, for many years the executive vice president of the Educational Records Bureau: "Only 10 percent of the graduating class of one of the most competitive schools started with them in kindergarten. Look at the school that is right for your child, not the school that has the name."

Beyond Nursery School: Considering What's Best for Your Child

With any decision about education, it's critical for you to know your child's needs and your own. David Hertz, an independent school consultant and the former assistant director of the Ethical Culture Schools, believes that "parents should think about their child's talents, skills, and interests. If you know that your child is extraordinarily happy painting and likes to muck up, find a place where he can do that."

Take a close look at your values and your home environment and how that affects your child. Sometimes parents who run a rather carefree home are tempted to put their child into a more rigid school environment to provide more "structure." That may seem appealing, but do you really want to make your child cope with two very different climates? Will your child find himself caught in between? Observes Hertz: "If it's foreign to you, your child will be more comfortable elsewhere."

To get you started thinking about schools, consider:

- How large a school—or class—will your child be comfortable in?
- Does your child need a structured day or class?
- What kind of classroom environment does your child need? If your child doesn't sit for forty minutes, find a class where children don't sit. You can tell by the furniture. You can tell by the movement.

- What type of help does your child require from the teacher? Will he need frequent one-on-one attention, which is most often found in smaller classes?
- How does your child work best—in a group or by himself?
- How does your child learn best—through personal experience, by listening to others, or by working on his own?
- If the school population appears rather homogeneous, how will your child feel if he is different?
- What do you expect from the school? What's most important to you?
- How will the school's location—and your home's proximity to it—affect your child's participation there? How much time will your child spend commuting? What transportation arrangements must you make? If you select a non-neighborhood school, will your lifestyle be able to accommodate the friendships that he forms through school?
- How much financial sacrifice will you have to make to send your child to this school? Will sending your child to this school create a budgetary strain that might affect the quality of your family life?
- What has your child's nursery or preschool teacher, or another person who has observed your child outside the home, recommended in terms of school environments?
- What are your "gut feelings" about the type of school that is best for your child?

Remember you are choosing a school for now, not for the next twelve years. You can always change. Don't try to look eight years into the future in making your decision. Says Hertz: "What makes you think you know the right high school for your preschooler?" Nor should you use another parent's judgment to make your choice. Howard Johnson, director of the Medical Center Nursery School, maintains that "the damaging part of the parent network is the comment: 'Oh, it is a fabulous school. This is where your child should go.' " Only you know what's best for your child. Don't be tempted by a school's reputation or prestige.

Beyond Nursery:
Taking the Measure of a School

How then do you evaluate a school? Use a three-pronged approach—marshaling facts from catalogues or other published data about a school, visiting the school, and interviewing the administration and teachers as well as the parents of children attending the school. Begin with some basic questions, many of which can be answered by reading the catalogues that schools distribute or by evaluating information that the New York City Board of Education can provide.

- What type of school is it? Coed? Single-sex? Religious? Five-year school? Six-year? Eight-year? Twelve-year?
- What demographic information is available about the students? What is the overall enrollment at the school? What are the enrollments by grade? What is the size of an individual class? How high is the student turnover from year to year? What is turnover attributed to?
- How are classes organized? By grades? By age? By ability? Developmentally? Do classes straddle grades? Are there special classes for the gifted, learning disabled, or bilingual?
- Does the school have a stated philosophy, such as progressive or traditional? What's the attitude toward homework? How does the school handle behavior or disciplinary problems? How are classrooms organized? Don't be surprised to find that public schools, like private schools, have strongly articulated philosophies.
- What's the "basic" curriculum at the school? When is reading taught? How? How is student's work evaluated?
- Is there a religious-education component to the school's curriculum? What is involved? If you enroll your child in a parochial school, you probably will get a clear sense of the curriculum. Some independent schools, however, may require that children attend chapel or expect that children participate in a special event—such as a Christmas pageant. How do you feel about that?
- What special services does the school offer? Does it have any "unique" aspects of its curriculum? Are foreign languages taught (and when)? What are its library resources? Are there joint programs with other schools in arts, academics, or sports? What "extras" is the school devoting its money to?
- How does the school handle students who are academically talented in one or several areas? Will it ever accelerate students permitting them to skip grades? If so, how many? If not, why not?
- What can you learn about the administration? Who are the teachers on staff? How high is the teacher turnover? If you are looking at a public school, you might ask about: the principal (tenured?), regular teachers (tenured, probationary, class, cluster?), additional school staff

(librarian, guidance, aides, paraprofessionals?) How fast are staff vacancies filled?
- Who is responsible for lunchroom monitoring, bus duty, playground, screening, or other supervision?
- What about parent involvement? What role do parents and the parents association play? When you talk with a member of a parents association, ask them what their priorities are for the school. In some public schools, the parents association raises funds—sometimes running into the tens of thousands of dollars—to pay for enrichment programs at the school.
- Who in the school is accessible to parents?
- If your child will not be able to walk to school, what are the transportation arrangements available? What will it cost you?
- If you need after-school care for your child, does the school have a program? What does it cost? If not, what is available near the school? Can the program pick your child up at school—or will you have to make arrangements?
- If you are looking at a middle or junior high school, particularly in the public school system, what's the school's size? Will your child be comfortable in a large intermediate school? Is there a specialty that's emphasized? Is the school curriculum tracked? What high schools do graduates typically attend?
- If you are looking at the upper grades, you may want to evaluate the advanced placement program, interschool or college-affiliated programs, the college admissions record, and students' test scores. Ask also about the dropout rate.
- If you are looking at a public school, get some facts about the building: What is its capacity? How does that compare to the enrollment? How many classrooms are there and how are they being used? If rooms are used for other purposes, what are they for? Is there a separate gym? Is there a library? Is there a multiuse room? What are the eating facilities (separate lunchroom)? What are the maintenance needs of the building?
- If your child will be attending an all-day kindergarten in a public school, find out how it's handled. Have they expanded the curriculum to account for the extra hours?

Visiting a school and talking with the principal or headmaster and teachers is mandatory. Observes one parent: "Look at the yards. Look at the playgrounds. Look at the teachers. Look at some classrooms. Watch some kids. You'll know in half an hour if your child should go there." Remember that "good" schools can look very different and your decision is subjective as well as objective. When you visit, ask yourself:

- How do the children appear? Happy? Involved? Orderly? Running around? Interacting with each other?
- What's on the walls of the school (artwork, announcements)? What is the message that comes across to you?
- What's going on in the halls? Who's in the halls? Do children say hello to teachers they pass in the halls? Are children running or walking? If you are looking at the upper grades, what are the halls like between classes?
- How secure is the school? Did you walk into the school without being stopped? Does the school have regulations about children going off the school's premises? What are they? Ask the principal about the school and safety and ask the head of the parents association.
- What are your impressions of the teachers?
- Where's the principal or headmistress? Does she know the kids? Is her door opened or closed? Many experts will tell you that the principal sets the tone for the school and its learning environment. A school is only as strong as its leader. One parent made her decision when she met the school's headmistress: "I went to the tea and thought that the headmistress was an idiot."
- Do your observations jibe with what you've read about the school in its literature or heard about it from others? If not, what's the discrepancy? How do you feel about that?

Finally, and most importantly, how do you feel about the school? If you were a child, would you want to spend your day there? If not, why are you thinking about sending your child there?

The Public Schools of New York City

The basic statistics about the New York City public school system are staggering. Its budget for the school year 1985–86 was $4.7 billion. Nearly a million students—including 464,097 in 623 elementary schools, 184,956 in 179 intermediate/junior high schools, and 272,457 in 111 high schools, as well as 14,721 in 55 special education schools—enrolled. Almost three quarters of them belonged to minority groups.

Class size averaged close to twenty-five students in grades kindergarten through second, but reached more than thirty in the upper grades. Some classrooms in the city were considerably more crowded. In some elementary schools, you might even find two classes, with two teachers and two aides, sharing the same classroom.

It is also a system constricted by shortages. Basic curriculum services taken for granted in other public school systems are not necessarily found in New York City schools. In 1985, a study done by the Educational Priorities Panel found that several hundred New York City schools had no librarians or functioning school libraries. The report said that "school libraries were an easy target for retrenchment in 1975 and 1976. So-called 'temporary' reductions have become standard operating procedures for school libraries." The problem appears to be most severe at the elementary school level.

Yet some schools are among the most renowned in the country. In 1981, *Money* magazine ranked the Bronx High School of Science as among the "twelve top public high schools," while in 1984, the U.S. Department of Education named Benjamin Cardozo High School in Bayside, Queens, one of 114 outstanding secondary schools in the country. Locally some schools—and districts—have also made the news. In 1985, the Mark Twain Junior High School (J.H.S. 239) in District 21 of Brooklyn, a school for the gifted, had the top junior high school ranking based on citywide reading scores—a position it has held for most of the past ten years. In 1985, every elementary and junior high school in Districts 25 and 26 in Queens and in District 11 in the Bronx had schoolwide reading scores above the national median. Of the ten highest-scoring elementary schools in the city, four (P.S. 4, 5, 26, and 54) were on Staten Island. Number one citywide was Public School 5 in Staten Island, with more than 99 percent of its students reading above the median. On the other hand, many New York City schools achieved the dubious celebrity in 1985 of falling on a state list of schools with the worst performance on reading and math tests. The State Education Department singled out nearly four hundred city public schools as low-performing.

The Board of Education at 110 Livingston Street in Brooklyn (718-935-2000), under the direction of the school chancellor, sets basic policy. But the daily business of the public school system at the elementary and intermediate school level takes place in thirty-two separate fiefdoms (called community school districts; see map, page 83, which also gives their addresses and telephone numbers). Each community school district has its own budget and administers the elementary, intermediate, and junior high schools in its area. A nine-member community school board, elected for a three-year term, as well as a community superintendent appointed by the board are in charge. Only the high schools are under the direct control of the Board of Education.

Restriction, not choice, is the fundamental precept on which the entire school system operates. Says Doreen DeMartini of the Office of Community School District Affairs: "Youngsters are zoned to New York City public schools on the basis of geographical boundaries. Within the school district, there may be optional programs, but children will go to schools within their school district. You don't come into the city and pick a school." To learn what the zoned school is for a particular address, contact the Office of Zoning and Integration (110 Livingston Street, Brooklyn, N.Y. 11201: 718-935-3070) or your local community school district.

If you are unhappy with your zoned school, your choices are most likely—at best—limited to a few schools within your own district. You can attempt to get an intradistrict zoning variance (from your principal and district) or even go outside your district by applying for an interdistrict pupil variance transfer by obtaining the approvals of the superintendent of the "sending" and "receiving" districts. Your chances of success are not great. (Some parents try a third option—falsifying their address. If caught, they could be subject to prosecution.) One exception: If you move, your child may remain in his school until his graduation. Don't expect bus service, however.

Given the lack of choices, it's critical for New York City parents to have a clearcut picture of what's available within their community school district. You can request their annual report (required by law) and minutes of the monthly public meetings of the community school board. You can talk with a staff that includes a school superintendent, curriculum coordinator, and director of elementary schools. Look at your community school district's budget to see what they're spending their money on. Ask about their programs for special education, talented and gifted, bilingual education and T.O.E.S.L. (Teaching of English as a Second Language). Find out which schools have enrichment programs (e.g., art and music) and after-school programs. Keep in mind that each school will have different programs. Be sure to inquire about "theme programs" emphasizing music, the arts, or science, and alternative schools at the elementary

THE COMMUNITY SCHOOL DISTRICTS

1. 80 Montgomery Street
   New York, N.Y. 10002

2. 210 East 33 Street
   New York, N.Y. 10016

3. 300 West 96 Street
   New York, N.Y. 10035

4. 319 East 117 Street
   New York, N.Y. 10035

5. 433 West 123 Street
   New York, N.Y. 10027

6. 665 West 182 Street
   New York, N.Y. 10033

7. 501 Courtlandt Avenue
   Bronx, N.Y. 10451

8. 650 White Plains Road
   Bronx, N.Y. 10452

9. 1377 Jerome Avenue
   Bronx, N.Y. 10452

10. 3961 Hillman Avenue
    Bronx, N.Y. 10469

11. 1250 Arnow Avenue
    Bronx, N.Y. 10469

12. 1000 Jennings Street
    Bronx, N.Y. 10460

13. 355 Park Place
    Brooklyn, N.Y. 11238

14. 215 Heyward Street
    Brooklyn, N.Y. 11206

15. 360 Smith Street
    Brooklyn, N.Y. 11231

16. 1010 Lafayette Avenue
    Brooklyn, N.Y. 11221

17. 2 Linden Boulevard
    Brooklyn, N.Y. 11226

18. 755 East 100 Street
    Brooklyn, N.Y. 11236

19. 557 Pennsylvania Avenue
    Brooklyn, N.Y. 11207

20. 1031 59 Street
    Brooklyn, N.Y. 11219

21. 345 Van Siclen Avenue
    Brooklyn, N.Y. 11223

22. 525 Haring Street
    Brooklyn, N.Y. 11235

23. 2240 Dean Street
    Brooklyn, N.Y. 11233

24. 67-54 80 Street
    Middle Village, N.Y. 11379

25. 70-30 164 Street
    Flushing, N.Y. 11365

26. 61-15 Oceania Street
    Bayside, N.Y. 11364

27. 90-15 Sutter Avenue
    Ozone Park, N.Y. 11417

28. 108-55 69 Avenue
    Forest Hills, N.Y. 11375

29. 221-10 Jamaica Avenue
    Queens Village, N.Y. 11428

30. 36-25 Crescent Street
    Long Island City, N.Y. 11106

31. 221 Daniel Low Terrace
    Staten Island, N.Y. 10301

32. 797 Bushwick Avenue
    Brooklyn, N.Y. 11221

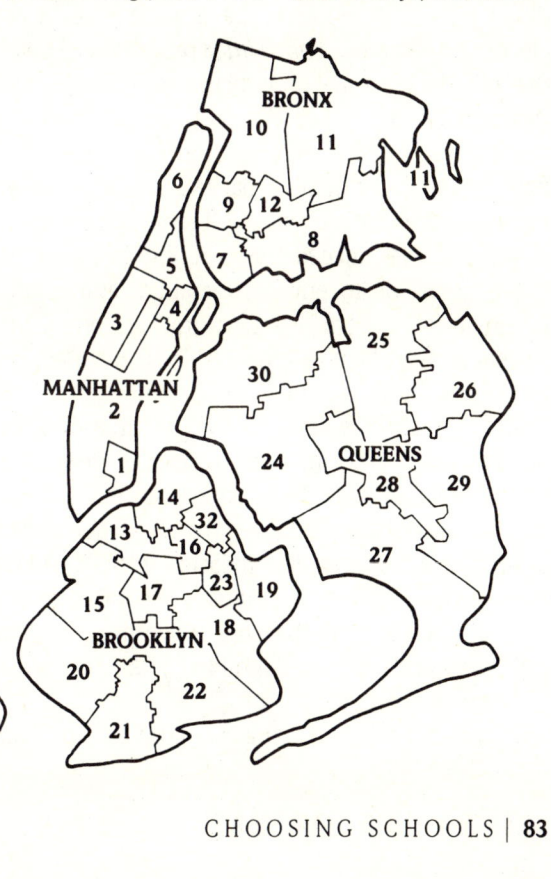

*Map courtesy of the
New York City Board of Education*

CHOOSING SCHOOLS | 83

or junior high levels. (District 4 in East Harlem, for example, has many alternative concept schools—including Central Park East I and II, River East, and the Maritime School—featuring open classrooms and minischools. Central Park East Secondary School for the upper grades is rooted in the educational philosophy of Professor Theodore Sizer of Brown University and is a member of the Coalition of Essential Schools. The district accepts students from other districts.)

Find out about special support systems within a school and the community resources schools take advantage of. Many schools participate in arts or museum programs. Others have links with universities. Teachers from Manhattan's P.S. 41 have participated in the workshops of the Teachers College Writing Project, while the Center School in Manhattan's Community School District 3 has had ties to Fordham University. Its students participate in performing arts activities. P.S. 183 in Manhattan incorporates science into its curriculum from kindergarten on and has turned to scientists at Rockefeller Institute, Sloan Kettering, and Cornell Medical Center for help. If you're unhappy with what you find, you can have a direct impact if you take the time to vote in community school board elections. *The New York Times* reported in May 1986 that "increasingly, the boards have become platforms not for parents but for teachers, supervisors, and other Board of Education employees." Only a small percentage of eligible voters in any one district usually take the time to vote, so that candidates backed by labor unions that turn out their members are often elected. Organized parents' slates in some districts, however, have succeeded in electing their candidates.

If you decide to enroll your child, admission at the elementary and intermediate school level is not a complicated procedure. Kindergarteners must be five years old by December 31. Registration is held in the spring before a child enters kindergarten (usually April and May; check the school your child will be attending for exactly when). You'll need to bring proof of birth, residence (lease, rent bill, or Con Ed bill), and immunizations. (New York State public health law requires that all children attending school—public, private, or parochial—be immunized against diphtheria, polio, measles, rubella, and mumps.) If you fail to register your child then, you can, of course, do so in the fall before school opens or at the time that you move into a neighborhood. School attendance is mandatory for all children, handicapped and nonhandicapped, at six years of age.

In the end, with a younger child, you'll probably be looking closely at your zoned school and those few other alternatives that may exist. To get information about individual schools, consult the Board of Education's book *School Profiles,* which compiles facts about the school districts as well as the individual schools within the district. The data for an individual school includes its physical facility (e.g., year of construction, capacity, utilization percentage), pupils (e.g., ethnic composition by grade, average class size, percent promoted, reading and mathematics scores), and staff (student/teacher ratio, percentage of teachers with five or more years' experience). Although the book is usually a few years out-of-date, it is a basic resource. *School Profiles* should be available at community school district offices and branches of the public library system. An employee in the Board of Education's Student Information Services at 110 Livingston Street (718-935-3841) will often give you the details for a specific school over the telephone or mail you a copy of a page in the book. If you're interested in learning about the current rankings of schools based on reading scores, the Office of Public Affairs (718-935-4320) can send you the *Annual Ranking of Schools by Reading Achievement.* Public Affairs can also provide you with a borough-wide list of schools and a wide range of other materials. (If you want an overview of the system, request from them a copy of the chapter on the Board of Education in *The Mayor's Management Report* and also *The Chancellor's Report Card.*)

Some schools will permit you to visit whenever you want; others will not. You can be assured access during "Open School Week" (in November and March), a time set aside by the New York City Board of Education for classroom visits in every school in the city. Some schools will also give tours for prospective kindergarten parents. It's advisable to call the school you're interested in before "Open School Week" to learn about their particular orientation programs. Ask the school to put you in touch with their parents association. (Official policy says that there must be a parents association or parent-teacher association in every public school.) The **United Parents Associations** (70 Lafayette Street, New York, N.Y. 10013: 212-619-0095), the citywide federation of public school parent associations and parent-teacher associations, will answer questions and refer you to local parents.

Unlike the elementary and intermediate schools, which operate under the decentralized system, the high schools, which start at ninth grade, are under the control of the Central Board. There are two kinds of public high schools in the city: the "lower" tier of zoned schools open to any student, and the "upper" tier of specialty and "theme" schools that recruit and select their students. These more selective schools offer both an abundance of riches—vocational-technical schools such as Aviation High School, specialized schools such as Stuyvesant High School and Fiorello H. LaGuardia High School of Music and the Arts, and alternative schools such as City-As-School—and, unfortunately for families trying to negotiate the system, an abundance of confusion.

The centralized admission process, with the overwhelming array of programs and details, leaves many students and parents adrift. Students use an official high school application in conjunction with the *Directory of the Public Schools* (available from the Division of High Schools, 110 Livingston Street, Brooklyn, N.Y. 11201: 718-935-3460), a 300-page book that lists all public high schools and gives information about the programs, entrance requirements, and deadlines. Applying to a particular program does not, however, guarantee a place. Entrance is often competitive and applicants have to take exams or audition for admission. Students who are not accepted to a specialty program or who do not apply attend their zoned high school.

Jill Blair of the Educational Priorities Panel has studied the confusion in the high schools and recommends that parents who want to explore the alternatives fully ask the Division of High Schools for every piece of information. Do this when your child is in seventh grade, since deadlines may be as early as October 15 of your child's eighth-grade year. You'll also want to attend the annual "September High School Fair." You'll have the chance to get to know all the programs available. Consider going twice—when your child is in *seventh* grade to shop around, and again when your child is in eighth grade so that you can concentrate on specific programs. If your child is applying to the four specialized high schools (Bronx High School of Science, Brooklyn Technical High School, Stuyvesant High School, or the Fiorello H. LaGuardia High School of Music and the Arts), be sure that by October 15 you get the special handbook describing the schools and the entrance exam given in December and January for the three science high schools.

Some students will prepare for the exam by enrolling in courses that focus on test-taking techniques and practice exams offered by the Stanley H. Kaplan Educational Center (131 West 56 Street, New York, N.Y. 10019: 212-977-8200) or by the GRF Tutoring Service (50 West 97 Street, New York, N.Y. 10025: 212-864-4085). Kaplan also provides preparation courses in the various boroughs for students who will be taking the standardized admission test used by many private schools or by the Catholic high school system. Finally, be aware that the public high school system has been under attack by educators and in 1986 the new executive director talked about a thorough reform of the two-tiered system.

GIFTED AND TALENTED PROGRAMS

One alternative you can explore is enrolling your child in the "gifted and talented" programs provided by each district. The criteria used by individual districts to define who is "gifted" varies. So do the specific programs districts offer. You may find that your district defines the top 15 percent of its children as "gifted" and has "pull-out" programs, focusing on enrichment activities and resource rooms. By contrast, District 18 in Brooklyn has full-time comprehensive programs. Says Joyce Rubin, director of gifted programs for District 18: "Our goal is to educate the top 3 percent of the population that needs a special environment. Gifted children need a differentiated curriculum. They don't only need faster. They need something different than what the average child is getting."

To learn about your district's programs, contact the co-ordinator for the gifted and talented. Since admission is selective, the co-ordinator can give you details about how children are chosen and where you can get your child tested. Be sure that you understand the exact nature of your district's gifted program.

If you live in Manhattan, your child may also apply for admission to Hunter College Elementary School, a public school with classes from nursery through sixth grade. Students enter at the four-year-old nursery level (about 32 students) and kindergarten (fifteen places). For information and an application, contact the **Hunter College Campus Schools** (94 Street and Park Avenue, New York, N.Y. 10128: 212-860-1262) the autumn before the school year your child would enter. The school will send you instructions about the preliminary admission test after they receive your completed application. There is a second round of testing for "finalists" at the school. Acceptance notices are sent out around April 15. Competition for admission is typically fierce. The upper school, Hunter College High School, admits students from all boroughs at the seventh-grade level. To take the entrance exam, students must have scores at least four years above grade level in both mathematics and reading on a standardized achievement test.

The **Center for the Study and Education of the Gifted at Teachers College, Columbia University** (Box 170, Teachers College, Columbia University, New York, N.Y. 10027: 212-678-3851) serves as a clearinghouse. It also runs the Hollingworth Preschool for "intellectually able" three- and four-year olds (admission based upon testing) and Saturday and summer enrichment courses for children from the ages of four to fifteen. Most nonpublic schools wouldn't describe themselves as developing curricula especially for gifted students. **St. Ann's School** in Brooklyn Heights is an exception, as is **Regis High School** in Manhattan. St. Ann's, which runs from preschool through high school, was established "with the express purpose of affording bright children an education specifically tailored to their needs." Regis High School, run by the Jesuits, each year admits 130 Catholic boys who test in the eighth grade as academically gifted. There is no tuition. Admission is at the ninth grade only.

If you're looking for a Saturday enrichment program, try Teacher's College or the St. John's University School of Continuing Education in Queens. Their program is for youngsters from the ages of ten to fourteen.

△ △ △ △ △ △ △ △ △ △ △

Nonpublic Schools

In the five boroughs, there are Roman Catholic, Jewish, Lutheran, Seventh Day Adventist, Episcopal, Greek Orthodox, Russian Orthodox, Baptist, Presbyterian, Quaker, Islamic, and Christian Fundamentalist schools, as well as independent schools with no religious affiliation. Of all these, more than half are Roman Catholic and a quarter are Jewish.

Roman Catholic schools come under the aegis of the **Archdiocese of New York** (Office of the Superintendent of Schools, 1011 First Avenue, New York, N.Y. 10022: 212-371-1000) and the **Diocese of Brooklyn** (Office of Catholic Education, 6025 Sixth Avenue, Brooklyn, N.Y. 12220: 718-492-1800). The Archdiocese of New York (encompassing Manhattan, the Bronx, and Staten Island) claims that its schools "educate approximately 15 percent of all school-aged children in New York City." The Diocese of Brooklyn covers Brooklyn and Queens. Neighborhood-based elementary schools go from preschool or kindergarten through grade eight. Each school handles its own admissions. Non-Catholics can apply—in 1985, 14 percent of the students in the Diocese of Brooklyn schools were non-Catholic—but preference is given to parishioners. The Archdiocese of New York estimates that tuition, which is set by the individual schools, ranges from $450 to $1,000, plus fees, while the Diocese of Brooklyn reports that the average tuition is $800 per child but can range from $600 to $1,000. There is usually a sliding scale for two or more children. With a maximum class size of thirty-six in Archdiocesan schools, classes can be large.

Admission to the predominantly single-sex high schools is also handled by the individual schools. Eighth-graders, however, take the Cooperative Admissions Examination Program as one basis for admission at many of the schools. This test is only given twice—in the fall. Students must apply to take the exam in September and October. For details about these schools, including which teaching community staffs them, their educational programs, tuition (most charge between $1,000 and $2,500), and size, contact the Archdiocese and Diocese.

Jewish schools range from Orthodox yeshivas, such as Salanter Akiba Riverdale Academy or the United Lubavitcher Yeshivoth in Brooklyn, to the nondenominational Abraham Joshua Heschel School in Manhattan. Most of the Jewish schools in New York are Orthodox. Many are Hassidic and Talmudic schools located in Williamsburg and Boro Park, Brooklyn. Each school has its own procedures for admission. Rabbi Joshua Fishman of Torah Umesorah warns that in certain neighborhoods, particularly in Flatbush or Boro Park, schools fill up early. "If you apply in November," he says, "you're late." The tuition in Orthodox schools can also vary, from the waiver of fees for an impoverished family to up to $1,800.

Two sources of information about Jewish schools are the **Board of Jewish Education of Greater New York** (212-245-8200) and **Torah Umesorah** (The National Society for Hebrew Day Schools, 160 Broadway, New York, N.Y. 10039: 212-227-1000). Both publish directories of schools. The Board of Jewish Education can also provide you with information about nursery programs, after-school programs, and special education programs.

There are also many nondenominational nonpublic schools in the City of New York. There are large coed schools, like Dalton or Riverdale Country, and intimate ones, like Corlears. There are schools just for girls—Spence, Chapin, and Nightingale-Bamford—and just for boys—Collegiate. Each is unique. French is spoken at the Lycée Français de New York. Students at the Manhattan Country School spend part of each year studying at a farm in upstate New York, where they develop proficiency in skills, such as milking a cow. The United Nations International

School, with one campus in Manhattan and another in Queens, prepares its students for an international baccalaureate, while the Professional Children's School takes as a given that its students may be acting in a Broadway play or training intensively with the New York City Ballet.

Nor are all the schools in Manhattan. Among the schools in the other boroughs are: the Berkeley–Carroll Street School and the Packer Collegiate Institute in Brooklyn, the Staten Island Academy on Staten Island, and Horace Mann in the Bronx. For a listing of all the nonpublic schools, contact the New York State Education Department (Publications Distribution Unit, Education Building Annex, Albany, N.Y. 12234: 212-488-3900) to request a copy of their annual *Directory of Nonpublic Schools and Administrators, New York State* ($1). This directory contains a county-by-county listing for New York State that gives the name of the school, its address, telephone number, and school administrator.

Many of the nondenominational schools (as well as some which are church-affiliated) belong to the Independent Schools Admissions Association of Greater New York (ISAAGNY). These schools have developed certain common application and testing procedures, although the admissions and the decision making is done by individual schools. The *New York Independent Schools Directory* describes individual schools. If you apply to an ISAAGNY school, your application may be due by December 1 or January 1. Most of the schools require that children be tested by the Educational Records Bureau. In addition, you'll be asked to visit the school (either for a group or a private tour) and most likely be interviewed by an admissions officer. Your child will also be interviewed ("observed"). Some schools will meet groups of children; others will see children individually. Each school has its own procedures for interviewing. Unlike the public schools, where kindergarteners must be five by December 31, most independent schools will require that a child be five by September 1 (some schools will have different birthday cutoff dates for boys and girls).

Tuition for most independent schools ranges between $5,000 and $9,000, with the charge rising by the grade. At Chapin, for example, in 1986–87 kindergarten cost $5,500, first grade $6,300, sixth grade $7,400, and twelfth grade $7,900. For the same school year, tuition at Dalton for the senior year was set at $8,630, at Columbia Grammar $7,366, and at Horace Mann $7,560. Tuition, however, is only part of the overall cost of independent school. Plan on possible expenses for lunch, uniforms, after-school enrichment activities (e.g., piano, dance), school trips, transportation, and tutoring. In the upper grades, there are book and lab fees. You may also be asked to make some voluntary contributions. There may, however, be financial aid.

The **Parents League** functions as a nonprofit service organization for ISAAGNY schools. Volunteer counselors will talk with you about member schools. You can purchase from them a copy of the *New York Independent Schools Directory* as well as their *Calendar*, which lists information on school vacation dates and after-school and weekend activities for children. Members also receive their newsletter and an annual journal. In October, the League holds an "Independent School Day," open to the public, where you can meet with representatives of the various schools. (This alternates annually with a "Boarding School Day.") The League is open during the school year, following the independent schools' calendar.

The **Educational Records Bureau** (3 East 80 Street, New York, N.Y. 10021: 212-535-0307), which administers tests for ISAAGNY, will also consult with you, for an additional fee, about school possiblities. The **Independent Educational Counselors Association** (38 Cove Road, P.O. Box 125, Forrestdale, Mass. 02644: 617-477-2127) has members in the New York area who can provide you with an alternative professional counseling service. Some of their counselors can administer tests and advise on day schools, boarding schools, and special educational needs. You pay their fee. Observes Patsy Wainwright, head of the Middle School at Nightingale–Bamford: "If you move in from out of town or are looking for a place beyond kindergarten, a consultant may save you a lot of phone calls." There are also some advisory services that, at no charge to you, will contact schools (or summer camps) on your behalf and ask them to send you an application (you'll be told that the school will probably waive the application fee). Keep in mind, however, that these services do indeed receive a commission from the school for each successful placement.

Where does all this knowledge about public and private schools leave a parent? Observed one Park Slope mother contemplating the future for her four-year-old: "The public school near us has just gotten funding for an arts program and it has an after-school program where I can send my child." But, she noted, "There are several private schools. Parochial school is an option because I'm Catholic. It's always a matter of trade-offs."

HAVE YOU WONDERED ABOUT PRIVATE SCHOOLS?

In certain neighborhoods of Manhattan, applying to private school becomes a central parental preoccupation and leads to great anxiety. Recalls a parent who submitted applications to a half-dozen schools and whose child now attends Nightingale–Bamford: "It was one of the worst experiences of my life. I was really uptight." Parents' concern is fueled by articles such as Dr. Beatriz Rubinstein's "Making the Private School Grade," which appeared in *New York* magazine in October 1986. In her provocative essay, Dr. Rubinstein tells parents how to prep their preschooler for the tests administered by the Educational Records Bureau. Dr. Rubinstein advises parents to work and play "with your child a few special minutes a day, using certain toys and materials that will help develop the skills being tested. The preparation I suggest here will bring out the skills he already has." Not everyone, however, shares this view.

The hysteria that seems to be gripping New York parents and the multiplication of applications now worries educators. Herewith some questions that parents often come up with—and the answers:

What's the First Thing That You Should Do When You're Thinking about Applying?

Admissions people recommend that you read the school's catalogue carefully. You may be able to weed out many schools that way. Make note of the cutoff date for applications, the fees and overall tuition, and the school's policy on testing and interviews. If you have more than one child whom you expect to send to independent school, you might want to inquire if there is sibling preference in admissions.

When Should You Start to Look for a Private School?

If your child will be applying for kindergarten admission, and if you have the time and fortitude and live in Manhattan, you might want to attend the Parents League's "Independent School Fair," even if your child is just three. You might also contact some schools in the spring of your child's third year—after independent schools have admitted their incoming classes. That is the "slowest" time of year for the admissions office and you might be able to take a tour then. You'll probably have to come back again in the fall, however, so if time is precious, don't bother.

Waiting until the fall of your child's fourth year is just fine.

How Many Schools Should You Apply To?

If you live in Manhattan, you might initially want to get information about as many as eight schools. Margaret Corey believes that "Four is a good number to apply to, if you're realistic in your four. If you're not realistic, then ten is not enough."

You should also be aware of the cycles of admission that schools go through. There are more spaces in the earlier grades. Many schools also expand at seventh grade. If you're applying to a benchmark grade (e.g., prekindergarten to second, seventh, or ninth grade), then you probably don't need to apply to as many schools as you might if your child will be trying to enter at grade five. Your need for professional counseling is also greatest if your child is applying for one of the "off" years.

I've Heard That the Competition for Admission Is So Keen That Children Are Turned Down for Admission.

David Hertz can't think of many situations where children do not get into a private school. Says he: "There is a sufficient number of private schools in the city to match the numbers of people applying." Howard Johnson, who has served on the board of ISAAGNY, reported that in 1985 many schools moved onto their waiting lists very quickly. He attributes this to families submitting multiple applications, leaving many independent schools unclear as to exactly how many children were seeking admission.

It's May and We've Just Learned That We're Moving to Manhattan This Fall. What Are Our Child's Chances of Admission?

Howard Johnson reports that "many schools have openings right up to the fall." An admissions specialist concurs: "I've never found a parent moving into the city who hasn't found a suitable place. Schools are well aware of the need to save places for those who find themselves relocated in the months of February or September. I would save places. Not everyone is in the position a year prior to know the school needs of their children."

Consult the Educational Records Bureau, the Parents League, or an independent counselor to learn about specific openings.

If I Ask Questions of the Admissions Staff about a School, Will It Negatively Affect My Child's Admission?

Patsy Wainwright believes that it's OK to ask questions. "People pull out their lists and I'm always impressed," she says. "The questions that I find inappropriate are those clearly answered in the catalogue."

I've Understood That My Child Will Have to Be Tested. What's Involved?

ISAAGNY, in cooperation with the Educational Records Bureau, has established a joint testing program. E.R.B. testing for kindergarten admission may sometimes be done at your child's nursery school, if the school is a member of ISAAGNY. If not, it will be done at the Educational Records Bureau. Other schools use different admissions tests. Check with them for specifics about where you should have your child tested.

Younger children are usually given an oral test. This academic aptitude test engages the child in conversation about the environment or in simple arithmetic tasks such as counting blocks. The examiner pays attention to the child's vocabulary, fine motor control, and appreciation of spatial relationships. Howard Johnson emphasizes that "you cannot prepare children to take intelligence tests. It's the kind of information that comes from the environment, growing up, and development." Children in grades three and up take written aptitude and achievement tests.

What about Financial Aid?

All schools have a commitment to financial aid but packages vary. Some find it difficult to provide aid at the lower grades. Keep in mind that if yours is a late admission you may find that the limited financial pool is exhausted.

There is no central clearinghouse for information about financial aid. Check with the schools that interest you. Ask about scholarships, loans and options for extended payment.

△ △ △ △ △ △ △ △ △ △ △

Special Education

Under U.S. Public Law 94-142, all children with handicapping conditions, including mental, physical, sensory, emotional, or speech and language difficulties are entitled to a free appropriate public education. The school system must provide it or alternatively pay an external agency for services. The handicapped child also has the right to instruction in the least restrictive environment, as well as the right of equal treatment and due process.

New York City has special programs for children with learning disabilities, mental retardation, and other handicaps. Some classes take place within the regular school setting, with children participating in a resource room at least one period a day or in a self-contained classroom.

Others are in separate facilities. Each school district has a Committee on Special Education (C.S.E.; known also as the Committee on the Handicapped). Its main function is to work with parents and professionals in developing recommendations to the Board of Education regarding the classification, evaluation, and educational programs of each handicapped child from the ages of five to twenty-one.

A request for services can be initiated by parents or by school personnel. Once this happens, state regulations stipulate that your child must be studied by the Committee or a school-based support team within thirty school days. You must, however, be informed about every step of the evaluation process. Your child cannot be evaluated or put into a special education program without your consent. Once the evaluation of your child is completed, the Committee recommends an appropriate individualized education program with learning goals for the year. Services must be offered to your child within thirty school days of the completion of the study. Despite these clear-cut guidelines, you may find that getting the services can be very time-consuming.

If you disagree with the school district about the provision of special education for your child, you have the right to challenge and to request an impartial hearing. At the hearing, both sides present their views to a hearing officer who then makes a recommendation.

Parents of children attending nonpublic school can also ask the Committee for services. In all likelihood, they may have to go to the public schools to get the services, which might be an after-school resource room or a speech and language program. There are also independent schools, such as the Stephen Gaynor School and the Gateway School of New York, which specialize in the education of the learning disabled. Tuition can be steep—as much as $9,000. If you can prove that the public education system cannot provide an appropriate education for your child, you may be able to get state support for sending your child to a private school. Not all special education schools, however, accept public education funding.

You don't have to wait until your child is elementary school-aged to avail yourself of special education facilities and programs. The New York State Education Department supports a network of Early Childhood Direction Centers for children ages birth through four (see Chapter Four) that help parents match the individual needs of young handicapped children to services within their region. These centers can make referrals on questions of diagnosis and service. Your child may also be eligible for a

Head Start program, since 10 percent of the enrollment must be reserved for handicapped children, and in such cases need is as much a criterion for eligibility as income. You may be able to educate your preschooler for free, even if he's attending a private program, since some special education programs can receive state funding if parents petition the Family Court to request these services. Most special preschools are equipped to do the petitioning of Family Court.

Resources for Children with Special Needs, Inc. (200 Park Avenue South, Suite 816, New York, N.Y. 10003: 212-677-4650) is a referral, advocacy, and support center that can help you take your bearings. Their computerized information includes public and private schools, educational resources, infant and preschool programs, day-care and child care services. You might also want to contact the **Foundation for Children with Learning Disabilities** (99 Park Avenue, New York, N.Y. 10016: 212-687-7211), which publishes a parent guide and a directory of schools. If your child is dyslexic, contact **The Orton Dyslexia Society** (80 Fifth Avenue, New York, N.Y. 10011: 212-691-1930). **Advocates for Children of New York** (24-16 Bridge Plaza South, Long Island City, N.Y. 11101: 718-729-8866) focuses on equal educational opportunities and due-process safeguards for New York City public school children. If you have a question on your child's rights, they can help.

Two booklets—*Special Education: A Guide for Parents* and *Special Education for Handicapped Children Birth to Five*—spell out much of the basic information (available free from the Office for Education of Children with Handicapping Conditions, New York State Education Department, Division of Program Development, Education Building Annex, Albany, N.Y. 12234: 212-488-3900). You should also be in touch with the Board of Education's Division of Special Education (718-596-8928). If your child is attending a private school, you may want to see *Placement and Education of Children with Handicapping Conditions in Private, State-Operated, and State-Supported Schools.*

Rights

Whether your child is attending public or private school, you have the right by law to see all of your child's official school records and to have them explained. You also can ask for standardized test scores. You can ask your school's principal to show them to you.

To get a copy of your child's computerized public school records from the New York City Board of Education, write to the **Office of Community School District Affairs** (Board of Education, 110 Livingston Street, Brooklyn, N.Y. 11201: 718-935-3050). Be sure you include your name, address, your child's full name, school, and borough. You will receive a form to complete. Under federal law, you must get a copy of the record within forty-five days.

If you have questions about your child's rights, or believe that your child has been unfairly treated, contact Advocates for Children.

Schooling at Home

Not every child in New York City attends a school. Sometimes, because of illness or other conditions, children are educated at home. The Board of Education has a special Office of Hospital and Home Instruction (212-534-0088). Some parents educate their children at home, however, not for reasons of health but of personal choice. New York State permits this, but you must prove that you are providing an equivalent education. Your first step is to contact your community school district, which is responsible for *all* the children in the district, and meet with the district superintendent. You must then submit a detailed contract which, if accepted, would be monitored by the district during the year. Expect that your child will be required to take any statewide test that is grade-appropriate. Says Dolores Murray of the New York State Education Department: "You have to make an excellent argument for not having the child in a public or private school setting." If home schooling appeals to you, contact **Holt Associates** (729 Boylston Street, Boston, Mass. 02116: 617-377-1550) which is a nationwide advocacy organization. They also publish a bimonthly newsletter, *Growing Without Schooling*.

▽ ▽ ▽ ▽ ▽ ▽ ▽ ▽ ▽ ▽ ▽

HOMEWORK HELP

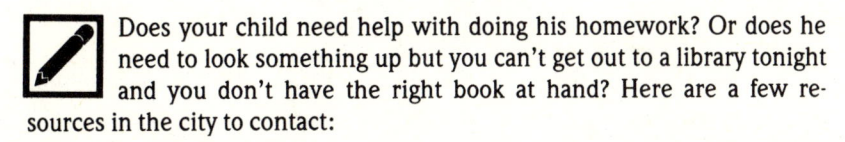

Does your child need help with doing his homework? Or does he need to look something up but you can't get out to a library tonight and you don't have the right book at hand? Here are a few resources in the city to contact:

- **Dial-A-Teacher: 212-777-3380:** Parents can call this hotline, developed by the United Federation of Teachers, Mon.–Thurs. 4–7 on school days.

- **Homework Hotline: 718-780-7766:** Operated by the Brooklyn Public Library, this hotline is for students and their parents, Mon.–Thurs. 5–8, while school's open.
- **Rewrite: 718-739-7483:** If you've got trouble deciding whether "is" or "was" belongs in the sentence, get grammar help from York College in Queens, on school days 1–4.
- **Homework Assistance Program** of the Langston Hughes Community Library and Cultural Center in Corona, Queens (718-672-2710): provides on-site adult supervision and local high school tutors for students in third through seventh grades. They serve also as the liaison for the students with their parents and local schools.

△ △ △ △ △ △ △ △ △ △ △

chapter 4
meeting your child's health care needs

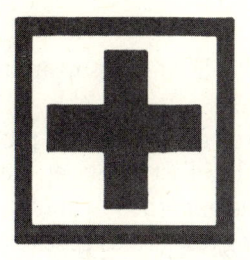

To get a sense of the vastness of New York's health care system, let's start with some statistics. In 1982, according to a survey done by the Greater New York Hospital Association, there were seventy-seven community hospitals in the city, 61 percent of them affiliated with medical schools. There were more than twenty-five thousand physicians working in the five boroughs, nearly half of them in private practice. The largest concentration of doctors was in Manhattan, followed by Brooklyn, Queens, the Bronx, and Staten Island.

New York City has its own public health system, designed to provide both well-child and sick-child care. The Department of Health operates both Child Health Stations and Pediatric Treatment Centers. Children up to the age of six receive free preventive health care, including checkups and immunizations, at the Child Health Stations. The Pediatric Treatment Centers see healthy children (infant to six years old) and sick youngsters (infant to twelve years old). The Department of Health also offers special immunization clinics for school-aged children that anyone can use. The Health and Hospitals Corporation, responsible for operating the city's general care and long-term hospitals, has Pediatric Clinics (located at the hospitals or at family care centers) that care for both healthy and sick children. While the Pediatric Treatment Centers and the Pediatric Clinics are open weekdays from 9:00 A.M. to 4:30 P.M., the Child Health Stations have a more limited schedule that you'll need to find out about in advance. To learn more about these facilities, and to locate the ones nearest you, call the Department of Health (212-566-7080).

There are other suppliers of free, primarily preventive, health care. The **Children's Aid Society** (105 East 22 Street, New York, N.Y. 10010: 212-949-4800), through its neighborhood centers, offers health exams, immunizations, and counseling, as well as special adolescent health services. **The Floating Hospital** (Pier 84, Hudson River, 44 Street and Twelfth Avenue, New York, N.Y. 10036: 212-736-0745) is a shipboard medical and dental center that primarily serves very low-income families. During the months of July and August, the ship makes day trips along the Hudson River. While on board, visitors are given extensive health screening for medical problems. Cruise tickets are distributed through Child Health Stations and community agencies. If you qualify, however, you can write to request tickets. From September to June, the ship is docked at Pier 84. Public school teachers can call about class trips to see a presentation by the children's health theater.

For many New Yorkers, however, health care comes via the private, rather than the public, sector through physicians in private practice and at voluntary non-profit hospitals or for-profit (proprietary) hospitals. What health care services people select, and how they use them, is closely linked to the health insurance that they have.

If you are employed full-time, chances are that you have health insurance coverage under an employer's group policy. If you are self-employed, then you may have signed up independently with a health insurance carrier. Or you may qualify to apply for the medical assistance program, Medicaid. Low-income people unable to pay for medical care or people with high uninsured medical bills are eligible (for an application, call 212-594-3050).

Health insurance has been based traditionally on fee-for-service. The client chooses his doctor and the nonprofit health insurance company, such as Blue Shield or the commercial health insurance company (for example, Equitable or Travelers), pays the physician or reimburses the patient for the expenses of the services provided. Linked to this coverage of doctor bills is usually a policy, such as Blue Cross, which covers hospital costs. The virtue of these plans has been that the patient decides which doctors to consult and where he will be hospitalized. Among the drawbacks: Out-of-pocket expenses can mount up, patients may skip checkups or find it frustrating to have to locate doctors. Well-baby visits, periodic checkups, and immunizations are usually not covered; deductibles must be met and only a percentage of the service—typically 80 percent—is covered.

As an alternative, some New Yorkers are looking to H.M.O.'s (Health Maintenance Organizations), which provide complete medical care for themselves and their families—covering everything from well-baby visits to major surgery to hospitalization—for a fixed fee. There are no out-of-pocket expenses and no claim forms to fill out. Often all the required services—doctors, labs, X rays, pharmacy—are centralized in one spot. In New York City, the Health Insurance Plan (H.I.P.) is one long-standing, nonprofit H.M.O. H.I.P. has medical groups that provide services through over sixty multispecialty and primary care centers. The centers are linked also to certain hospitals in the metropolitan area. Medical groups are staffed by physicians, nurses, optometrists, laboratory and X-ray technicians, social workers and health educators. You select a primary pediatrician for your child from the panel of physicians on staff and can expect continuity of care. H.I.P.'s Medical Director Dr. Isobel Pollack believes that "from the point of view of parents with young children, H.I.P. is super. We cover routine immunizations, well-baby care, and provide round-the-clock coverage."

Empire Blue Cross/Blue Shield operates another H.M.O. plan. There's likely to be an expansion in the number of H.M.O.s in the New York area as for-profit groups such as Humana Health Care, Maxicare, and U.S. Healthcare enter the New York market. An expanding H.M.O. option is the I.P.A. (Individual Practice Association). The I.P.A. contracts with doctors in individual practice to provide health services to H.M.O. members. The doctor cares for the patient in his own office, instead of at a group, and the H.M.O. pays the doctor.

New York City employees have still another possibility: Group Health Incorporated/Blue Cross. Under the G.H.I. component, participating providers (physicians, nurse-midwives, or chiropractors, for example) agree to charge the patient just $5 for an office or home visit and then to accept G.H.I.'s payment for the rest. Medical care in hospitals and dental care is also covered. If you see a "nonparticipating physician," G.H.I. reimburses you, rather than the doctor, based on a set fee schedule (your out-of-pocket expenses could be as much as 50 percent here). You also have hospitalization coverage through Blue Cross.

Whether you join an H.M.O., use doctors in private practice, or visit a clinic in the public system, you should be an informed, inquisitive consumer of health care. Questions can be asked—and concerns raised—

about all of them. Says one mother who's used H.I.P. for more than fifteen years: "You can shop just as hard in H.I.P. as you might for a doctor in private practice."

Choosing a Physician for Your Child

If you're the parent of a new baby, observes parent educator Gloria Rubin, "the relationship with your child's physician is intense." At the minimum, you'll see your doctor for frequent well-baby checkups in the first year, but there's a good chance that you'll make additional office visits for the occasional bout of diarrhea, diaper rash, or earache. Add to that some telephone discussions about feeding or your baby's fussiness and you could be seeing your doctor as much as some friends. Given these circumstances, says Rubin, the co-author of *Living with Your New Baby* (New York: Berkley Books, 1980), "you're buying a physician's philosophy as well." Ideally, you'd like to say about your child's doctor what Adrienne Fuller says about hers: "I feel comfortable with her practice and comfortable with the decisions she's made. I feel like she's a friend now."

The physician's hospital affiliation should be a first consideration in your choice. Says Dr. James Lione, chairman of the Department of Pediatrics at Flushing Hospital: "You want your doctor to be affiliated with a not-for-profit community hospital and an institution which has a residency training program." Observes Dr. Louis Z. Cooper, director of Pediatric Service at St. Luke's–Roosevelt Hospital Center: "New York pediatricians are linked to big institutions—to teaching institutions." Why is this so critical? Queens pediatrician Dr. Ivan Koota feels: "When you need to hospitalize a child, you are usually hospitalizing very sick children. It's nice to have the highest technology available. In pediatrics, there's the potential for something going horribly bad at the last moment."

Although your child is not likely to be hospitalized, you want to be assured that, should the need arise, he will get the best care possible. Your doctor's hospital affiliation is likely to determine where your child is sent for a medical workup, for hospitalization, or for emergency treatment. It will also influence his physician referrals. Before you settle on a doctor, gather some information about the hospitals where he's affiliated. Most doctors are affiliated with just one or two hospitals. Is the hospital part of a medical school? Does it have a pediatric residency program? A full range of pediatric services? At pediatric teaching hospitals, you'll find not only general pediatric services but specialty units in, for example, cardiology, gastroenterology, hematology, and oncology. Many of the city's hospitals have separate pediatric emergency rooms or areas set aside in the general emergency room to handle pediatrics. Recommends Elizabeth Sommers of the Greater New York Hospital Association: "Keep in mind the quality of the hospital as a safety net if your child should really get sick."

You've also got to decide what *you* want from your child's doctor, aside from a satisfactory hospital affiliation. Do you expect the doctor just to provide medical care, or are you looking for guidance and parental education as well? Have you considered a specialist in family practice as an alternative to a pediatrician? How much hand-holding do you need? How do you feel about a doctor's availability in case of illness? Do you want *your* doctor to be on call the majority of times that your child is not well, or is a "covering" doctor—an associate or another physician affiliated with the center—acceptable? How far from home do you want to travel to obtain medical care? What do other parents—friends, neighbors, and colleagues—tell you about their doctors? What do they like? What bothers them?

You may want to interview several doctors in advance, so that you have a sense of them, their office, and its procedures. Plan on paying for this visit, since you are taking up the doctor's time. Try to come when there are patients around, so that you can observe other parents and children in the office. How are sick and well children handled? In some areas of the city, and in some practices, pediatricians have two separate waiting rooms. Some even have lab facilities on the premises. In this brief meeting, try to get a sense of whether you'd be comfortable with the physician. Listen carefully to the answers. How do you feel, for example, about a doctor who tells you: "I always prescribe vitamins . . ." Recommends Dr. Richard K. Stone of the Metropolitan Hospital: "Think about the three A's and the two C's. That is—Affability, Availability, Accessibility, Comprehensiveness, and Continuity." There's a third C, also: Convenience.

Finally, if you are unhappy with your pediatrician at a later point, remember that you can always make a change. Says Dr. Cooper: "In a city like New York, you don't have to settle. You can find the style that suits you." Concurs another pediatrician: "No doctor can be all things to all patients."

To locate a doctor you can:

- Get recommendations from your obstetrician, midwife, another physician or childbirth educator.
- Check with the County Medical Societies. You can also contact the American Academy of Pediatrics (141 Northwest Point Boulevard, Elk Grove Village, Ill. 60007: 312-228-5005) or the American Academy of Family Physicians (1740 West 92 Street, Kansas City, Mo. 64114: 816-333-9700).
- Contact the directors of pediatrics at hospitals. Says Dr. Cooper: "They'll tend to give the names of junior faculty. Ask for several names."

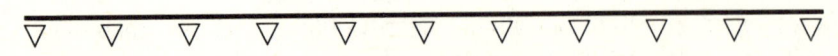

FIND OUT ABOUT

Ask the Doctor

- How are the phone calls handled? If I call, will I speak with you or the nurse? If you cannot talk with me, when am I likely to hear back?
- Do you have "call-in" hours? Some doctors set aside special times when you can phone in with questions. These sound great, but be prepared for a busy signal when you try.
- What happens if my child is sick at night or on a weekend? How do I reach you? Do you make house calls? Some pediatricians and family physicians do!
- What are your office hours? Maintains Diana Simkin of Family Focus: "Office hours are a reflection of the philosophy of the doctor."
- What are your fees? How do you handle medical insurance?
- How do you treat a common cold? What medicines do you often prescribe? Will you prescribe medication over the telephone?
- If both parents work: How do you feel about working mothers? How do you feel about having someone other than a parent bring my child for checkups or for sick-child visits?
- If the doctor is part of a medical group: How often will I be seeing your associates?
- If you are the mother of a newborn: How do you feel about breast-feeding? What percentage of your patients breast-feed?

Ask Other Parents

- How long do patients typically wait when they come to the office before they are seen?
- How available is the doctor by telephone?
- Does the doctor listen to a parent's intuition about the child? Recalled one mother: "My son had recurrent ear infections. We noticed that he tended to have nosebleeds before he complained of ear pain. We discovered that this was of no consequence, but when I first suggested it, my pediatrician was willing to take my observation seriously."
- How does the doctor get along with children?
- How willing is the doctor to answer questions?
- How much time does the doctor routinely take with your child and with you?
- Are you comfortable with your doctor's backup and the arrangements?
- If the doctor is part of a medical group: How often has your child been seen by his associates? Under what circumstances? How do you feel about them?
- How well does the doctor—or doctors—know your child?
- If you were to move, what would you look for in your next doctor: Knowing what you know about Dr. X, would you choose him again? Why? Why not?

△   △   △   △   △   △   △   △   △   △   △

Children in Hospitals

Your child may have to visit an emergency room or possibly have a lab test or X ray done at a hospital, but the chances are that your child will not be hospitalized overnight. Reports one Manhattan pediatrician: "In my practice, I might have one patient a year who will be hospitalized for an extended period of time." Visit any hospital's pediatric floor and you'll see that the majority of the children there are chronically ill or suffering from serious medical problems or disabilities. Says Dr. Cooper: "In a hospital, you get sick kids."

Hospitals' inpatient pediatric populations have changed so dramatically because many common pediatric problems—hernia repair, tonsillectomy, cystoscopy, myringotomy (ear draining with tubes), extropia (crossed eyes), biopsies, and removal of cysts—are now handled in ambulatory, also known as day or walk-away, surgery. You'll find these walk-away centers in hospitals, although in the years to come New York is also going to have freestanding clinics. Empire Blue Cross/Blue Shield and other health insurers have created lists, which they have sent to physicians and institutions, recommending which procedures should be done on a one-day basis. The pressure for cost containment, coupled with the belief that hospitals are not good for children, has led to the flourishing of day surgery. Says Queens pediatric surgeon Dr. Jerrold Becker: "Nowadays any hospital that doesn't have an ambulatory unit is left behind."

Any time your child must be involved with a hospital, you'll want to get answers to some basic questions. Just as in maternity care, you're likely to find that the hospital's "official" policies may be different from what your doctor or you can negotiate. "Why, for example, does a child have to go to the hospital for some hospital procedures the night before?" questions Dr. Marji Gold, an attending physician and faculty member in the Montefiore Family Medicine residency program. "Is it because the pediatrician has to give 'clearance,' saying that the child is 'medically clear' and the blood count done? That could be done the night before at the physician's office. Don't settle for the assumption that your child has to be in the hospital overnight." Perhaps your child has an orthopedic problem that requires traction. Suggests Dr. Gold: "You might even ask if traction could be done at home. Can you get a hospital bed and hook it up?" Don't assume that your child *has* to be hospitalized for a procedure to be done. As your child's primary advocate, push your doctor and the hospital. Says Dr. Gold: "You have to be very careful. You have to be sure that somebody is meeting your needs."

Not only should you have some basic data available about your hospital from the start, but you should be prepared to ask questions. Almost all hospitals have unlimited visiting hours for parents and permit one parent, and often both, to spend the night. Space limitations, rather than medical philosophy, are often the determining factor. Sleeping accommodations for parents run the gamut from beds to cots to pull-out chairs. If your child is in the pediatric intensive care unit, your visiting time may be restricted. Rules for sibling visitation vary by the hospital. Most area hospitals ban children under the age of twelve or fourteen, but a few do welcome younger siblings. Don't expect your child's friends to visit unless they are teenagers. If your child is suffering from a life-threatening illness that requires extended hospitalization or treatment, you might want to find out about the Ronald McDonald Houses at 419 East 86 Street in Manhattan (212-876-1590) and at Schneider Children's Hospital in New Hyde Park (516-694-1919). You—and if it's possible, your child—can stay there for $10 per night. The House is particularly attractive for out-of-town parents and children or for metropolitan area families shuttling between home and hospital for a period of time for a specific treatment such as chemotherapy.

The questions listed below apply specifically to situations where children stay overnight. Some, however, are relevant for day surgery, lab tests, and X rays. Don't hesitate to ask them.

- What type of preadmission preparation program for both parent and child does the hospital offer? Can we visit the hospital before he's admitted to look around? Whether your child is having a brain tumor or a tonsil removed, he needs to know ahead of time what can happen. University Hospital, for example, takes parents and children on a tour on the day of admission and gives the child a coloring book, *My Stay in the Hospital.* Other hospitals provide orientation programs before the day of admission.
- What are the procedures for admission and discharge?
- Can my child wear her own clothes in the hospital? Can she bring toys and clothes from home?
- For what procedures can the parent be present? Parents are usually permitted to stay with their children for laboratory tests. You can probably accompany your child to X ray but may have to step outside when the procedure is done. You may be able to accompany your child to the operating room, but don't expect to be with him during surgery. At some hospitals, you can join him afterward in the recovery room.
- If your child is an adolescent, how will he be handled? Some hospitals, such as Mount Sinai, have special adolescent facilities; others lump adolescents in with general pediatrics.
- If your child is school-aged and will be spending an extended period of time in the hospital, what are the arrangements for school? The Board of Education's home instruction program deploys more than three hundred teachers who travel around the city to teach home-bound and hospitalized children. Many of the hospitals have their own schoolrooms. Check with the hospital, or the Board of Education, for details.
- What type of support services are there? Many of the hospitals have staff, known as pediatric recreational therapists or child life specialists, who work with children to ease the emotional trauma of being in the

hospital, as well as the medical trauma. These specialists are attuned to the special needs of children in the hospital setting. Says child life specialist Diana Cassidy: "We see very few appendectomies and tonsillectomies. University Hospital sees life-and-death situations, so that the support network is extensive." Where there are child life programs, you'll find playrooms stocked with games, toys, and puzzles, and at New York Hospital, even the Last Elegant Bear Library, a book nook with several hundred children's books. The child life program at most area hospitals is designed for hospitalized children, not for day surgery or periodic outpatient visits.

In addition to child health specialists and hospital social workers, there are also parent support groups. Parents for Parents, a support group for parents of hospitalized children that is based at Babies Hospital (125 Northmore Drive, Yorktown Heights, N.Y. 10598: 914-962-3326), connects parents of hospitalized children through telephone support and monthly meetings. They'll put you in touch with parents of children suffering from the same illnesses. At other hospitals, you'll find similar groups.

If you'd like further general information about children in hospitals, contact the **Association for the Care of Children's Health** (3615 Wisconsin Avenue N.W., Washington, D.C. 20016: 202-244-1801). This organization is concerned about issues of medical care for children and can send you, for a small fee, recommended reading lists and pamphlets for both parents and children (available also in Spanish).

Using a Hospital's Emergency Room

What is an emergency? According to Eileen Hansen of New York City's Emergency Medical Service (E.M.S.), an emergency is a situation where "someone is going to die if he doesn't get help immediately." Severe trauma, shock, loss of blood, difficulty in breathing, and poisoning are emergency conditions. Says Dr. Koota: "If you are in a critical care situation, don't fool around. If your child needs immediate care, go to the nearest hospital."

If it's not a true emergency, however, call your doctor first—even if you're not in your own neighborhood or it's a weekend. Don't just head blindly to an emergency room. "Having a contact someplace," says Dr. Gold, "is better than coming in at random. It's much better for you to have a contact who calls in to the hospital." Ask yourself, says Dr. Gold, "how much do you really need an emergency room?"

Emergency rooms are designed to handle medical traumas and situations that can't wait. As we have noted, to treat children most New York hospitals have set aside an area in their emergency room or even created separate pediatric emergency rooms staffed by pediatric residents and pediatricians. Most hospitals will permit you to stay with your child, although, observes Dr. Koota, "one parent may be permitted to stay rather than both."

If you use an emergency room without consulting with your doctor, your child will be seen by whoever is available. You have to accept what is offered rather than what might be available to you under nonemergency situations. Be aware, therefore, of the realities of a hospital's house staff. New interns and residents join in July. If you show up on July 5, your child could be seen by a doctor fresh out of medical school and new to the hospital who's just learning his way around. By May that same doctor will be a seasoned veteran.

You should nevertheless find out about your neighborhood's emergency rooms and their services. It's a good idea to carry your hospital insurance card with you and to know the history of your child's immunizations. If you are a member of an H.M.O., such as H.I.P., learn their special procedures for emergencies. Says H.I.P. Medical Director Dr. Pollack: "We're moving to keep groups open until eleven at night, so patients don't have to go to emergency rooms. We have a central answering service that's manned by doctors and nurse-practitioners. You may be given advice or the emergency room is called."

Summoning an Ambulance

What happens if it is an emergency and you feel that you need an ambulance? To contact New York's Emergency Medical Service, simply dial 911. You'll reach a police department operator at One Police Plaza in Manhattan who'll ask for basic information—your address, the nature of the emergency, and your *call-back* number. The call is then passed on to the Communications Center of the Emergency Medical Center in Maspeth, Queens, where you'll speak with the complaint receiving operator (C.R.O.), an emergency medical specialist, or a paramedic. While the police department operator stays on the line, the C.R.O. asks you a few medi-

(continued on page 120)

PEDIATRIC CARE IN THE HOSPITALS OF NEW YORK CITY

The information in these charts comes from a survey sent to area hospitals with pediatric beds. It did not include specialty hospitals such as Memorial Sloane-Kettering. The survey, done in summer, 1986, was mailed to the chairman of the Department of Pediatrics. I followed up by telephone and mail in the fall of 1986 repeatedly in an attempt to reach all hospitals. Where a section is blank, I did not receive an answer.

Hospital (Medical School)	Ped. Res. Prog.	EMERGENCY ROOM No. of Patients Seen Annually	How E.R. is set up	Pediatric Ambulatory Surgery Unit?
BRONX				
Bronx Municipal Hospital Cntr. (Albert Einstein College of Medicine)	Yes	59,800	Pediatric E.R.	
Montefiore Medical Cntr. (Albert Einstein)	Yes	22,700	Separate area in E.R. for pediatrics.	No, but day surgery done.
North Central Bronx (Albert Einstein)	Yes	24,800	Pediatric E.R.	
Jack D. Weiler Hospital (Albert Einstein)	Yes			Yes
Bronx-Lebanon Hospital Cntr.				
Lincoln Medical and Mental Health Cntr. (N.Y. Medical College)	Yes	60,000	Pediatric E.R.	Yes
Our Lady of Mercy Medical Cntr. (N.Y. Medical College)	Yes	15,000	Pediatric E.R.	Yes
BROOKLYN				
Baptist Medical Cntr. (New York College of Osteopathic Medicine)	No	5,000	Separate area in E.R. for pediatrics	Yes

A few basic points for clarification:

- The medical school with which a department is affiliated is put in parentheses.
- Res. Prog. means "Pediatric Residency Program."
- Any material in quotation marks comes directly from the survey and was said or written by hospital personnel.

WHEN A CHILD IS HOSPITALIZED

Visiting Hrs. for Parents	Parent Sleepover?	Sibling Visits	Child Life?	Other information:
Flexible	Yes. Chairs.	Not under fourteen.	Yes	**For the affiliated hospitals:** R.F. Kennedy Center for Child Development. Mental Retardation, and Developmental Disabilities; LIFE Program.
Flexible	Yes. Chairs.	Not under fourteen.	Yes	
Flexible	Yes. Chairs.	Not under fourteen.	Yes	
Twenty-four hrs.	Yes. Chairs.	Not under fourteen.	Yes	
Twenty-four hrs.	Yes. Chairs.	Yes	Yes	Grandparent support group. "Largest pediatric in-patient service in NYC. 10,800 pediatric admissions per year. Pediatrics is integrated with Metropolitan Hospital and overall with N.Y. Medical College."
All day	Yes. Cots, chairs.	No small siblings.		Playroom.
11 A.M.–8 P.M.	Yes. Chairs.	Not under twelve.	No	

HEALTH CARE NEEDS | 111

Hospital (Medical School)	Ped. Res. Prog.	EMERGENCY ROOM No. of Patients Seen Annually	How E.R. is set up	Pediatric Ambulatory Surgery Unit?
BROOKLYN				
Brookdale Hospital Cntr. (SUNY Health Science Cntr.–Brooklyn)	Yes.	11,000	Triage system. Separate examining room for pediatrics.	Yes. "We like very young children to stay over."
Brooklyn Hospital Cntr. (SUNY)	Yes	17,829	Separate area in E.R. for pediatrics.	Yes
Coney Island Hospital (SUNY)	Yes	20,000	Separate area in E.R. for pediatrics.	Yes
Interfaith Medical Cntr. (SUNY)	Yes	15,000	Separate E.R. for pediatrics.	Yes
Kingsbrook Jewish Medical Cntr.	No	ca. 3,000	General E.R. and pediatrician on call.	No, but day surgery permitted.
Kings County Hospital Cntr. (SUNY)	Yes	500,000 in E.R. and walk-in clinics and patients with appointments. 100,000 seen in E.R.	Pediatric E.R.	No, but day surgery done.
Long Island College Hospital (SUNY)	Yes	9,000	Separate area in E.R. for pediatrics.	Yes
Lutheran Medical Cntr. (SUNY)	Yes	10,000	Separate area in E.R. for pediatrics.	No
Maimonides Medical Cntr. (SUNY)	Yes	18,250	Pediatric E.R.	Yes
Methodist Hospital (SUNY)	Yes		Separate area in E.R. for pediatrics.	No, but day surgery permitted.
St. Mary's Hospital (Cornell Medical School)	No	8,000	Separate area in E.R. for pediatrics.	No, but day surgery permitted.

WHEN A CHILD IS HOSPITALIZED

Visiting Hrs. for Parents	Parent Sleepover?	Sibling Visits	Child Life?	Other information:
2–4 P.M. and 7–9 P.M.	Yes. Pull-cots and chairs. Only one parent.	Not under sixteen.	No	Adolescent lumped into pediatrics. Cardiology, oncology, sickle-cell, diabetes parent support groups.
Twenty-four hrs.	Yes. Chairs. One parent.	Yes	No	
11:30 A.M. –2:30 P.M.; 6:30 P.M. –8:30 P.M.	Yes. Chairs.	No	No	
11 A.M. –8 P.M.	Yes. Reclining chairs. One parent.	By arrangement.	No	"Full-time specialists available in major disciplines of pediatrics."
Anytime	Yes. Chair beds.	Not under fourteen.	No	
2 P.M. –8 P.M.	Yes. Beds.	Not under fifteen.	Yes	Playrooms on each patient unit. "Grandmas" on each unit.
All day	Yes	Not under fourteen unless permission.	Yes	Pediatric and adolescent playrooms. Parent support groups.
Unlimited	Yes. Lounge chairs.	No	No	
Anytime	Yes. Cots.	Extended care only; sibling must be four; Sundays.	No	
Twenty-four hrs.	Yes. Cots. One parent.	Yes: by permission.	No	Asthma support group.
	Yes		Yes	

HEALTH CARE NEEDS | 113

Hospital (Medical School)	Ped. Res. Prog.	EMERGENCY ROOM No. of Patients Seen Annually	How E.R. is set up	Pediatric Ambulatory Surgery Unit?
BROOKLYN				
SUNY Health Science Center—University Hospital: also known as Downstate (SUNY)	Yes	40,000	Separate area in E.R. for pediatrics	Yes
Woodhull Medical and Mental Health Cntr. (SUNY)	Yes	40,000	Separate area in E.R. for pediatrics.	No
Wyckoff Heights Hospital (SUNY)	Yes	16,000–17,000	Separate area in E.R. for pediatrics.	No, but day surgery permitted.
MANHATTAN				
Babies Hospital at Presbyterian (Columbia University College of Physicians and Surgeons)	Yes	65,000	Pediatric E.R.	Yes
Bellevue Hospital Cntr. (New York University)	Yes		Pediatric E.R.	No, but day surgery permitted
Beth Israel Medical Cntr. (Mount Sinai)	Yes		Until 8 P.M. patients go to ped. clinic; after 8 P.M. separate area in E.R.	No, but day surgery permitted.
Harlem Hospital Cntr. (Columbia University)	Yes		Pediatric E.R.	No
Joint Disease, North General Hospital (Mount Sinai)	No	3,000	Separate area in E.R. for pediatrics.	Yes
Lenox Hill Hospital (N.Y. Medical College)	Yes	3,553	Mon.–Wed. Pediatric attending in E.R. evenings; at other times the house staff covers.	Yes

114 | THE NEW YORK PARENTS' BOOK

WHEN A CHILD IS HOSPITALIZED

Visiting Hrs. for Parents	Parent Sleepover?	Sibling Visits	Child Life?	Other information:
Noon–8 P.M. All-day pre-op and intensive care.	Yes. Cots, chairs. "Nominal" charge.	Not under sixteen.	Yes	Leukemia, hemophilia support groups; cardiac surgery, renal transplant and dialysis. "Only dept. in NYC with accredited training in all subspecialties that can be accredited."
Unlimited	Yes. One parent.	Must be fourteen.	No	Asthma self-management. In-patient support group.
Unlimited	Yes. One parent.	Must be fourteen.	Yes	
Unlimited	Yes. Bed or cot. One parent.	Over fourteen unlimited; usually no visiting for acute patients; long-stay patients can be visited.	Yes	Parents for Parents support group. Re: pediatric care—"It is first-rate."
	Yes. Cots.		Yes	
Anytime	Yes. Cots.	Not under one year.	Yes	Psychiatric liaison. Difficult child program.
2 P.M.–4 P.M.; 6 P.M.–8 P.M.	Yes. Chair beds. One parent.	None; special permission possible.	No	"Open door policy" in pediatric clinic to try to provide a private patient environment.
Anytime	Yes. Chair beds. One parent.	None	Yes	
8 A.M.–8 P.M. and as per parent request.	Yes. Chair beds. If private room, both parents can stay.	Not under twelve. Special permission for others.	Yes	Communication disorders, speech and hearing. Orthopedics for pediatrics. Skhool for Parents.

HEALTH CARE NEEDS | 115

Hospital (Medical School)	Ped. Res. Prog.	EMERGENCY ROOM No. of Patients Seen Annually	How E.R. is set up	Pediatric Ambulatory Surgery Unit?
MANHATTAN				
Metropolitan Hospital Cntr. (N.Y. Medical College)	Yes	21,000	Pediatric E.R.	Yes
Mount Sinai Medical Cntr. (Mount Sinai School of Med.)	Yes	31,000	Pediatric E.R.	Yes
New York Hospital– Cornell Medical Cntr. (Cornell Medical School)	Yes	14,000	Pediatric E.R.	Yes. "We do a lot of these cases."
N.Y. Infirmary–Beekman Downtown (N.Y.U)	Yes	4,000	Pediatric E.R. within E.R.	No, but day surgery permitted.
St. Luke's—Roosevelt Hospital Cntr. (Columbia)	Yes	St. Luke's: 20,000 Roosevelt: 8,000	St. Luke's: Pediatric E.R. Roosevelt: Separate area in E.R.	Not a separate unit, but day surgery done.
St. Vincent's Hospital and Medical Cntr. (N.Y. Medical College)	Yes	over 6,000	Pediatric E.R.	No, but day surgery permitted.
N.Y.U. Medical Cntr., University Hospital (New York University)	Yes		Pediatric E.R.	Yes
QUEENS				
Booth Memorial Medical Cntr. (Dept. of Pediatrics is affiliated with North Shore and Cornell)	Ambulatory Pediatric Fellowship	10,000	Separate area in E.R. for pediatrics.	No, but day surgery permitted.
City Hospital Cntr. at Elmhurst (Mount Sinai)	Yes	40,000	Pediatric E.R.	Yes

WHEN A CHILD IS HOSPITALIZED

Visiting Hrs. for Parents	Parent Sleepover?	Sibling Visits	Child Life?	Other information:
Flexible	Yes. Chairs.	Yes	Yes	
Twenty-four hrs.	Yes. Cots, sofas.	No siblings on infant-toddler, school-age, adolescent floors. Over fourteen OK.	Yes	Oncology parent support. Weekly parent conferences on each unit. Adolescent center.
Unlimited	Yes. Chair beds.	Yes	Yes	Parent groups: talking about toddlers child development program, hematology, allergies and asthma, COPE program. Hematology has day hospital for malignancies. Special nurse for coordination of chronic care. "We have strong local affiliations with Hospital for Special Surgery and Memorial Sloane-Kettering."
Anytime	Yes. Cots. One parent.	Over twelve; others by special permission.	Yes	
Twenty-four hrs.	Yes. Beds, chairs, cots.	By arrangement.	Yes	All programs with chronic illnesses have parent support groups. St. Luke's has sickle-cell program. Roosevelt has Developmental Disabilities Cntr.
Anytime	Yes. Beds.	By arrangement.	Yes	Parenting groups: cystic fibrosis and rape crisis. Separate adolescent recreational lounge.
Unlimited	Yes. Parents' room and lounge chair.	On individual basis.	Yes	Rusk Institute of Rehabilitation Medicine; Pediatric neurosurgery; Institute of Reconstructive Surgery; day hospital for oncology patients; parent support group
Twenty-four hrs.	Yes. Chaise longue. One parent.	Over fourteen daily; others on Sundays.	Yes	Special program for obese children combined with sports medicine dept. Presurgical classes for kids and their parents.
Twenty-four hrs.	Yes. Cots.	"Same as parents."	No	Developmental Evaluation Clinic.

HEALTH CARE NEEDS | 117

Hospital (Medical School)	Ped. Res. Prog.	EMERGENCY ROOM No. of Patients Seen Annually	How E.R. is set up	Pediatric Ambulatory Surgery Unit?
QUEENS				
Flushing Hospital and Medical Cntr. (Albert Einstein)	Yes	15,000	Pediatric E.R.	Yes
Jamaica Hospital	No	over 1,500	Separate area in E.R. for pediatrics.	No
LaGuardia Hospital (Cornell)	Yes	ca. 10,000	General E.R. patients seen by pediatrician.	No, but day surgery permitted.
Mary Immaculate Hospital (Cornell)	No	6,000–7,000	Separate area in E.R. for pediatrics.	Yes
Peninsula Hospital				
Queens Hospital Cntr. (SUNY—Stonybrook)	No	ca. 25,000	Pediatric E.R.	No, but day surgery permitted.
St. John's Episcopal Hospital (Cornell)	Yes	14,000	Separate area in E.R. for pediatrics.	No, but day surgery permitted.
St. John's Queens Hospital (Cornell)	No		Pediatric E.R.	Yes
Schneider Children's Hospital Long Island Jewish Medical Cntr (SUNY—Stonybrook; Mount Sinai)	Yes	12,635	Pediatric E.R.	Yes
STATEN ISLAND				
St. Vincent's Medical Cntr. (N.Y.U.)	Yes	22,000	Pediatric E.R.	No
Staten Island Hospital (Suny—Brooklyn)	Yes	10,000	Pediatric E.R.	Yes

WHEN A CHILD IS HOSPITALIZED

Visiting Hrs. for Parents	Parent Sleepover?	Sibling Visits	Child Life?	Other information:
Twenty-four hrs.	Yes. Cots. One parent only.	No	Yes	Infant apnea monitoring program.
11 A.M. –1 P.M.; 2 P.M. –7:30 P.M.	No	Over sixteen.	No	
Twenty-four hrs.	Not routine. One parent. Fold-out chairs.	Over sixteen.	No	"The only true pediatrics is nursery and some surgery. Anything else is referred elsewhere."
Noon–8 P.M.	Yes. Chairs. One parent.	No	No	
2 P.M.–4 P.M.; 6 P.M.–8 P.M.	Yes. Chair bed. One parent.	Must be fourteen.	No	
Twenty-four hrs.	Yes. Cot, lounge chair. One parent.	Daily.		"This is a small community hospital with rotating residents from North Shore University Hospital."
Twenty-four hrs.	Yes. Cots, daybeds.	Yes	Yes	
Twenty-four hrs. Routine except psychiatric and I.C.U.	Yes. Parents' suites. (seven rms.); chair beds next to child's.	11–8:30; must be over twelve on oncology service.	Yes	Parent support groups: oncology, cystic fibrosis. Orientation programs; closed-circuit TV. Outdoor facilities including atrium and garden. "The facilities and environment are planned to meet the special needs of sick children, so that colors, wall decorations, ceilings have been selected accordingly."
Noon–8 P.M.	Yes. Cots.	None	No	
Flexible	Yes. Chair beds.	Not under twelve.	Yes	Parent support groups: asthma, diabetes.

HEALTH CARE NEEDS | 119

(continued from page 109)

cal questions and assigns a priority to your call. Calls are given numbers: from one, "the most life-threatening," to eight, the least. "Many callers mistake this process to be a delay in ambulance dispatching," says Eileen Hansen. "It is not. As the caller and the C.R.O. are on the line together, the C.R.O. is entering information into a computer, which is sending it to a dispatcher. The dispatcher is choosing the ambulance to respond and may indeed already have sent one while the caller is on the line."

There are many 911 receiving hospitals in the New York area capable of treating and admitting patients with any injury or illness. There are also "Specialty Care Referral Centers" that have set aside an area in their emergency room, labs, and intensive care unit for the treatment of a particular "classification." The classifications are major trauma, burns, replantation (to reattach a severed limb), snakebite, and hyperbarics—smoke inhalation and diving accidents. These hospitals have specially trained doctors, nurses, and support staff for their particular classification.

Do you have a say as to which hospital your child will be taken to? Can you get into an ambulance and order them to head for one hospital or steer clear of another? E.M.S. pays attention to the condition of the patient and the nature of the injury or illness. Says Hansen: "If the patient is in critical or unstable condition, the patient and family have no choice, he goes to the nearest receiving hospital" or to a Specialty Care Referral Center. "The last consideration," she says, "is the request of the patient or family member." Under less dire circumstances, however, you may be able to express your opinion. Says Hansen: "We have what is called a ten-minute rule." *If* the patient is stable, *if* the area can be covered by another unit while your child is being transported (the ambulance checks back with the dispatcher), and *if* the hospital you request is within a ten-minute drive, in the same borough, and is a receiving hospital, then the crew can take your child to the hospital you requested. Warns Hansen: "If all these circumstances are not favorable, the patient will be taken to the nearest receiving hospital. You have the option of hiring a private ambulance to transfer your child to another." The priorities of the Emergency Medical Service are: first, the patient's condition; then, the closest and most appropriate hospital; and finally, the request of the family and patient.

If you need to summon an ambulance:

- Stay calm and answer all questions.
- Give the address and location of the patient—not where you are calling from if that is different.

- Don't hang up. Let E.M.S. hang up on you first.
- After your call is completed, stay off the phone in case E.M.S. wants to call you back.
- Give a call-back number.
- Call only in an emergency. According to Hansen, over 250,000 of the more than 700,000 calls E.M.S. receives each year are unnecessary.

Poisoning

"My two-year-old just drank some furniture polish," reports the worried mother at the other end of the telephone line of New York City's Poison Center. "What do I do?" That situation, unfortunately, happens all too often in New York City. The New York City Poison Control Center (reached simply by dialing 212-POISONS) gets more than seventy thousand calls each year relating to accidental and intentional exposures to hazardous and poisonous substances. Poisoning is one of the most common accidental forms of death, and children under the age of five are the most frequent victims. Says Dr. Mary Ann Howland of the Poison Control Center: "Fifty percent of our calls involve children with accidental ingestion." They've sampled soaps and detergents, cosmetics and colognes, plants, various creams and ointments, suppositories, insecticides, alcohol, paints, lacquers, and household cleaning products—all sorts of products found around the house but not meant to be eaten. Sometimes they've even overdosed with aspirin, acetaminophen, or vitamins.

If a poisoning occurs, call the Poison Control Center: 212-POISONS, which is manned round-the-clock. Says Dr. Howland: "We are immediately accessible." The Center is staffed by information specialists trained in pharmacy and chemistry and draws upon physicians, pharmacists, and clinical toxicologists.

If you call, remain calm, and be prepared to answer a few questions:

- What is your phone number?
- How is the person doing?
- What was the substance ingested? How much? How long ago? Have you done anything at home for it? (It helps to have the product at hand.)
- What is the medical history?

Based on the information you supply, the staff at the Center will advise you on treatment or, perhaps, tell you that no treatment is needed. If warranted, they can also dispatch an ambulance. If something spills into your child's eye or onto the skin, however, rinse with tepid water first for fifteen minutes (if there is clothing on, get it off), and then call because the danger can be immediate.

Know what to do if a poisoning occurs. Have on hand a bottle of syrup of ipecac (it causes the child to vomit), but use it only when you're told to by the Poison Control Center or your physician. The best solution, however, is to practice prevention. Keep these items out of your child's reach and get rid of paints and other solvents when you finish with them. You can also write to the New York City Poison Control Center (New York City Department of Health, 451 First Avenue, New York, N.Y. 10016) for poison control information and stickers to attach to your telephone.

▽ ▽ ▽ ▽ ▽ ▽ ▽ ▽ ▽ ▽ ▽

LEARNING ABOUT FIRST AID

The stories send shivers up your spine. You hear about the baby who suddenly stops breathing or chokes on the piece of bread. Or perhaps it was the one-year-old who drowned in the bathtub when his mother briefly turned her back to get a towel. What would you have done?

Parents in the New York area have been trying to find out some answers. Over the past few years, many have signed up for "Baby + Life" courses offered at Y's, churches, and family centers in New York. The single four-hour course developed by Noel Merenstein teaches simple lifesaving techniques for parents of infants and young children. You learn about infant/child CPR, poison emergencies, household safety, and emergency first aid. Part of the class is a lecture but much is a practicum in which you attempt, for example, CPR on a doll.

"Baby + Life" is not the only program in the area, but it's probably the most widespread (to find out about classes and fees, contact them at 344 East 78 Street, New York, N.Y. 10021: 212-744-0805). The 92 Street Y periodically offers "A Medical Guide for Parents" taught by Dr. Richard Stone of Metropolitan Hospital. You can also take "Tot-Savers" through the Emergency Care Consultants (241 Sixth Avenue, New York, N.Y. 10014: 212-243-9123). To learn CPR, you can also check with the American Heart Association (212-661-5335), which will refer you to organizations that offer courses covering techniques for both adults and children.

△ △ △ △ △ △ △ △ △ △ △

For Your Information

Need some basic medical information? Here are some places designed especially to provide you with that:

- **Center for Medical Consumers** (237 Thompson Street, New York, N.Y. 10012: 212-674-7105): This is a free medical library with an extensive clippings file as well as reference books and periodicals. Its purpose is "to encourage people to make a critical evaluation of all treatment recommendations, to use medical services more selectively, and to understand the limitations of modern medicine."

- **Health Education Center** (Blue Cross and Blue Shield of Greater New York, 3 Park Avenue, New York, N.Y. 10016: 212-481-2323): Here you'll find a reference library, booklets to take home, and health workshops, offered lunchtimes and after work, covering everything from nutrition to back care to family mental health and parenting.

- **Lenox Hill Hospital's Health Education Center** (1080 Lexington Avenue at 76 Street, New York, N.Y. 10021: 212-439-2980): There are a multitude of community health programs including free health screenings, such as a hearing test, brochures, nutrition counseling, and the "Skhool for Parents." Want to browse by telephone? Try **Tel-Med**, the free telephone library offering more than 100 tapes on medical and health topics. Among your choices: "Aspirin for Children," "Earache in Children," "Chickenpox," "Should I Keep My Child Home from School?"—even "Let's Find Out About the Hospital." All the tapes are numbered and to use one, dial 212-439-3200 (Mon.–Fri. 9:30–4:30) and request a specific tape or topic. If you really want to take advantage of the offerings, get a brochure—available by mail through the Health Education Center—listing all the tapes.

Special Needs, Special Concerns

Do you need help in locating specialists or advice on the latest treatments? Or just the chance to talk with other parents? The resources in New York are quite overwhelming.

The **Early Childhood Direction Centers** provide free information and referral for children up to the age of five who are known, or suspected, to have handicapping conditions. These centers will help you locate evaluation services that can diagnose disabilities. New York has four centers:

- Early Childhood Direction Center (New York Hospital, 525 East 68 Street, New York, N.Y. 10021: 212-472-6535)
- Early Childhood Direction Center of Brooklyn and Staten Island (Interfaith Medical Center, 1545 Atlantic Avenue, Brooklyn, N.Y. 11213: 718-604-6412)
- Bronx Early Childhood Direction Center (Lincoln Hospital, 234 East 149 Street, Bronx, N.Y. 10451: 212-579-5778)
- Queens Early Childhood Direction Center (United Cerebral Palsy of Queens), 82-25 164 Street, Jamaica, N.Y. 11432: 718-380-3000, ext. 265)

You'll also want to be in touch with **Resources for Children with Special Needs** (212-677-4650), an information, referral, advocacy, and support center for parents and professionals. Their computerized information includes everything from medical and health services to educational programs to camp and summer programs to sources for toys, equipment, and educational materials.

You can also turn to hospitals that offer pediatric residencies and have an array of subspecialty clinics. Count on the university teaching hospitals for sophisticated programs that treat the complex disorders of childhood. In addition to handling specific medical ailments, they often have multidisciplinary centers to diagnose and treat learning disabilities.

Here are some specific organizations and programs that can help. For:

- **Asthma:** Mount Sinai has a comprehensive pediatric pulmonary center. The New York Lung Association (22 East 40 Street, New York, N.Y. 10016: 212-889-3370), Queensboro Lung Association (112-25 Queens Boulevard, Forest Hills, N.Y. 11375: 718-263-5656) and the Brooklyn Lung Association (165 Cadman Plaza East, Brooklyn, N.Y. 11201: 718-624-8531) can refer you to specialists. They also run special family asthma programs for school-aged youngsters which stress asthma self-management. The Brooklyn Lung Association also has a physical conditioning and recreation program for children with asthma called "Super Kids" that meets at a local Y. Queensboro has a similar program. You can also call "Lung Line" at the National Jewish Hospital and Research Center, National Asthma Center (3800 East Colfax Avenue, Denver, Colo. 80206: 800-222-LUNG).
- **Blind or Visually Impaired:** There are several organizations here in New York. You could get in touch with the American Foundation for

the Blind (15 West 16 Street, New York, N.Y. 10011: 212-620-2000) and the National Society to Prevent Blindness (79 Madison Avenue, New York, N.Y. 10016: 212-684-3505). The Lighthouse/New York Association for the Blind (111 East 59 Street, New York, N.Y. 10022: 212-355-2200) works with all ages of children throughout the metropolitan area and provides comprehensive services to them and their families. Says one staffer: "We work with infants from day one." Their Child Development Center prepares children for school. The special programs for youth, ages six to twenty-one, include Saturday sports, arts, and field trips for partially sighted and blind children. They also have an extensive lending library of materials: large-print, cassettes, and regular print books.

- **Cerebral Palsy:** Check with United Cerebral Palsy of New York City (122 East 22 Street, New York, N.Y. 10010: 212-677-7400) and United Cerebral Palsy of Queens (81-15 164 Street, Jamaica, N.Y. 11432: 718-380-3000). You'll find comprehensive services—from infant stimulation to education to health and dental care to recreation—provided from infancy on up.

- **Cystic Fibrosis:** For general advice, get in touch with the Cystic Fibrosis Foundation (60 East 42 Street, New York, N.Y. 10165: 212-986-8783). Several area hospitals—among them, St. Vincent's, Mount Sinai, and Babies Hospital in Manhattan, Long Island College Hospital in Brooklyn, and Long Island Jewish in New Hyde Park—have special treatment centers.

- **Down Syndrome:** The National Down Syndrome Society (141 Fifth Avenue, New York, N.Y. 10010: 212-460-9330) offers general information, parent support, and help in finding infant stimulation programs at area hospitals.

- **Epilepsy:** Contact the New York State Epilepsy Association (60 Madison Avenue, New York, N.Y. 10010: 212-684-3344).

- **Hearing Loss:** There are many speech and hearing clinics. Two places to check with are the New York League for the Hard of Hearing (71 West 23 Street, New York, N.Y. 10010: 212-741-7650) and the Lexington Center for the Hearing Impaired (Thirtieth Avenue and 75 Street, Jackson Heights, N.Y. 11370; 718-899-8800).

- **Hemophilia:** The National Hemophilia Foundation (110 Greene Street, New York, N.Y. 10012: 212-219-8180) makes referrals to treatment centers, local chapters, and even special summer camps. New York Hospital, Mount Sinai, and Long Island Jewish have comprehensive hemophilia treatment centers.

- **Juvenile Arthritis:** Try the New York Arthritis Foundation (115 East 18 Street, New York, N.Y. 10003: 212-477-8700). Many area hospitals have arthritis clinics. The foundation will send you a list of clinics, as well as a list of physicians with an interest in arthritis.

- **Juvenile Diabetes:** Contact the Juvenile Diabetes Foundation (432 Park Avenue South, New York, N.Y. 10016: 212-889-7575 or 800-223-1138). Many of the area hospitals have special treatment clinics.

- **Sickle Cell Anemia:** The Sickle Cell Anemia Foundation of Greater New York (209 West 125 Street, New York, N.Y. 10027: 212-865-1201) provides counseling and referrals to hospitals.

- **Sleep Disorders:** There's a range of sleep disorders now recognized in children, including infantile apnea, insomnia, night terrors, somnambulism, and nocturnal eneuresis. You can check with the Sleep-Wake Disorders Center at Montefiore Medical Center (212-920-4841) and the Sleep Disorders Center at Presbyterian Hospital (212-305-1860).

- **Spina Bifida:** The Howard A. Rusk Institute of Rehabilitation Medicine at New York University has a major treatment clinic (212-340-6113). To locate a parent group, contact Spina Bifida Information and Referral (1700 Rockville Pike, Rockville, Md. 20852: 800-621-3141).

- **Ulcerative Colitis and Crohn's Disease:** Turn to the National Foundation for Ileitis and Colitis Foundation (444 Park Avenue South, New York, N.Y. 10016: 212-679-1570). They sponsor parent workshops and support groups for parents and children and can refer you to pediatric gastroenterologists.

Prescription Drugs

When was the last time that you bought a generic drug, a drug known by its chemical name, rather than by a brand name? New York State has a law requiring your pharmacist to substitute less expensive generic drugs for brand name drugs *if* your doctor indicates this on the prescription slip. Generics, although expected to be chemically equivalent with brand names, typically cost much less. Ask your physician to indicate that a generic drug is acceptable. And look for them over the counter too. Acetaminophen by another name is Tylenol, for example.

If you need to get a prescription filled late at night or on a Sunday, you may find that your neighborhood drug store is closed. Two pharmacies open round-the-clock seven days a week are Neergaard in Brooklyn (454 Fifth Avenue: 718-768-0600) and Kaufman (50 Street and Lexington Avenue: 212-755-2266) in Manhattan.

Dental Care

Your own dentist may treat your child or you may decide that you'd prefer him to see a pedodontist, a dentist with special training in children's dental care. For referrals, check with your dentist, pediatrician, or family physician. You can also contact the local dental societies. They will give you the names of several dentists (or pedodontists), using your ZIP code as the basis. The local societies are: the **Bronx County Dental Society** (212-733-2031), the **Second District Dental Society** (for Brooklyn and Staten Island: 718-522-3939), the **First District Dental Society** (for Manhattan: 212-889-8940), and the **Queens County Dental Society** (718-454-8344). The First and Second Districts also operate emergency hotlines with tape-recorded messages. If you need a dentist and can't reach yours (or don't have one), the hotlines list dentists or clinics able to see you on an emergency basis. For Brooklyn and Staten Island, call 718-852-2022; for Manhattan, call 212-679-3966 or 212-679-4172.

The **Department of Health's Bureau of Dental Health** treats children at no cost in clinics around the city. For details, contact the Tremont District Health Center (212-583-5500) in the Bronx, the Fort Greene (718-643-7563) and Homecrest (718-645-8280) District Health Centers in Brooklyn, the Lower Manhattan (212-239-1792) and Upper West Side (212-927-6300) District Health Centers in Manhattan, and the Jamaica (718-658-6600) District Health Center in Queens. Staten Island residents should get in touch with the Lower Manhattan Center.

You can also get free dental care from the **Children's Aid Society** (212-949-4800) in its neighborhood centers in Manhattan and Staten Island. A dentist at the neighborhood center offers general care, while a central clinic provides orthodontic and prosthodontic care. (You don't have to be poor to use their services.) You can also bring your child for free care to the dental clinics run by the city's two dental schools, New York University and Columbia. If you use their programs, your child may be seen by dental students under the supervision of faculty. Both have special children's clinics. Lenox Hill Hospital also does pediatric dentistry.

Whatever you do, choose a dentist who is good with children. Be sure that he uses a "tell-show-do" approach that gives your child a chance to be prepared. In the beginning, it's as important for your child to develop a feeling of ease around the dentist as it is for the treatment to take place. Avoid a situation where your child is kept waiting or where she observes anyone who is upset—either you or another child.

Mental Health

If you have a mental health concern, your child could be seen by a variety of professionals, including a social worker, family therapist, guidance counselor, child psychologist, or a child psychiatrist. You might use graduate schools at universities, hospitals, freestanding clinics, or social service agencies. In Manhattan, for example, you could turn to Mount Sinai or Bellevue, which have well-known child and adolescent psychiatry departments, the Postgraduate Center for Mental Health, the New York State Psychiatric Institute, or the Jewish Board of Family and Children's Services.

Among the sources for referrals:

- **Your local mental health association:** the Brooklyn Association for Mental Health (30 Third Avenue, Brooklyn, N.Y. 11217: 718-624-5191); the Mental Health Association of New York and Bronx Counties (235 Park Avenue South, New York, N.Y. 10003: 212-254-0333); the Queens County Mental Health Society (235-61 Hillside Avenue, Queens Village, N.Y. 11427: 718-479-0030); the Staten Island Mental Health Society (669 Castleton Avenue, Staten Island, N.Y. 10301:718-442-2225). The Staten Island Society sponsors a call-in parents' "Help Line" (Mon.–Fri. 11 A.M. to noon: 718-720-0771).
- **Individual counselors:** The American Psychological Association (212-725-8177) is a membership organization of psychologists that has a referral service for the five boroughs and outlying areas. You'll be

offered several names. The American Psychiatric Association (212-421-4732) has on file the names of Board-certified psychiatrists and you'll be told about three. Check with them for New York and Staten Island. You can also call: Brooklyn (718-855-3030), Queens (718-461-8413), and the Bronx (914-946-9008). The National Association of Social Workers (212-903-4707) will give referrals to certified social workers.

chapter 5
meeting the challenges of living in new york city

When was the last time you ate lunch with a chimpanzee? Justin Frey of Manhattan did last year when he attended the fifth birthday party of a friend. Zippy the Chimp was there, dressed in a red tuxedo and brown leather shoes. Zippy tucked a napkin under his plate for the crumbs, rode a little bicycle around the living room, and did tricks on roller skates. Keeping twenty five-year-olds at bay during a birthday party in an apartment poses just one of the many challenges of raising children in New York. Planning parties, tackling the space crunch, instilling "street smarts," even just getting around town with toddlers in tow . . . and keeping your sanity—such are the unsung acts of heroism that distinguish the New York parent. This chapter provides a rundown of what to expect and how to tackle it.

Making Space

"New York children sleep in dining rooms, living rooms, lofts above parents' bedrooms, even walk-in closets," observed Linda Wolfe in *New York* magazine. Family planning New York-style is much more than birth control. It involves devising a strategy for creatively turning the studio, one-, or two-bedroom apartment into a space where both adults and children can flourish.

The solutions are sometimes quite simple. The foot of the L-shaped thirty-foot living room is lopped off to become the small second bedroom. Some families undertake major construction projects, hiring the superintendent or a contractor to put up Sheetrock walls and hang doors; others rely on bookcases or wall and storage units to do the trick. Within bedrooms, they may use combination units available at stores such as Conran's, Workbench, or Bon Marché, or perhaps turn to wall system designers such as Lockwood. Another technique, suggests interior decorator Joan Wolf, is to visit "the wonderful stores around town that specialize in formica work, cabinetry, and custom-made furniture. For little, tight areas they come in very handy."

As you fashion a child's room, think carefully about how the space will be used. Architect Sarah Brezavar recommends that you "write down what activities are going to happen." With children, those activities include sleeping and playing, of course, but also storing toys and clothes, doing schoolwork or art projects, entertaining friends, and possibly using a computer. Brezavar then has her clients write down next to the list of activities what they will need—be it a bed or a closet—to accomplish them. "The big bugaboo," she says, "is storage space."

No doubt, friends and neighbors will be delighted to show you how they transformed their apartment. Consider also talking to a professional. The New York chapter of the American Society of Interior Designers (200 Lexington Avenue, New York, N.Y. 10016: 212-685-3480) has a referral service. The New York chapter of the American Institute of Architects does not, although you can use their files to do research. Brezavar suggests that you might check with local architectural schools for a referral to someone, perhaps a recent graduate, who'd be willing to consult on your small job. Says Brezavar: "You may get wonderfully creative ideas about how to deal with a space problem." You'll also want to spend some time browsing through magazines and books. Three good surveys are *Sunset Ideas for Children's Rooms and Play Yards* (Menlo Park, Calif.: Lane Publishing Company, 1980), *Sunset Children's Furniture* (Menlo Park, Calif.: Lane Publishing Company, 1985), and Mary Gilliatt's *Designing Rooms for Children* (Boston: Little, Brown, and Company, 1984).

While it's tempting to think about tucking your child into a handy closet, windowless alcove, or hallway, don't do it. New York City's housing maintenance code requires that all rooms used as "living" spaces have a window. If you're thinking about adding on a room, be aware that you're also expected to file papers with the Department of Buildings. You may have to alter a Certificate of Occupancy and you need to find out the requirements for zoning resolutions and building code. Finally, if your children are under eleven years old, New York's Health Code requires that there be guards on the windows to prevent youngsters from accidentally tumbling out.

BUNK BEDS

Bunk beds are common space solvers when two children need to share one room. While most parents buy the beds at stores, others design their own. In the Dworkin house, there's a homemade outsized bunk bed unit featuring a bookcase that runs along one side and a clothes closet at the foot.

If you're planning on incorporating bunk beds into your design plan, beware. The U.S. Consumer Product Safety Commission estimates that in 1984 approximately twenty thousand children under the age of fifteen were treated at hospital emergency rooms for bunk-bed-related injuries. It offers the following suggestions about the beds. (For their complete recommendations about bunk beds, call them: 800-638-CPSC).

- Choose beds that have a guard rail on each side that can be screwed, bolted, or otherwise firmly attached to the bed structure. The rail should not permit a space more than three and a half inches above the bed frame and should extend at least five inches above the mattress to prevent the child from rolling out. The rail should be in place at all times because children roll during their sleep.
- Be sure that cross ties under the mattresses are securely attached.
- Ascertain that ladders are securely attached to the bed frame. (Have your child try the ladder. Just before buying a bed, one mother discovered that her four-year-old son couldn't climb the built-in ladder of a well-known children's bunk bed because his legs were too short. The bed was clearly designed for an older child.)
- Check that there is a feature that permits you to make the bed into two single beds if you have young children.
- Do not let very young children—who could fall or roll between the bed and the wall, between the guard rail and the mattress, or between the ladder and the mattress—use the "bunk" part of the bed. (In its *Product Safety Fact Sheet on Bunk Beds,* issued in October 1985, the U.S. Consumer Product Safety Commission stated that: "The Commission knows of twenty children three years and younger who have died in this matter.")
- Children should be taught that rough play is unsafe around and on bunk beds.

Playgrounds and Playrooms

If once the sidewalks of New York were the focus of a child's activities, today it's the playgrounds. New York has an infinite variety. The Parks Department oversees more than eight hundred playgrounds, ranging from the tiny vest-pocket playground, with the old-fashioned swing set, jungle gym, sliding pond, and seesaws, to the "adventure" playgrounds with their wooden or stone structures, tire swings, moats, and ropes. They're continually building new ones and redesigning older ones. That's just the beginning. You'll find playgrounds in schoolyards, between buildings in a housing project, even on rooftops. The New York City Housing Authority, the Department of Housing, Preservation, and Development, and the Board of Education also have a role in playground construction.

The condition of these playgrounds, however, can vary dramatically. In August 1986, *The New York Times* reported that on the basis of a survey of Parks Department playgrounds "there is a wide disparity" in conditions. "While many are clean, leafy places of joy, excitement, and safety, others are filthy, ugly places of boredom, danger, and fear. The city's best-kept playgrounds are on Staten Island and in Queens and the worst are in Brooklyn." The *Times* also found that the "best playgrounds were in the higher-income neighborhoods." The survey revealed that although almost all the playgrounds had usable slides, less than half had all their swings working. Other maintenance problems included missing safety padding, trash, and glass. The comfort stations at 34 percent were closed (27 percent had none in or near them) and at 47 percent of the playgrounds there were no water fountains (or none that were working).

The sad fact about some playgrounds is that they're filthy and poorly maintained. If that's the case with your neighborhood playground, speak up. Contact the agency that's responsible for administering it (at the Parks Department, start with your borough commissioner) and your local **Community Board.** If you're interested in getting your local playground spruced up, you'll find helpful "A Step-by-Step Guide to Playground Renovation," which appeared in the fall 1986 issue of *Parents' Resources.* The Parks Department's Volunteer Program (212-360-8284) lends supplies and equipment for volunteer clean-ups.

While most of the time you'll content yourself with using what's available locally, there are several innovative playgrounds in the city that warrant an out-of-neighborhood visit. Manhattan's **Central Park** has an abundance of riches. Among them: the Heckscher playground at 62

Street and Seventh Avenue, the West 68 Street playground (with, in nondrought years, its running water) at Central Park West, the 67 Street playground at the East Side's 67 Street entrance, the playground at Fifth Avenue between 84 and 85 streets, the playground between 85 and 86 streets off Central Park West (best for school-aged children, since the equipment is large), and the Diana Ross Playground at 81 Street and Central Park West.

It's worth knowing, however, that the West 68 Street playground and the playground at 84 Street on the East Side do not have comfort stations on their premises, so you've got to be prepared to walk a few blocks to take your child to the bathroom. In Flushing Meadows–Corona Park in Queens, you'll find the **Playground for All Children** (111 Street and Corona Avenue), created for handicapped as well as able-bodied children from the ages of three to twelve. It features swings and seesaws with safety belts, slides that can be ascended by crawling or climbing, bars with multilevel platforms, and a wheelchair-accessible rocking bridge. The sand play area has large sand tables equipped with a conveyor belt that children can use to move sand from one location to another. Open April through November; call 718-699-8283 to learn about community hours (weekday mornings are reserved for groups) and scheduled special events. If you're in Manhattan's Tribeca, preschoolers will enjoy the **Washington Market** park (Greenwich and Harrison streets) at Independence Plaza.

Although public playgrounds predominate, there are also some private ones. People affiliated with New York Hospital–Cornell Medical Center can join the cooperative Play Area Association. P.A.A. operates an outdoor playground called "Woodchips" and two locked indoor play areas in residence halls. In the summer, the P.A.A. sets up several small baby wading pools and one larger four-foot pool. They also run toddler classes (open to nonmembers). Some apartment complexes also have outdoor playgrounds or indoor playrooms whose use is restricted to residents. If you live in a co-operative and would like to create a playground or playroom, you'll need to mobilize parents in your building, find the appropriate space, get insurance coverage (a rider to your building's policy probably), and set up a stringent set of rules. The Council of New York Co-operatives in Manhattan and the Federation of New York Housing Co-operatives in Queens can give you basic advice and steer you to co-ops that have succeeded.

Wherever your child plays, it's up to you to ensure that he does so in a safe environment. "Sending your child to a playground can be a hazardous thing to do," observes playground designer Lauren Martelli. Both you and your child need to learn about playground safety. Nationwide, many thousands of children under the age of four are injured on playgrounds every year, some of them very seriously. According to studies of playground injuries by the U.S. Consumer Product Safety Commission, the most common injuries to children are caused by falls.

The type of injury, and the severity of it, has been shown to be directly related to the surface on which the fall occurred. Avoid equipment built over concrete or asphalt. Remove any glass shards or other debris before you loose your child. Look for sharp edges, broken swings or seesaws, bolts that aren't tightened, missing screws, rust and peeling paint. If there's a wall or fence nearby, check that the equipment is positioned far enough away that your child can't strike it if he falls or swings. If you find defects, contact the borough office of the Parks Department and your local community board. If you have no success, call your local city council member.

Make sure that your child is fastened in the baby swing before you send him flying. Climbing bars and rings should be easily grasped. Be certain that no bar or ring could entrap a child's body or head. Teach your child playground basics: how to use the equipment properly (slides, for example, are for going down, not up), how to sit on swings, seesaws, and a merry-go-round, how to get off the equipment and walk away safely, and how to take turns. The U.S. Consumer Product Safety Commission will send you at no charge its *Handbook for Public Playground Safety* (800-638-CPSC; in New York City: 212-264-1125; federal budget cuts eliminated the printing of several other safety booklets, including coloring books for children on playground safety, but it's worth asking what else is available.)

Getting Around

Children six and under ride for free on city subways and buses and on the Staten Island Rapid Transit. After that age, they must pay full fare. To get a map of the subways or a borough-wide bus map, write to the New York City Transit Authority (370 Jay Street, Brooklyn, N.Y. 11201). For travel information, call 718-330-1234. Weeknights and weekends, if you're taking a group of children on a recreational outing (and your group is nonprofit and tax-exempt), they can go for free if you've been issued an identification card. For details, send your request (on a group letterhead) to the Office of the Mayor, New York City Youth Bureau (44 Court Street, Brooklyn, N.Y. 11201). Don't plan on using a bathroom facility in a subway station. According to a spokesman for the New York City Transit Authority, only 10 percent of the system's 462 stations, have bathrooms that are open.

Children under five ride for free on the Long Island Rail Road and Metro-North. Half fare is charged for children from the ages of five to eleven. If you are traveling with a group, contact the group sales departments about special reduced rates.

Whether your child is attending *public, private, or parochial* school, he may be eligible for a pass (at no cost or reduced fare) to ride on a subway or bus between home and school or on a yellow school bus under contract to the Board of Education. The same rules apply to all youngsters. Children in kindergarten through grades two receive free transportation if they live half a mile or more from their school. Free rides are given to children in grades three to six if they live a mile or more from school. Students in grades seven to twelve are eligible for reduced fare privileges on public transit if they reside a mile and a half or more from school. Check with your school or the Office of Pupil Transportation (28-11 Queens Plaza North, Long Island City, N.Y. 11101: 718-784-3313) for full details.

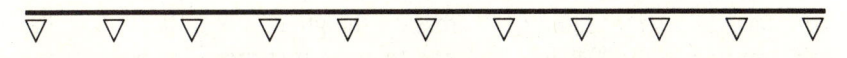

▽ ▽ ▽ ▽ ▽ ▽ ▽ ▽ ▽ ▽ ▽

BUCKLE UP

New York State mandates that all automobile passengers riding in the front seat fasten their seat belts. Children under ten must be belted, and any child under four should be secured in an approved child safety restraint device. You can get a list of approved car seats from the Governor's Traffic Safety Committee (Empire State Plaza, Albany, N.Y. 12228: 518-474-5777) or the National Highway Traffic Safety Administration in Washington, D.C. (800-424-9393). You can purchase a car seat at some children's furniture and toy stores and department stores. CAUTION: Although it is often tempting to accept a hand-me-down seat from a friend or relative, be sure that it meets current federal standards. To check on the car seat, send the make and model number, along with a self-addressed stamped envelope, to the National Child Passenger Safety Association (1705 DeSales Street N.W., Washington, D.C. 20036).

Westchester County has a pioneering car seat "loaner" program. Residents of the county, whether they are parents or grandparents, can borrow, free of charge for up to six months, a car seat from the Traffic Safety Board in White Plains. Nothing like this exists in the five boroughs. In Brooklyn, the Sunset Park Family Health Center, with state funding, has lent car seats to low-income families in the neighborhood. If you're renting a car, several of the car rental agencies, including Avis, Hertz, and National, will provide car seats (for an additional charge) with two days' advance notice. Automobile Club of New York members can borrow seats for up to two weeks for visiting children through its Child Restraint Loan Program. Call the Club's Traffic Safety Department (212-586-1166 or 516-746-7730) about a week in advance.

△ △ △ △ △ △ △ △ △ △ △

Street Smarts

As you travel with your child around the city, you've got to begin to teach him safety rules for the street. What does he need to know?

When he's ready, teach him his name, address, phone number, your names, work numbers, and whom to contact in an emergency, including phone numbers. Practice a few scenarios that might crop up: For example, what if he gets off the school bus and you're not there to meet him? Even before he starts walking around the neighborhood on his own, get him started on street safety: to "cross on the green, not in between," to pay attention to the "Walk" sign, and to cross at corners. Sounds simple enough until you realize that every day parents are undermining this lesson. When they're in a hurry and pushing their child in the stroller, how many observe these rules? There are some other basics to hammer home: "walk, don't run," "look both ways before you cross," and, particularly on Manhattan streets, watch out for bicycles (they are notorious for ignoring traffic lights, one-way street signs, and other rules of the road).

If your child will be walking to school on his own, work out the route and go over the rules. If he will be taking public transportation on his own, then he'll need to learn how to use the bus pass, handle extra money, and call for help. There are other basic concerns. How do you teach him to deal with strangers, prevent muggings, avert sexual abuse or a child-snatching? No New York parent can forget the tale of Etan

Patz, who disappeared on the first day he was allowed to walk alone to the school bus stop in SoHo. In her book *How to Raise a Street-Smart Child* (New York: Facts on File, 1984) New Yorker Grace Hechinger goes over this and much more. Although written for a national audience, *Street-Smart Child* draws heavily upon New Yorkers' experiences.

While much of the job of instilling "street smarts" lies with you, don't hesitate to turn to others for some tips. You can:

- Ask the crime prevention officer in your police precinct to talk to a group about safety or contact the Police Department's Office of D.C.C.A., Crime Prevention Section (120-55 Queens Boulevard, Kew Gardens, N.Y. 11424: 718-520-9300) and request a speaker.
- Contact the Parents League of New York, which dispenses safety information to members and conducts parent workshops.
- Enroll your child in a workshop at **S.A.F.E., the Safety and Fitness Exchange** (541 Avenue of the Americas, New York, N.Y. 10011: 212-242-4874). S.A.F.E. offers classes in personal safety promoting a self-defense program for toddlers on up. These strategies are outlined in Flora Colao and Tamar Hosansky's book *Your Children Should Know* (New York: Harper & Row, 1987). SAFE's representatives also visit schools.
- Arrange for a presentation to a group by **L.I.A.I.S.O.N., the Long Island Association to Increase Security in Our Neighborhoods** (Herricks Community Center, Herricks Road, New Hyde Park, N.Y. 11040: 516-741-0620). It created a free program, "Playing It Safe," for preschoolers and kindergarteners. Hand puppets bring the message about safety, abduction and sexual abuse. L.I.A.I.S.O.N. has concentrated on bringing its program to groups in Long Island and Queens.
- Call New York City's Victim Services Agency (212-577-7700), which gives free assistance to victims of crime. Their services range from providing speakers to counseling to preparing court cases for child victims to operating a twenty-four-hour Crime Victim Hotline (212-577-7777).

Several neighborhoods in the city have even organized "*safe haven*" programs in which local merchants or other community resources agree to be identified, often with a decal, as sanctuaries where a child "in distress" on the street can turn in an emergency. The Safety Net program on Manhattan's Upper East Side, which extends from 59 Street to 97

Street and from Fifth Avenue to the Harlem River in Police Precinct 19, has put up decals, painted crosswalks in front of schools, and put up signs near schools warning that children are in the area. Parent safety patrols are also active around several independent schools during specific after-school hours. For some advice on how to organize your own "safe haven" program, you can turn to the community affairs officer in your neighborhood police precinct and the New York City Police Department's Community Affairs Division (One Police Plaza, New York, N.Y. 10038: 212-374-3804), which will mail you a pamphlet describing the Safe Haven Program. But the legwork requires a large community effort, including fundraising, lobbying, and enlisting parent power to keep things going.

Perhaps you'd feel better knowing that your child has been fingerprinted. The Police Department will not fingerprint children, but the Board of Education will, at no charge to you, through your community school district. Each district has its own procedures. There are also organizations such as Long Island's International Documentation Center, Inc. (P.O. Box 65, West Hempstead, N.Y.: 516-538-5411), which fingerprint children individually or in groups for a fee. Often they're hired by a local Y or school for a day-long session. Be sure that you use a method that produces clear and classifiable prints (do-it-yourself is not advised). Many experts also advise that you, rather than someone else, keep the prints.

Sports: Indoors and Outdoors

"New York has everything, except a lot of wide open spaces," report Jane Goldman and Laetitia Kennedy in their book *The New York Urban Athlete* (New York: Simon and Schuster, Inc., 1983). Having said that, Goldman and Kennedy go on to chronicle an astonishing array of recreational choices for the adult, particularly the Manhattanite—everything from swimming and squash to croquet and Frisbee. City kids too have much to choose from—if their parents know where to look.

For starters, ask the youth co-ordinator of your local **Community Board.** The city's fifty-nine community boards play an advisory role in zoning and land-use matters, but also direct their attention to the co-ordination of municipal services. The youth co-ordinators keep track of youth services. Whether it's a question about what sports activities are available, or how to organize a program for your neighborhood, the co-ordinator can help. In fact, many of the local boards have published directories of youth services—including everything from recreational facilities to cultural resources to health and education resources—for their area. Request one (available to you free, or at minimal cost) and you've got a capsule portrait of what's going on in your community. To locate your community board, contact your borough president's office or check in the telephone book's White Pages in the "Blue Pages" under "New York City Government Offices, Community Boards."

The New York City Department of Parks and Recreation, with its major recreation and play centers throughout the five boroughs, is another primary resource. You'll find that there are programs in tennis, baseball, soccer, basketball, golf, swimming, and track and field, as well as special offerings for the handicapped through R.E.A.C.H. (212-860-1842). During the summertime, the Parks Department runs special play camps for youngsters, and year-round there are competitions, such as the annual Youth Games, which draw thousands of city kids from the ages of nine to fifteen for competition in basketball, bowling, swimming, tennis, track and field, and volleyball.

Other major resources for recreational programming for youth are Y's and community centers, the Police Athletic League (P.A.L.) and the citywide Catholic Youth Organization (C.Y.O.). Check also with any neighborhood after-school programs. Don't forget to call the continuing education departments of local colleges—you may turn up anything from swimming lessons to specialized summer camps. In Manhattan, you'll also find special sports clubs for kids.

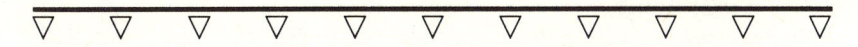

▽ ▽ ▽ ▽ ▽ ▽ ▽ ▽ ▽ ▽ ▽ ▽

GETTING A HANDLE ON THE PARKS DEPARTMENT

The Department of Parks and Recreation oversees the parks, beaches, playgrounds, recreation facilities—golf courses, swimming pools, tennis courts, skating rinks—and public spaces of New York. It's in charge of some 24,600 acres of land, including parks and playgrounds. The headquarters of the Parks Department is in Manhattan's Central Park at The Arsenal (212-360-8111). Each of the boroughs has a borough office with a borough commissioner in charge. For details about particular sports and recreation programs, call the borough offices (Bronx: 212-430-1800; Brooklyn: 718-965-8900; Manhattan: 212-408-0100;

Queens: 718-520-5900; Staten Island: 718-390-8000). You can also contact the Sports and Fitness Division (718-699-4225) and the Aquatics Program (718-699-4219).

The principal recreational centers of the Parks Department are:

Bronx

Mullaly Play Center (164 Street and Jerome Avenue: 212-822-4382)
St. Mary's Recreation Center (145 Street and St. Ann's Avenue: 212-822-4681)

Brooklyn

Betsy Head Recreation Center (Hopkinson and Livonia, Dumont avenues: 718-965-6550)
Brooklyn War Memorial (Cadman Plaza, Fulton and Orange streets: 718-965-6584)
Brownsville Recreation Center (155 Linden Boulevard: 718-965-6583)
Red Hook Recreation Center (Bay and Clinton streets: 718-965-6500)
St. John's Recreation Center (1251 Prospect Place: 718-965-6574)
Sunset Park (43 Street and Seventh Avenue: 718-965-6578)
Von King Recreation Center (670 Lafayette Avenue: 718-965-6567)

Manhattan

Alfred E. Smith Recreation Center (80 Catherine Street: 212-397-3090)
Carmine Street Recreation Center (Clarkson Street and Seventh Avenue: 212-593-8309)
East 54 Street Recreation Center (348 East 54 Street: 212-397-3148)
Highbridge Recreation Center (173 Street and Amsterdam Avenue: 212-927-9737)
Jackie Robinson Play Center (Bradhurst Avenue and West 145 Street: 212-307-3152)
John Rozier Hansborough, Jr., Recreation Center (35 West 134 Street: 212-397-3083)
Mount Morris Recreation Center (Mount Morris Park West and 122 Street: 212-397-3135)
West 59 Street Recreation Center (533 West 59 Street: 212-397-3170)

Queens

Lost Battalion Hall (93-29 Queens Boulevard: 718-520-5366)
Roy Wilkins Recreation Center (119 Avenue and Merrick Boulevard: 718-276-4630)
Sorrentino Recreation Center (18-48 Cornaga Avenue, Far Rockaway: 718-471-4818)

Staten Island

Cromwell Recreation Center (Murray Hulbert Avenue and Hannah Street: 718-720-6863)

You must have a permit to use certain city facilities. For information about permits for golf, tennis, field events, and special events, call the borough offices. They can refer you to the correct permit office. If you have difficulty obtaining a permit for an event, ask your community board for help. To find out what's happening, dial the Parks Department's **Free Events Message:** 212-360-1333. For a rundown of important phone numbers, call the Department of Parks Directory (212-360-3444). Be forewarned: Numbers change frequently at the Parks Department.

△ △ △ △ △ △ △ △ △ △ △

Here's a brief look at some sports and how you can learn more about what's going on:

◆ **Baseball:** In 1986, Little League Baseball, with eight teams and more than 125 boys and girls from the age of eight to twelve participating, came to Manhattan's Upper West Side. The first game pitted the H&H Bagels team against the Fairway Fruits and Vegetables. Reported *The New York Times:* "On the Henry Hudson, where traffic was stalled, a carload of commuters cheered a hit by Ian Berger of the H&H Bagels team." Quipped a coach: "This is really city baseball." Said one mother, "Now we don't have to move to the suburbs."

The Upper West Side League may be the newest Little League, but it's not the only baseball league around. (On Staten Island alone you'll find Babe Ruth Leagues, Little Leagues, the Kiwanis Grasshopper League, and other local programs.) The youth co-ordinator of your community board should know exactly who's running programs. You can also contact the Little League (Box 3485, Williamsport, Pa. 07701: 717-326-1921), Babe Ruth Baseball (Box 5000, Trenton, N.J. 18638: 609-695-1434), and the American Amateur Baseball Congress (215 East Green Street, Maurhall, Mich. 49068: 616-781-2002). They can direct you to local groups or help you organize a team. For the baseball enthusiast, there are several local summer baseball camps (intensive week or more long sessions, usually for ages eight and up). Check with St. John's University and Queens College in Queens and Fordham University in the Bronx. In some areas of New York, baseball's hard to get going because of the shortage of playing fields.

If you'd like to take a group of children to a ballgame, both the Mets and the Yankees have special programs. The Mets' Community Relations Department at Shea Stadium in Queens provides reduced rate tickets for 25 cents per child on certain days. The "Yankee Juniors" program at Yankee Stadium in the Bronx features complimentary tickets to a ballgame plus a two-hour clinic before the game in which kids meet with Yankee coaches to learn about baseball fundamentals. Write to the teams on your group's stationery. The teams recommend that you contact them at the beginning of the baseball season, since their programs are popular. If you are in Con Edison's service territory, you can call the Community Relations Department (212-460-6917) and ask them to supply your youth group (up to 25 children) with free tickets (these are tickets that Con Edison has purchased) to Yankee ballgames.

◆ **Basketball:** This sport's king in certain neighborhoods in New York City and the eager seven-year-old can begin with the Biddy Basketball League of the Children's Aid Society. Several Y's also start this young, while the Parks Department begins at nine. There's no shortage of basketball leagues—progressing from biddy to midget to juniors and seniors—in the city. Among the more well known: C.Y.O., P.A.L., Public School Athletic League (P.S.A.L.), Manhattan's Children's Aid Society, Riverside Church and Holcombe Rucker Community League, Brooklyn U.S.A., the Bronx's Gauchos, and Queens' E.L.M.C.O.R. The Department of Parks and Recreation also has leagues and sponsors various competitions. You'll find several local basketball camps. Check with St. John's University and Wagner College on Staten Island and Fordham University in the Bronx.

If you're interested in complimentary tickets to take your youth group to a New York Knicks game at Madison Square Garden, write to the Knicks' director of communications at the Garden, outlining your request. He'll try to oblige.

◆ **Gymnastics:** Many of the Y's have progressive gymnastics programs for children, as do some of the independent schools (during school hours and after school). If you prefer a private club, Paul Spadaro of the Richmond Gymnastic Center (718-816-6287) can tell you about clubs affiliated with the United States Gymnastic Federation. If your child wants an intensive summer camp program, try the Y's (among them: Brooklyn's YWCA, the Flatbush YMCA, and the Greenpoint YMCA, as well as Manhattan's YWCA, the McBurney YMCA and the West Side YMCA), Queens College, York College, and private clubs.

◆ **Horseback Riding:** Although some stables will give lessons to very young children (Van Cortlandt in the Bronx says that they will teach a child as young as five to ride), many others start with youngsters around the age of nine. Among the places to check: Van Cortlandt Stables (West 254 Street and Broadway: 212-543-4433) and Pelham Bit Stables (9 Shore Road: 212-885-9723) in the Bronx; Jamaica Bay School of Equitation (7000 Shore Parkway: 718-531-8949) and Culmitt Riding Stables (51 Caton Place: 718-438-8849) in Brooklyn; and Claremont Riding Academy (175 West 89 Street: 212-724-5100) in Manhattan. For summer camp, check with Claremont and Jamaica Bay. Be forewarned: Horseback riding can be pricey.

◆ **Ice Skating:** During the wintertime, it's occasionally possible to skate on city lakes and ponds, including Van Cortlandt Park Lake in the Bronx, Conservatory Lake in Central Park, Alley Pond and Kissena Lake in Queens, and Martlings Pond in Staten Island. Since skating conditions vary, check with the Borough Offices first. Try also the Parks Department's Free Events message number (212-360-1333). If your child is interested in playing ice hockey (this is a sport where costs can mount up), check with the local rinks or contact the **Greater New York City Ice Hockey League** (P.O. Box 252, Brooklyn, N.Y. 11214-0252: 718-643-6722). For a summer camp program, contact the Staten Island Veterans Sports Complex.

▽ ▽ ▽ ▽ ▽ ▽ ▽ ▽ ▽ ▽ ▽

FINDING AN ICE SKATING RINK

Among the places for rink skating are:

Brooklyn

Abe Stark Ice Skating Rink, Boardwalk at West 19 Street, Coney Island, Brooklyn: 718-965-8196: City-owned, indoor, admission fee and skate rental. Season runs from October through March.

Kate Wollman Memorial Skating Rink in Prospect Park, 718-965-6561: City-owned, admission fee for children and adults and skate rental. (Season runs from November through March.)

Manhattan

The Ice Studio, 1034 Lexington Avenue, Manhattan, 212-535-0304: Private, indoors, admission fee, skate rentals, skating lessons. Year-round.

Lasker Memorial Rink, 106 Street in Central Park, 212-397-3142: City-owned, outdoors, admission fee, and skate rental. Season runs from November through March.

Rivergate Ice Rink, 401 East 34 Street, Manhattan, 212-689-0035: Private, outdoors, admission fee, skate rental, skating lessons. Season runs from November through March.

Rockefeller Center Skating Rink, 1 Rockefeller Plaza, Manhattan, 212-757-5731: Outdoors, admission fee, skate rental, skating lessons. Season runs from mid-October through April.

Sky Rink, 450 West 33 Street, Manhattan, 212-695-6555: Indoors, admission fee, skate rental, skating lessons. Year-round.

Wollman Memorial Rink, East 64 and Fifth Avenue in Central Park, 212-734-4843: City-owned, admission fee, skate rental, skating lessons. Newly reopened in 1986, season runs from November through March.

Queens

World's Fair Ice Skating Rink in Flushing Meadows Park (in New York City Building), 718-271-1996: Indoor rink, city-owned, admission fee, skate rental, classes and private lessons. Season runs from October for about twenty-six weeks.

Staten Island

Staten Island War Memorial Ice Skating Rink in Clove Lakes Park, 718-720-1010: City-owned, outdoors, admission fee, skate rental. Season runs from fall through spring.

Staten Island Veterans Sports Complex, 835 New Dorp Lane, 718-667-7541: Admission fee, skate rental, private and group lessons. Year-round.

△ △ △ △ △ △ △ △ △ △ △

◆ **Running and Track and Field:** The Parks Department offers many programs, including track meets. Call the borough offices for details. The New York Road Runners Club (9 East 89 Street, New York, N.Y. 10128: 212-860-4455) runs a year-round free "Urban Running Program" in parks in the five boroughs for youth ages fourteen and under. Check with them (send a self-addressed stamped envelope) for details.

◆ **Soccer:** While the Parks Department has offered some programming in soccer, you'll find that the majority of the activity is organized by private organizations. To get your child involved in a soccer program, contact the American Youth Soccer Organization (P.O. Box 5045, 5403 West 138 Street, Hawthorne, Calif. 90251-5045: 800-421-5700) and the United States Soccer Federation (The Viscount Hotel, J.F.K. International Airport, Jamaica, N.Y. 11430: 718-917-8484), which will give you the current address and phone number for the Eastern New York Youth Soccer Association (whose headquarters move when the presidency turns over). These groups will tell you about the teams, clubs, and leagues active in your community. Try also your local community board, and in Manhattan the sports clubs. During the summer, you'll find several nonresidential soccer camps on Long Island and in New Jersey. Check with the associations or with *Soccer Week* (124 Front Street, Massapequa Park, N.Y. 11762).

◆ **Swimming:** The Parks Department has both indoor and outdoor pools that come in three sizes—mini, intermediate, and Olympic. While the serious swimmer will need to head to a larger pool, the outdoors aboveground mini pools (twenty feet by forty feet), dispersed on schoolyards and playgrounds, are great for children ages three and up.

Many of the Y's and community centers have pools for recreational swimming and lessons. They often also have swim teams for youngsters to join. Thirty-five public schools—elementary, intermediate, and high schools—scattered throughout the five boroughs also have indoor swimming pools. Several of the independent schools, including Manhattan's Trinity, have swimming pools open, for a fee, at certain hours to the public. Try also apartment complexes (some will permit nonresidents to swim for a fee) or hotels (in Manhattan, for example, the Ramada Inn, the Days Inn of America, and the Sheraton City Squire Inn). There are even churches, such as the Madison Avenue Presbyterian Church and St. Bartholomew's Episcopal Church and Community Center in Manhattan and St. Sebastian's Roman Catholic Church in Queens, whose pools are open to nonparishioners. Your community board may be your best source for exactly what's nearby.

If you're interested in swimming lessons, don't overlook the continuing education offices of local colleges and universities. Swim lessons for children are part of the curriculum at Borough of Manhattan Community College and Marymount Manhattan College; Queens College, St. John's University and York College in Queens; and Brooklyn College. Several health clubs also have swim classes; check the Consumer Yellow Pages under "Swimming Instruction."

CAUTION: You'll find "water baby" or "teeny tot" or "toddler swim" classes around the city, some of which emphasize "drown-proofing" children. Exactly when, and how, children should be taught swimming is controversial. There have been articles that raise questions about the risk to young children who swallow water, suggesting that this could lead to the spread of infection, the erosion of dental enamel, and hyponatremia (water intoxication). The American Academy of Pediatrics' Committee on Accident and Poison Prevention has stated: "Organized group swimming instructions for children under three years of age is *not* recommended. Learning to swim at this age does not make your child water-safe. Infants and toddlers in swimming programs are at increased risk of infection and convulsions from swallowing large quantities of water. Total submersion should be prohibited and YMCA guidelines for infant swimming should be followed." Consult your physician before you sign up.

▽ ▽ ▽ ▽ ▽ ▽ ▽ ▽ ▽ ▽ ▽

THE PUBLIC POOLS OF NEW YORK CITY

Outdoor pools are open from the end of June through Labor Day usually from 11 A.M. to 7 P.M. The indoor pools, often located at major recreational centers, are open year-round with hours varying depending upon the pool. For full information, contact the Borough Offices. There's no charge for admission.

The Parks Department's Aquatics Division offers free *Learn-to-Swim* classes for children at a few pools in each borough during the summer mornings (two three-and-a-half week sessions) and weekends during the school year. They also hold some periodic competitive swim meets. Check with the Aquatics program (718-699-4219) or your Borough Office to find out where and when.

These are New York's indoor and outdoor public pools:

Bronx

Bronx River (174 Street and Bronx River Avenue): mini
Castle Hill (Olmsted and Turnbull Avenue): mini
Crotona Park (East 173 Street and Fulton Avenue): outdoors
Claremont Pool (East 170 Street and Clay Avenue): outdoors
Edenwald (Schieffelin Avenue and 229 Street): mini
Gouverneur Morris (Third Avenue and St. Paul's Place): mini
Haffen Park Pool (Ely and Burke avenues): outdoors
Mapes Pool (Prospect Avenue and 180 Street): outdoors
Mathews and Mullimer (Morris Park Avenue): mini
Mullaly Play Center: outdoors
P.S. 16 (East 239 Street and Matilda Avenue): mini
St. Mary's Recreation Center: indoor
Van Cortlandt Pool (West 244 Street east of Broadway): outdoors
Williamsbridge Oval (208 Street and Bainbridge Avenue): mini

Brooklyn

American Playground (Noble, Franklin and Milton streets): mini
Betsy Head Memorial Playground (Hopkinson, Livonia and Dumont avenues): diving, outdoors
Brownsville Recreation Center: indoors
Bushwick Pool (Humboldt, Bushwick, and Flushing avenues): intermediate, outdoors
Commodore John Barry (Flushing Avenue, Park, Navy and North Elliot Place): intermediate, outdoors
Crown Heights/Lincoln Terrace Park (East New York Avenue, Eastern Parkway, Rochester Avenue and Lincoln Terrace): mini
Douglass Pool (Third Avenue between Douglass and DeGraw streets): intermediate, outdoors
Howard Houses (East New York and Stone avenues): intermediate, outdoors
David A. Fox Memorial Park (Avenues H and I, East 54–55 streets): mini
Kosciusko Street Pool (between Marcy and DeKalb avenues): outdoors
Alex Lindower Park (Mill and Strickland avenues): mini
Glenwood Houses Playground (Ralph Avenue and Farragut Road): mini
McCarren Park (Lorimer and Bayard streets): diving, outdoors
Metropolitan Avenue Pool (at Bedford Avenue): indoors
Playground at P.S. 26 and JHS 57 (Stuyvesant and Lafayette avenues): mini
Playground at P.S. 44 (Sumner Avenue): mini
Playground at P.S. 20 (Adelphi Street to Clermont Avenue): mini
Red Hook Park (Clinton, Bay and Henry streets): outdoors

St. John's Recreation Center: indoors
Sunset Park (Seventh Avenue and 43 Street): outdoors

Manhattan

Abraham Lincoln Houses Playground (Fifth Avenue and East 135 Street): mini
Alfred E. Smith Recreation Center: mini
Carmine Street Recreation Center: indoors
Jackie Robinson Play Center: outdoors
Dyckman Houses Playground (West 204 Street and Nagle Avenue): mini
East 54 Street Gym and Pool: indoors
East 23 Street (East 23 Street and Asser Levy Place): indoors and outdoors
Frederick Douglass Houses Playground (Amsterdam Avenue between West 100 and 102 streets): mini
Hamilton Fish Park (East Houston and Pitt streets): diving, outdoors
Highbridge Park (West 173 Street and Amsterdam Avenue): mini, outdoors
John Jay (East 77 Street at Cherokee Place): intermediate and diving, outdoors
John Rozier Hansborough, Jr. Recreation Center: indoors
Lasker Memorial (Central Park opposite West 110 Street and Lenox Avenue): outdoors
Marcus Garvey Memorial Park (East 124 Street and Fifth Avenue): mini, outdoors
William H. Seward Park (Canal, Hester, Essex and Jefferson streets): mini
Sheltering Arms (West 129 Street and Amsterdam Avenue): outdoors
Szold Place Pool (10 Street and Szold Place): outdoors
Thomas Jefferson Park (First Avenue and East 111–112 streets): outdoors
Thompson Street Playground (Thompson Street between Spring and Prince streets): mini
Tompkins Square Park (Avenues A to B, East 7 to East 10 streets): mini
Wagner Houses (East 124 Street between First and Second avenues): intermediate, outdoors
West 59 Street Gym and Pool: indoors and outdoors

Queens

Astoria Heights Recreation Park (30 Road, 45–46 streets): mini
Astoria Park (19 Street, opposite 23 Drive in Astoria): Olympic, diving, outdoors
Fisher Pool (32 Avenue and 99 Street in Elmhurst): intermediate, outdoors
Liberty Park Pool (172 Street and 104 Avenue): intermediate, outdoors

Playground at P.S. 186 (Little Neck Boulevard and 252 Street): mini
Playground at J.H.S. 158 (47 Avenue near 211 Street): mini
Roy Wilkins Recreation Center: indoor
Queensbridge Park (21 Street, Vernon Boulevard, East River): mini
Windmuller Park (52 Street, Woodside Avenue, 39 Road, 39 Drive and 54 Street): mini

Staten Island

Beach Houses Playground and P.S. 46 (Parkinson Avenue, Kramer Street): mini
Berry Houses/General Douglas MacArthur Playground (Dongan Hills Avenue and Jefferson Street): mini
Faber Park (Richmond Terrace and Faber Street): intermediate, outdoors
Hylan Pool (Joline Avenue and Hylan Boulevard): intermediate, outdoors
Joseph H. Lyons Pool (Pier 6 and Victory Boulevard): outdoors
Mariners Harbor Houses Playground (Grandview Avenue, Continental Place), mini
Michael J. Mahoney Memorial Playground (Beechwood Avenue, Crescent & Cleveland Streets), mini
Stapleton Houses Playground and P.S. 14 (Tompkins Avenue, Broad and Hill streets), mini
Lawrence C. Thompson Memorial Park (Broadway and Chappell Streets), intermediate, outdoors

△ △ △ △ △ △ △ △ △ △ △

If you prefer beach swimming in the summertime, you've got several choices. The city's beaches are free and open from Memorial Day through Labor Day. At some beaches, in recent years, swimming has been prohibited because of pollution. (South and Midland Beach on Staten Island have been closed for swimming by the Department of Health.) If you've got questions about conditions at public beaches, contact the Parks Department's public information office at 212-360-8141. The Parks Department's events message also mentions swimming conditions during the summer. Be forewarned: not all beaches have facilities for changing but there are public bathrooms. For directions to the beaches, call the **New York Transit Authority Travel Information Bureau:** 718-780-1234. New York's swimming beaches are: Orchard Beach in the Bronx; Brighton Beach, Coney Island Beach, and Manhattan Beach in Brooklyn; the Rockaway Beaches and Jacob Riis

Park in Queens; Great Kills Beach and Wolfe's Pond Park Public Beach in Staten Island.

If you want to venture farther out, try Jones Beach State Park (516-785-1600) in Nassau and Robert Moses State Park (516-669-0449) on Fire Island. Weekends at Jones Beach come early as traffic backs up and the beach gets crowded.

◆ **Tennis:** You'll find tennis programs in the parks, the schoolyards, and private clubs of New York City. During the summer, the Parks Department offers free tennis clinics for youngsters who are between the ages of eight and eighteen and with no previous experience in the sport. The Youth Tennis program has been held two days a week, usually for three hours daily, at various sites throughout the city. There is no charge and racquets and balls are included. More advanced players may try out in May for the Urban Youth Tennis Academy. The Academy is a nonprofit scholarship tennis program that gives city kids the opportunity to develop their skills under specialized supervision. Successful applicants receive a year of free tennis coaching, tournament expenses, and equipment. For full details on both programs, contact the director of tennis in the Sports and Fitness Division, 718-699-4225.

The nonprofit New York Junior Tennis League (25 West 39 Street, Suite 1402, New York, N.Y. 10018: 212-302-5030) has as its goal to "make it possible for metropolitan area children to learn, practice, and compete in tennis regardless of their economic level." They have developed, in conjunction with community school districts and the Board of Education, a springtime Schoolyard Program that utilizes portable net posts and permanent lines. In the summertime, they run a free structured program, three days a week, three hours a day, at various locales in the city. Racquets, coaches, courts, balls, and team T-shirts are provided. There's also special instruction for the handicapped. During the wintertime, any youngster who wishes is welcome to play for twenty-two weeks from 6 A.M. to 8 A.M. on weekends at one of the N.Y.J.T.L.'s winter indoor program sites (e.g., the U.S.T.A. National Tennis Center in Queens). They'll be glad to tell you about their programs and send you a free *New York Junior Tennis League Journal/Directory* that includes information about programs and lists facilities, both public and private, around the city. For an intensive summer program at a private club, contact Skip Hartman's Junior Tennis Camp (c/o Stadium Tennis Center, 11 East 162 Street, Bronx, N.Y. 10452: 212-293-2386). The camp is held at the Horace Mann School of Riverdale. You may also want to contact the United States Tennis Association Education Center (729 Alexander Road, Princeton, N.J. 08540: 609-452-2580).

▽ ▽ ▽ ▽ ▽ ▽ ▽ ▽ ▽ ▽ ▽

RECREATION FOR THE TINIEST TOTS

Your child's barely crawling, walking, or running. But you think that he needs to shape up. Around the city you can sign him up for baby in diaper gyms, parent/infant exercise classes, rock 'n' roll movement programs, or tumbling tots. Chances are you need look no further than your local Y, community center, synagogue, or church. In Manhattan Family Focus, the Elisabeth Bing Center for Parents and the Walden School are other places that have led the way in developing these programs.

Two franchise companies, **Playorena** (800-645-PLAY) and **Gymboree** (consult your local telephone directory), have penetrated the metropolitan area. In their exercise classes (for ages three months to four years), children wriggle through tunnels, roll, bounce, and jump on dozens of brightly colored, smooth, soft materials such as foam-rubber logs. While the teensiest ones are flexing and stretching fingers and toes, three-year-olds in Gymgrad, a class at Gymboree, are practicing skills such as throwing a basketball, jumping distances, and walking the balance beams.

Before you sign up your tot for any exercise program, do some basic research. Observe a class. Look for classes that emphasize a child's natural pattern of development and don't require too much. Be sure that the staff is trained in teaching young children and that there is adequate supervision. Do parents participate? While the emphasis may be on movement education and developing basic skills (avoid classes that emphasize mastery of any piece of equipment), the keynote should be having fun. Check that there is proper matting, appropriately placed, and examine the equipment carefully. Don't hesitate to ask your physician for an opinion.

Perhaps you'd like to consider infant massage as a way to enhance muscle tone? One massage instructor claims that "The stimulation of baby massage can increase your baby's motor, mental, and social development." Another sees it as a way of promoting bonding between parent and child. For information about massage and where classes have been offered, check with the Y's, local parenting centers, or the International Association of Infant Massage Instructors (c/o Laurie Evans, P.O. Box 298, New York, N.Y. 10272: 718-596-9658).

△ △ △ △ △ △ △ △ △ △ △

Celebrating a Birthday

Brooke Hampton, age eight, hasn't lunched with Zippy the Chimp yet, but in her years of partygoing on Manhattan's Upper East Side she's been to many of the juvenile party hot spots. One year she hosted her own birthday celebration at the razzle-dazzle Jeremy's Place (price tag: about $450 for 15 children), the next at Jodi's Gym (price tag: $200 for ten children to do an hour of gymnastics), and the year after that at the Ice Studio (price tag: $210 for an hour). She's also baked a cake with Birthdaybakers . . . Partymakers (price tag: $350) and eaten birthday cake decorated with a Dutch windmill and wooden shoes at the Museum of the City of New York (price tag: $15.00 per child for a minimum of ten).

Josh Laughton, also eight, lives in Greenwich Village, and the parties he's been to have been decidedly less upscale. He's had his share of burgers and fries at McDonald's equipped with an indoor playground (price tag: about $4.50 per child for a minimum of ten children) and eaten birthday cake served onstage after a performance at the Courtyard Playhouse of the Little People's Theater (price tag: $5.00 per child). He's also been to several parties held in space rented from local independent schools. His four-year-old sister's social life has so far been more modest—mostly a round of at-home parties sparked only by the desperate ingenuity of the birthday child's parents—but she's just had her first taste of the high life: a party at the Children's Museum of Manhattan (price tag: $175 uncatered).

Children's birthday parties are big deals in New York, whether parents live in a cramped apartment in Manhattan or a detached house in Queens. For some parents, the choice is to take the party outside the home; for others, to import some entertainment to keep the guests amused. The costs vary dramatically, depending upon the neighborhood you live in and the kind of party you have in mind.

If you're interested in booking an entertainer in your home, start by talking to other parents. "One year it seemed that every child in my daughter's nursery school had YoYo the Clown," remembers one mother. "They saw each other so much they were on a first-name basis." You'll also find entertainers listed in the Yellow Pages (under "Clowns, Entertainers, and Puppeteers and Marionettes") and in the classified sections of magazines and newspapers (*New York* magazine has a special section, "Entertainment/Kids"). Some of the performers who advertise also have places where they will throw the party for you for an additional fee. To find a puppeteer you can also contact the Puppetry Guild (Box 244, New York, N.Y. 10016), which publishes a membership directory. If you're a member of the Parents League of New York, check their birthday file for ideas and services. You might also try local colleges—either their employment services or their performing arts programs—for less expensive entertainers. Local high schools are another resource. Take a look also at the *New York Party Directory* (published by the New York Party Directory Associates, 123 East 54 Street, New York, N.Y. 10022: 212-486-0410), which gives party ideas, including places, caterers, supplies, and entertainment, and features a special section on "Children's Parties."

The choices are many if you're thinking about an out-of-home party. You might rent space in a local community center or nursery school or even a community room in an apartment building. Restaurants, such as pizzerias or fast-food emporia, are other possibilities. Hosting a party at a neighborhood McDonald's or Burger King is quite common. Not all branches of these restaurants will be willing to accommodate your group, but some have their own party rooms or indoor playgrounds just for this purpose. The price of the party usually includes the meal, cake, and party favors. Be forewarned, however, that at some McDonald's there may be more than one party taking place at the same time and in the same area. Observes one Queens parent: "Weekend parties are an abomination. All different age groups are thrown in together, a three-year-old party mixed with an eight-year-old party." If you're concerned, check before you book.

Ice cream parlors are also popular. At Jahn's in Richmond Hill, you can run a two-hour birthday party in a private room (meal, cake, and party hat included) for $5.00 per child. A birthday in one of the famed Manhattan parlors is more expensive: At Serendipity 3, it's likely to cost you about $17.50 per child for a minimum of 20 children for one of their scrumptious desserts served up in their private room.

An outing of roller skating, ice skating, or bowling, or an activity at a gymnastics or dance studio, health club, karate or judo club, gymnasium, Y, tennis or sports club are other possibilities. The Brooklyn YWCA offers "Pool Parties," which includes time in the pool and the use of a room for games, dancing, and refreshments ($90). You can also head for video arcades or amusement parks, such as Brooklyn's Nellie Bly. The popular

Chuck E. Cheese in Brooklyn offers an hour-and-a-half birthday party package that includes the table trimmings, pizza, an ice cream sundae, and game tokens for about $6.00 per child.

Another possibility would be to attend a magic show at Mostly Magic or the Magic Towne House in Manhattan. Or you might consider a "theater party" (for a more detailed discussion of entertainment, including phone numbers and addresses, see Chapter Six). Some performance halls—Radio City Music Hall or Madison Square Garden, for example—will sell a block of tickets for a group at a discounted price. You can also look into the following birthday deals:

- "Family Time" performances at the Brooklyn Center for the Performing Arts of Brooklyn College. If you purchase ten or more tickets to the show, your child's name is put in the program, there's a birthday banner hung in the lobby, and your child receives a small gift.
- Children's Theater Festival at Kingsborough Community College: Season subscribers are entitled to the birthday bonus. Their children receive a gift and are feted on stage by "Friendly Fran the Clown." Before the show, you can arrange to use a private room on campus and pay for lunch to be served.
- Little People's Theater Company, Off Center Theater, 4th Wall Repertory Company, Thirteenth Street Repertory Company, and Michael Taubenslag Productions in Manhattan: For the price of admission, the children can mingle with the actors after the show in a space provided by them. You provide the refreshments.

Perhaps you'd prefer to mix museums and birthdays. Several museums have come up with special birthday packages (for information about addresses and telephone numbers, see Chapter Six). The programs at some of these museums are big hits. Count on booking months—or even years—in advance. Intrigued? Get in touch with these:

- Alley Pond Environmental Center in Queens: Children five and up can participate in a two-hour program involving an introduction to pets, walks outdoors, and a craft project. You bring the food and the charge is just $4.50 per child.
- American Museum of Natural History: Members can sign up for "Dinosaur Birthday Parties" for children from the ages of five to ten. In addition to a tour of the Dinosaur Halls, children handle fossils, create an origami birthday hat, play dinosaur bingo, and pin the tail on the

dinosaur. You're charged a basic $195 for the program, plus an additional $10.00 per child (minimum, ten; maximum, twenty) to pay for all materials, decorations, the special favor bag, and ice cream and juice (cake extra).
- Children's Museum of Manhattan: Members' children, as part of the birthday package, can explore a museum exhibit, investigate the animal collection, and do an art activity. The charge is $15.00 per child with a minimum of ten children and a maximum of fifteen.
- Museum of Broadcasting in Manhattan: How about watching the original *Peter Pan* with Mary Martin for birthday entertainment? Or perhaps a pastische of children's programs, including "The Muppet Show," "Captain Kangaroo," "Sesame Street," "Howdy Doody," and "Doctor Seuss"? At this museum, the education staff will put together an hour-and-a-half ($40) or two-hour ($60) television or radio program just for your group. No food or drink permitted on the premises; you'll have to go somewhere before or after to cut the cake.
- Museum of the City of New York: Children from the ages of six to twelve take a tour of a gallery and participate in a "Please Touch Demonstration," where they handle antique objects and try on costumes. You're provided with a cake, ice cream, candy, balloons, and souvenirs. The cost: $12.00 per child with a minimum of ten and a maximum of fifteen.
- New York Aquarium: You'll attend a performance in their theater at which the dolphin and the trainer salute the birthday child. There's also some arts and crafts programming for the group. Cake and juice served. The cost: $100 for a group of fifteen.
- New York Hall of Science: School-aged children at specified hours receive an orientation, see demonstrations and use the hands-on exhibit. The charge is $10.00 per child, with a minimum of ten children. You bring the food; the museum decorates the place where you eat, supplies paper goods and a party bag filled with items from their shop.
- Staten Island Children's Museum: As part of your membership, plus an additional $50 plus $2.00 per child, you can purchase a birthday party which includes a tour of the exhibit and a workshop. The birthday child must be at least four years old.
- Staten Island Museum: Children ages four to ten take a tour of the museum and participate in a workshop. The museum provides the "goody" bag, while you bring the refreshments. The charge is $5.00 per child for nonmembers and $3.00 for members.

- The Brooklyn Children's Museum: For $100, members can book parties for children ages five to twelve in the "birthday party space." The museum provides table settings and a balloon party favor, while you bring the refreshments. Your group is given a schedule and is encouraged to split into small groups to explore the museum.

Whatever direction your party planning takes, be sure that you talk with the booker in advance and understand all the arrangements. Establish exactly what's provided for free or in the basic package price and what "extras" you will be charged for or have to bring yourself. Ask about their policy on deposits, refunds, and cancellations, in case the birthday boy should come down with the flu on the morning of the big bash. Don't hesitate to solicit recommendations or to ask whether you might observe another party in progress before you book. And be sure to get your child's opinion about the arrangements before you sign up. You don't want to discover too late that little Benjamin thinks dinosaur fossils are "yucky" or that Melissa is certain she will throw up the moment she is forced to see the sharks.

Perhaps you'll decide that the home party, sans professional entertainment, best suits your family. If so, and the children are preschool or elementary-school-aged, you'll want to plan the party carefully. Don't hesitate to keep it short: an hour and a half is plenty long for excited children. Before the guests arrive, put away any special toys that your child does not want to share. If you serve a meal—either lunch or a hearty after-school snack—plus cake, the children remain quiet at the table for a sizable stretch of time, rather than wandering around your house. You'll also want to come up with a selection of party games. While musical chairs may be great fun for large suburban recreation rooms (musical statues, which requires no props, works well in small spaces), you'll probably be tempted by quieter indoor games, such as "Indian Chief" or "Hot Potato." Ask your child, and his teacher, to suggest some favorites. You can also check special game books, or party books, for ideas. Consider a very simple crafts activity (decorating party bags may appeal to young children), but pre-test it with your child to ensure that it's age-appropriate. Be sure you leave plenty of time for opening presents, since everyone delights in ogling new toys. Don't fret if your party seems humdrum by adult standards. Observes Jean Marzollo in *Birthday Parties for Children* (New York: Harper & Row, 1983): "It seems to me that the most successful birthday parties are often the least elaborate. They follow the basic steps in the ritual: invitations, decorations, presents, desserts, games, treat bags for everyone, good-byes, and it's over. The ritual need not be jazzed up, but if it is, only one or two special things are added. Too many things are just that: too much. For the best time, keep the party simple."

▽ ▽ ▽ ▽ ▽ ▽ ▽ ▽ ▽ ▽ ▽

IS YOUR CHILD WELCOME HERE?

Knowing the rules of the city—where, and when, children are welcome—is important. Here's what to expect:

- **Museums:** The Frick Collection does not permit children under the age of ten. The Solomon R. Guggenheim Museum and the Whitney Museum of American Art do not permit strollers, although the Whitney provides backpacks free of charge (see Chapter Six for a more complete rundown of policies at selected museums).
- **Movies:** Bringing an infant or toddler with you for an adult movie can be problematic. Although none of the movie chains will turn you away, the theater manager may ask you to pay for your child—even if he's asleep in a frontpack. Don't be surprised if you're told to sit in the back on an aisle or are required to leave—or step into the lobby—if your child vocalizes.

  Nor should you count on sending your school-aged child to a movie without you. The City of New York has regulations governing attendance at theaters. Youngsters under the age of sixteen must be accompanied by a parent, guardian, or other adult unless the theater is licensed by the Department of Consumer Affairs, employs a licensed matron, and has set aside a separate seating area for unaccompanied minors. Unescorted children cannot be admitted during school hours or after 6 P.M. In July and August, the rules change and children may attend every day until 7 P.M.

  Most theaters don't have a matron on hand daily, although a district manager for the United Artists chain reported that his theaters have matrons on duty on weekend afternoons, summers, and holidays. Other theaters, however, will engage a matron only for films designed to draw the young set or for special matinees. If you're tempted to drop your children off, check with the theater before you do.
- **Live Theater:** Infants, toddlers, and preschoolers are not wanted on Broadway. Children four years and under will not be admitted to any of the Shubert-owned theaters. Your five-year-old can attend, but you'll be charged full price for the seat. A spokesman for the Nederlander organization reported that admission to their theaters was at the discretion of the

management, but "we don't really want infants in the theater at all. If a child opens his mouth, he's out." The rule of thumb: *If* your child's let in, you'll pay full price and there's no refund if you're asked to leave.

Off-Broadway and Off-Off Broadway theaters have less clear-cut policies and some even cater to children. The wise parent, however, checks with any theater—on, off, or off-off Broadway—before showing up with a youngster, particularly an infant or toddler, in tow.

◆ **Restaurants:** The tip-off as to a restaurant's attitude toward children is often in the services it provides. When you find high chairs, booster seats, and special children's menus, you know kids are welcome. You'll find these services at fast-food joints, delicatessens, pizzerias, neighborhood coffee shops, diners, and "family-style" restaurants. Chinese, Greek, Indian, and Italian—among the ethnic restaurants—seem the most friendly to youngsters.

If you like eating out and plan on regularly taking your child along, start at an early age but be careful where you pick. Begin by eating near your home in a restaurant you know and where the service is fast. Dine when the restaurant is least crowded and at times when your child is at his best. Enforce some restaurant manners. Don't let your child become rowdy or wander around the room. If you have any doubts about the restaurant's policy toward children, call ahead to find out if your child is welcome.

One additional caveat: In selecting a restaurant, you may also want to look at its bathroom facilities, since youngsters frequently have to go—often more than once during the course of a meal just for the adventure—and there's nothing more awkward than telling a young child he has to "hold it." Some fast-food places don't have public bathrooms at all, while the facilities at other less fancy establishments around the city may be such that you don't want to use them. In the case of one, otherwise quite decent, Indian restaurant (now closed), your trek to the fetid lavatory led into the kitchen, around the boiling caldrons, through a trap door in the floor, and down a treacherously narrow flight of stone stairs to the unfinished basement to a tiny lavatory that had obviously been used much more frequently than cleaned by the employees.

△ △ △ △ △ △ △ △ △ △ △

Shopping

There are innumerable places to shop in New York City: the five-and-dime store, the discount shop, the outlet, the department store, the specialty boutique. If you have your heart set on the twenty-four-karat, gold-plated Solange crib, then head for the renowned Lewis of London, which also offers everything from diaper changing tables to wall hangings to strollers and car seats. If your taste (or the size of your checkbook balance) is more modest, there is a great variety of other stores in New York for your children's shopping. In Manhattan, you'll find clothing boutiques clustered on the Upper East and West Sides, in Greenwich Village, and in SoHo in addition to the large midtown department stores, while the other boroughs offer their own wide selection of neighborhood shops, discount outlets, and malls. You'll find a surprising selection of the basics at your five-and-dime store.

Most department stores in New York carry infant's and children's clothing. Abraham & Strauss, B. Altman & Company, Alexander's, Bloomingdale's, Lord & Taylor, Saks Fifth Avenue, and Macy's have sizable, varied collections in both their flagship and branch stores. Macy's Herald Square has an added bonus: the specialty haircutter Kenneth for Kids. (If you want to combine a haircut with toy shopping, you can also visit *Shooting Star,* 212-758-4344, at F.A.O. Schwarz.) If you're looking for a Sears, with its sturdy, dependable clothing, there are stores in the Bronx, Brooklyn, and Queens. Century 21 in Lower Manhattan and in Bay Ridge, Brooklyn, is a lesser known department store that carries name brands, such as Health-Tex, Absorba, and Carters, at reduced prices. People flock from all boroughs to the chain stores Kids "R" Us (in Brooklyn and in Staten Island). Here you'll find first-quality brand-name clothing "off-priced" between 20 and 30 percent. Reports one mother: "It's good if you're looking for fashionable 'in' children's clothing, but a party dress is hard to find." Don't count on much sales help, however. There's also a separate Buster Brown shoe store and photo studio within the stores. Your child will also like shopping at Kids "R" Us since Toys "R" Us is nearby.

If you're looking for baby items, particularly furniture, you'll probably visit specialty stores. While many have a sizable inventory in stock, the stores recommend that you visit in advance, since some cribs may have to be special-ordered as much as three months ahead. Most have policies like Ben's Babyland: "We deliver when the customer delivers."

The shopping lists that follow are by no means inclusive and are intended solely as a *sampling* (admittedly, Manhattan-skewed) of what's available around New York. They are not intended as an endorsement of one store over another (some stores are omitted from this section solely because of the limitations of space within this book, not because of issues of quality). In your New York shopping, you'll no doubt find some stores on your own that are truly distinctive and others that are not. No doubt you have your own neighborhood, and borough, favorites. You'll probably also discover that the knowledgeable small retailers willingly take the time to provide the advice that the larger supermarket retailers don't.

Before you head out, though, do some reading and talk to seasoned veterans about what's generally recommended. Inform yourself about the potential safety hazards of the items you intend to buy, especially if you're in the market for toys, cribs, or other children's furniture. Some products have been recalled for being dangerous to young children, and others are sold with accompanying warnings about the age or size of the child for whom the product is unsafe. Jack Gillis and Mary Ellen R. Fise's *The Childwise Catalogue* (New York: Pocket Books, 1986) is a helpful consumer guide to purchasing everything from cribs to sleepwear for newborns through age five. For a quick fix on toys, see Helen Boehm, *The Right Toys* (New York: Bantam Books, 1986). When looking at toys, keep in mind the ages of *all* children who may use the toys. Your two-year-old is likely to try the toy with a thousand small pieces that you've selected for your six-year-old. The results can be lethal. If "hand-me-down" furniture, toys, or clothing interests you, find out if these older goods conform to current product standards.

Clothing and Furniture

BROOKLYN

Abel's (515 Fifth Avenue, 718-788-0640): Furniture and accessories with more than forty different cribs in stock. Their slogan is: "We deliver everything but the baby."

Berman's Furniture (4415 Thirteenth Avenue, 718-438-1323): A large selection of furniture, strollers and accessories.

MB Discount Furniture (2309-11 Avenue U, 718-332-1500): Nursery and juvenile furniture, including bunk beds.

Natan Borlam (157 Havemeyer Street, 718-782-0108): This store, like its Lower East Side cousins, discounts clothing for tots to teens. The bargains are greatest as the season winds down. Closed Saturdays and open Sundays. Cash and checks with I.D. only.

Quiltex (168 39 Street, 718-788-3158): Factory outlet that sells discounted and seconds in outerwear (jackets, pram suits), bunting and bedding for sizes baby to 6X. Open Mon.–Thurs. 10–3, Fri. till noon. Cash only.

The Blossom Shop (486 Fifth Avenue, 718-768-7893): You can find the traditional "party dress" here, as well as other children's clothing.

Widensky's (1811 Schenectady Avenue, 718-253-5045): Children's wear but also an extensive layette collection make it, according to one mother, "the place to go."

MANHATTAN

Albee's (715 Amsterdam Avenue, 212-662-5740): This large children's store on the Upper West Side carries everything from cribs to carriages to high chairs to dressers to clothing to toys.

Au Chat Botte (903 Madison Avenue, 212-772-3381): A selection of imported nursery furniture and children's clothing.

Bellini (1305 Second Avenue, 212-517-9233): Nursery furniture from West Germany and Italy that's adult-sized and can be used by older children.

Ben's Babyland (81 Avenue A, 212-674-1353): Infants' furniture and clothing. This is just one of the children's specialty furniture stores on the Lower East Side (**Schneider's** at 20 Avenue A, 212-473-9251 and **Lederman's** at 200 Orchard Street, 212-529-2922). These stores are chock full of name-brand cribs, changing tables, strollers, and other accessories. Some items are discounted.

Ben's for Kids (1380 Third Avenue, 212-794-2330): Infants' furniture, accessories, clothing, and toys makes this a popular shopping spot on the Upper East Side.

The Chocolate Soup (946 Madison Avenue, 212-861-2210): Small boutique packed with merchandise, one-of-a-kinds, and prices to match. Other Madison Avenue children's clothing boutiques include: **Cerutti** at 807 Madison Avenue, 212-737-7540; **Glad Rags** at 1007 Madison Avenue, 212-988-1880; **Le Monde des Enfants** at 870 Madison Avenue, 212-772-1990; **Petit Bateau** at 930 Madison Avenue, 212-288-1444, which specializes in the manufacturer's clothing; and **Tim's for Boys** at 878 Madison Avenue, 212-535-2262.

The Children's Room (318 East 45 Street, 212-687-3868): Children's furniture, including versatile bunk beds, trundles and lofts, and even expandable beds.

Conway Stores: The atmosphere at these stores, clustered around 34 Street and Herald Square, is decidedly downscale, but the merchandise, including Shands, French Toast, and Crayons, is heavily discounted. Why pay full price for name-brand cartoon-character underwear when you can get it here for much less? You'll also find great buys on hand-smocked girls' dresses. There are similar stores, and similar brands, along 14 Street between Union Square and Eighth Avenue.

M. Kreinen Sales Co. (301 Grand Street, 212-925-0239): The boxes are piled high and you've got to wade through the seeming disarray, but here you'll routinely get between 15 and 30 percent off high-quality infants' and children's clothing, including designer labels. This is the place for successful shopping when you need a bathing suit in December or a snowsuit in June. You can make quite a day shopping on the Lower East Side. There's also **Rice and Breskin** at 323 Grand Street, 212-925-5515; and **Klein's of Monticello** at 105 Orchard Street, 212-966-1453. Remember: closed Saturdays and don't be embarrassed to negotiate on prices. It's traditional.

Lewis of London (215 East 51 Street, 212-688-3669, 72-17 Austin, Forest Hills, 718-544-8003): European imports abound and some parents swear by the selection—but beware, the store is pricey. Mindy Isacoff, the manager of the Manhattan store, says about her clients: "My average order for furniture and bedding is $2,000. That's not everything. They're just buying furniture." There's also a catalogue to tempt you.

Melnikoff's (1594 York Avenue, 212-288-3644): When the list from the sleep-away camp arrives specifying what your child is required to bring, this store or **The Camp Shop** (41 West 54 Street, 212-505-0980) or **Morris Bros.** (2322 Broadway, 212-724-9000) can help. Whether it's the duffel bag, the canteen, or the camp T-shirt, they stock it. Once you're done shopping, they'll sew in the name tags.

R. G. Crumbsnatcher (254 Columbus Avenue, 212-724-8681): A West Side clothing boutique carrying sizes from infant up to size six, including imported and one-of-a-kind handmade items.

Richie's Discount Children's Shoes (183 Avenue B, 212-228-5442): The price reductions at this store are sizable and the merchandise is name-brand, so families head here to stock up on sneakers, party shoes, snow boots, slippers, and other items that push the annual shoe bill sky high.

Scandinavian Design (127 East 59th Street, 212-755-6078): Nursery and children's furniture in natural birchwood and painted white, including bunk beds, storage and wall units.

This End Up (1139 Second Avenue, 212-755-6065; 89 South Street, 212-406-0055): Solid, sturdy wood furniture that looks like it's made from packing crates. The selection is limited but the prices are very reasonable.

Wendy's Store (131 Wooster, 212,533-2305): This SoHo boutique features expensive—but cute—items. In Greenwich Village: **Kids, Kids, Kids** (436 Sixth Avenue, 212-533-3523) and **Peanut Butter and Jane** (617 Hudson Street, 212-620-7952). For staples, including shoes, parents in SoHo and the Village turn to **Lewis Children's Shop** (264 Bleeker Street, 212-242-5033).

Wicker Garden's Baby and **Wicker Garden's Children** (both at 1327 Madison Avenue, 212-348-1166): Choose from wicker baby furniture to hand-smocked clothing to children's accessories.

Workbench (470 Park Avenue South, 212-481-5454; 2091 Broadway, 212-724-3670; 1320 Third Avenue, 212-734-5106; and 60 Clinton Street in Brooklyn, 718-625-1616): A selection of modernistic, often wooden, children's furniture.

QUEENS

Berns Juvenile Furniture (57-20 Myrtle Avenue, Ridgewood, 718-821-1000): Several floors of furniture, including cribs, strollers, and high chairs.

Cooper's Youngland (212-27 26 Avenue, 718-631-1179): Name-brand clothing sold here at reduced prices. Watch for their periodic sales when you'll find great bargains. Another store is **Young World** (97-09 Queens Boulevard: 718-896-0105) and when you're looking to dress your child up in special party clothes, try **Little Royalty** (116-18 Queens Boulevard: 718-263-5999).

Hush a Bye (107-16 Queens Boulevard, 718-268-6305; there's a smaller store at 1459 First Avenue in Manhattan, 212-988-4500): Nursery furniture and accessories, including quilts and crib bumpers.

Juvenile Mart (158-05 Northern Boulevard, Flushing, 718-353-8759): Nursery and children's furniture.

Most (210-15 Horace Harding Expressway, 718-225-3455): The clothing's out on sawhorses and you find what you want but name brands are discounted here.

Murray's (160-13 Northern Boulevard, 718-463-6644): A giant clothing emporium that takes up the whole block.

Got company coming and need to rent a crib for two weeks? **Keefe and Keefe Crib and Carriage Rental Service** (429 East 75 Street, Manhattan, 212-988-8800) will provide stainless steel cribs if you give them a day's notice.

Books

Many bookstores in New York City have children's sections that stock both hardbacks and paperbacks. You can usually find a limited selection of books and records at toy stores. However, there are a few bookstores that cater to parents and children.

Bank Street College of Education Bookstore (610 West 112 Street, 212-663-7200): At this teacher's college store, there's a strong emphasis on parenting books.

Barnes and Noble Sales Annex (Fifth Avenue at 18 Street): The selection in the second floor children's section is sizable and the prices are discounted. Children's programming the first Sunday of the month during the school year.

Books of Wonder (464 Hudson Street, 212-645-8006; 132 Seventh Avenue, 212-989-3270): Large selection of new children's books. You can also find that out-of-print childhood favorite. Storytelling, special events, and a free mail-order catalogue.

Corner Bookstore (Madison Avenue at 93 Street, 212-831-3554): This store has developed charge accounts for kids. Parents can set up an account (usually $10 or more) for their children and the store keeps a record of the child's purchases. When the account runs low, the child is told. The accounts, reports the store, are "well used."

Cousin Arthur's (82 Montague Street, Brooklyn, 718-643-1232). A children's bookstore with Saturday storytelling.

Eeyore's Books for Children (2212 Broadway, 212-362-0634; 1066 Madison Avenue at East 81 Street, 212-988-3404): Weekly Sunday story hours for children ages three to six. There are also some periodic special events, such as book signings. You can be put on their mailing list.

Metropolitan Museum of Art's Children's Bookshop (Fifth Avenue at 82 Street, 212-570-3726): There's a lot more than books here. The **Brooklyn Museum** (200 Eastern Parkway, 718-638-5000) also has a children's shop, artSmart. You'll also find children's shops in the children's museums.

For some suggestions about current books to read or purchase, contact **The Children's Book Council** (67 Irving Place, New York, N.Y. 10003 212-254-2666), which publishes several lists annually, including *Children's Choices,* and a pamphlet, *Choosing a Child's Book.* (Be sure to include a self-addressed, stamped envelope.) The public library systems also distribute lists of recommended reading for young children (available at the branches). If your child wants to read about another country, you can contact **The Information Center on Children's Cultures** (U.S. Committee for UNICEF, 331 East 38 Street, New York, N.Y. 10016: 212-686-5522). For the price of a self-addressed, stamped envelope, they'll send you free book lists that describe materials about various countries. The U.S. Committee for UNICEF also has other free publications and sells their own children's books and records.

There's one special annual book event that kids always enjoy. On a Sunday in mid-September the "New York Is Book Country" fair is held on Fifth Avenue, and publishers set up booths where kids play games and receive free posters and bookmarks.

Toys

There's nothing to beat browsing in the doll, games, or robot collections of Manhattan's legendary **F.A.O. Schwarz** at Fifth Avenue and 58 Street to find that special toy for your child. But when it comes to large-scale holiday or birthday shopping, you may be tempted to head for a discount toy emporium such as **Toys "R" Us** (in Brooklyn, Queens, and Staten Island) with its rows upon rows of the latest "hot" toys, be they Transformers, Popples, or Pound Puppies, or **Kay Bee Toy and Hobby Stores** (in Brooklyn and Queens). At Toys "R" Us, you can also stock up on diapers by the box or carton, or if you prefer, load onto the top of your car a child-sized swimming pool. Local five-and-dime stores, such as Lamston's and Woolworth's, have a surprising selection of basics, as do some drugstores. You can also turn to museum shops, many of which stock unusual items for children. If you want to stock up on art supplies, try **Pearl Paint Company** (308 Canal Street, 212-431-7932; no charge cards accepted), where the selection of watercolors, tempura paints, markers, crayons, and even school glue is extensive and discounted.

A **sampling** of where to find the toy to dazzle the child:

BROOKLYN

The Gifted Child (385 Seventh Avenue, 718-768-4245): Games and educational materials, toys, books, records, and tapes.

MANHATTAN

Babyland (Fifth Avenue and 41 Street, 212-213-1404): All the Cabbage Patch Kids you ever wanted.

Childcraft Center (150 East 58 Street, 212-753-3196): Their assortment of educational toys, particularly for preschoolers, is extensive so teachers, as well as parents, come here to stock up. Watch for their sales in February and June. You can also ask to be put on their mailing list and shop by mail.

Children of Paradise (154 Bleecker Street, 212-473-7148): The space is small but the collection of trendy toys is sizable. Around the corner at 496 LaGuardia Place, you'll find **Jamie Canvas** (212-505-1256), with its collection of unusual toys.

Compleat Strategist (11 East 33 Street, 212-685-3880 and 320 West 57 Street, 212-582-1272): Games—fantasy, mystery, history—galore.

The Doll House and Manhattan Doll Hospital (176 Ninth Avenue, 212-989-5220): Collection of dollhouses and miniatures. You can leave a broken doll or favorite stuffed animal off for repair. The **New York Doll**

Hospital (787 Lexington Avenue, 212-838-7527) also does repairs. For special dolls, try **F. A. O. Schwarz** and **Macy's**. Stuffed animals overrun the **Enchanted Forest** (85 Mercer Street, 212-925-6677).

Forbidden Planet (821 Broadway, 212-473-1576 and 227 East 59 Street, 212-751-4386): The emphasis here is on science fiction, and there are books, robots, and other wonderful objects, including an amazing collection of masks. At **Star Magic** (743 Broadway, 212-228-7770; 275 Amsterdam Avenue, 212-769-2020), you can be tempted by kits that create erupting volcanoes and space paraphernalia.

Go Fly a Kite (1201 Lexington Avenue, 212-472-2623): Specializing in kites and kits.

Madison Lionel Trains (105 East 23 Street, 212-777-1110): They've been selling Lionel trains since 1909. Check also the **Red Caboose** (16 West 45 Street, 212-575-0155) and the **Train Shop** (23 West 45 Street, 212-730-0409), which has a variety of HO trains.

Penny Whistle Toys (1283 Madison Avenue, 212-369-3868; 448 Columbus Avenue, 212-873-9090; 132 Spring Street, 212-925-2088): Lots of educational, imported, and old-fashioned wooden toys.

Tannen's Magic (6 West 32 Street, 212-239-8383): The magic here is sure to spellbind.

Toy Park (112 East 86 Street, 212-427-6611): Look here for your basics.

QUEENS

Carol School Supply Company (185-04 Union Turnpike, 718-454-0050): Educational supplies.

chapter 6
utilizing cultural resources

Adults who want to keep up on what's going on in New York check the pages of *The New York Times, The New Yorker,* or *New York* magazine. Looking for children's programming begins there, but sometimes takes a little more ingenuity. What you'll quickly discover, however, is that New York is as much the cultural capital for kids as it is for adults. Here's a basic kids'-eye-view of the ongoing cultural resources that you can take advantage of.

Libraries

New York City has three separate public library systems—the Brooklyn Public Library, the New York Public Library, and the Queens Borough Public Library. Each has its own central library and a long list of neighborhood branches. These three library systems operate independently of each other and have different rules and policies. You must have their individual library cards—good for any library within their network—to borrow books. However, as a holder of one system's card, you may apply to the other two for borrower's privileges. To obtain a library card from any of the systems, you don't need to be a New York City resident. *You only have to show that you live, work, go to school, or own property in New York State.* You must, however, show proof of your name and address.

Before visiting any library, call to check if it's open, since the hours of service vary daily.

BROOKLYN PUBLIC LIBRARY

The major facility of the Brooklyn Public Library is the Central Library at Grand Army

Plaza. Here you'll find the Central Children's Room (718-780-7717), with its extensive collection of children's books, including foreign language children's books, materials for partially sighted and deaf children, and reference books for both children and adults. You'll also find films, filmstrips, records, and the only collection in the system of audio cassettes. There's also a special poetry section.

To obtain a library card, children must be able to write their first and last names. The Brooklyn Public Library has a policy of complete open access for children. Children can use the adult collection without the librarian's or parent's permission. This policy, observes Co-ordinator for Programming Services Marguerite Dodson, reflects "the child's right to read."

Books circulate for three weeks and can be returned to any branch library. During the summer, there's a special "vacation loan" entitling children to borrow up to ten books for a period of more than two months. If you can't find a book at a branch library, you can request an interlibrary loan. You can also make a "reserve" request for a children's book.

Every branch except the Business Library also has a children's collection. The Central Children's Room has frequent picture book and storytelling hours. All the branches have some kinds of children's programming during the year. To find out the month's activities, you can pick up a free monthly calendar of events at any branch library. You can also call your local branch.

The Brooklyn Public Library has several special programs that may interest you:

- **The Child's Place** (for children two and a half to six): Libraries that feature more than just books. On hand are toys, crafts, films, and storytelling programs, and educational games as well as programs for adults. Three branch libraries are centers: the Williamsburgh Library, the New Lots Library, and the New Utrecht Library. Over the years, there have been several smaller centers, which are subject annually to funding renewal. For full details, check with the Programming Services Office at the Brooklyn Public Library (718-780-7781).
- **Reading Is Fundamental:** Clubs for youngsters through the eighth grade. The goal: To nurture a love of reading. Members receive free paperback books five times a year. Any child with a Brooklyn Public Library card can join the R.I.F. program. Sign up at the Central Library and all branches.

- **Books by Mail:** Available for both adults and children. Homebound individuals can register for the service and the library will send books to them. Call the Central Library (718-780-7723).
- **Telephone Reference:** Answers to factual questions while you wait: 718-780-7700. At certain hours, you call Library-On-Call: 718-780-7817. There's also a special **Homework Hotline** (for students and their parents, Mon.–Thurs. 5–8 P.M., while school's open: 718-780-7766).

The branch libraries (with any special features noted) are:

Arlington, 203 Arlington Avenue at Warwick Street (718-277-0160)
Bay Ridge, 7223 Ridge Boulevard at 73 Street (718-748-3042)
Bedford, 496 Franklin Avenue at Hancock Street (718-638-9544)
Borough Park, 1265 43 Street near Thirteenth Avenue (718-435-3375). Records available.
Brighton Beach, 16 Brighton First Road near Brighton Beach Avenue (718-266-0005)
Brooklyn Heights, 280 Cadman Plaza West at Clinton Street (718-780-7778)
Brower Park, 725 St. Mark's Avenue near Nostrand Avenue (718-778-6262)
Brownsville, 61 Glenmore Avenue at Watkins Street (718-345-1212)
Bushwick, 340 Bushwick Avenue at Siegel Street (718-443-1078)
Canarsie, 1580 Rockaway Parkway near Avenue J (718-257-2180)
Carroll Gardens, 396 Clinton Street at Union Street (718-625-5838)
Clarendon, 2035 Nostrand Avenue near Farragut Road (718-434-3620)
Clinton Hill, 380 Washington Avenue near Lafayette Avenue (718-857-8038)
Coney Island, 1901 Mermaid Avenue at West 19 Street (718-266-1121)
Cortelyou, 1305 Cortelyou Road at Argyle Road (718-462-4200)
Crown Heights, 560 New York Avenue at Maple Street (718-773-1223)
Cypress Hills, 465 Fountain Avenue near Hegeman Avenue (718-277-8257)
DeKalb, 790 Bushwick Avenue at DeKalb Avenue (718-452-5678)
Dyker, 8202 Thirteenth Avenue at 82 Street (718-748-1395)
East Flatbush, 9612 Church Avenue near Rockaway Parkway (718-498-0033)
Eastern Parkway, 1044 Eastern Parkway at Schenectady Avenue (718-756-5150)

Flatbush, 22 Linden Boulevard near Flatbush Avenue (718-282-2017)
Flatlands, 2065 Flatbush Avenue at Avenue P (718-252-6115)
Fort Hamilton, 9424 Fourth Avenue at 95 Street (718-745-5502)
Gerritsen Beach, 2712 Gerritsen Avenue at Everett Avenue (718-743-3040)
Gravesend, 303 Avenue X near West 2 Street (718-376-9311)
Greenpoint, 107 Norman Avenue at Leonard Street (718-383-6692)
Highlawn, 1664 West 13 Street at Kings Highway (718-837-1700)
Homecrest, 2525 Coney Island Avenue near Avenue V (718-645-2727)
Jamaica Bay, 9727 Seaview Avenue at East 98 Street (718-531-1602)
Kensington, 410 Ditmas Avenue near East 5 Street (718-436-0525)
Kings Bay, 3650 Nostrand Avenue near Avenue W (718-332-5656)
Kings Highway, 2115 Ocean Avenue near Kings Highway (718-375-3037)
Leonard, 81 Devoe Street at Leonard Street (718-387-3800)
McKinley Park, 6802 Fort Hamilton Parkway at 68 Street (718-748-5800)
Macon, 361 Lewis Avenue at Macon Street (718-453-3333)
Mapleton, 1702 60 Street at Seventeenth Avenue (718-232-0346)
Marcy, 617 DeKalb Avenue near Nostrand Avenue (718-858-1828)
Midwood, 975 East 16 Street near Avenue J (718-377-7972)
Mill Basin, 2385 Ralph Avenue at Avenue N (718-763-8700)
New Lots, 665 New Lots Avenue at Barbey Street (718-649-3700). Includes The Child's Place.
New Utrecht, 1743 86 Street at Bay 17 Street (718-236-4086). Includes The Child's Place.
Pacific, 25 Fourth Avenue at Pacific Street (718-638-5180)
Paerdegat, 850 East 59 Street near Flatlands Avenue (718-763-4848)
Park Slope, 431 Sixth Avenue at 9 Street (718-768-0593)
Red Hook, 7 Wolcott Street at Dwight Street (718-875-4412)
Rugby, 1000 Utica Avenue near Tilden Avenue (718-345-9264)
Ryder, 5902 23rd Avenue at 59 Street (718-232-5064)
Saratoga, 8 Hopkinson Avenue at Macon Street (718-455-3078)
Sheepshead Bay, 2636 East 14 Street near Avenue Z (718-743-0663)
Spring Creek, 12143 Flatlands Avenue near New Jersey Avenue (718-649-0020)
Stone Avenue, 581 Stone Avenue at Dumont Avenue (718-385-3737)
Sunset Park, 5108 Fourth Avenue at 51 Street (718-439-8846)
Ulmer Park, 2602 Bath Avenue at 26 Avenue (718-266-7373)

Walt Whitman, 93 St. Edwards Street at Auburn Place (718-855-1508)
Washington Irving, 360 Irving Avenue at Woodbine Street (718-386-6212)
Williamsburgh, 240 Division Avenue at Marcy Avenue (718-782-4600). Includes The Child's Place. Home also of El Centro Hispano de Información, with a bilingual staff able to give help in translating material in English and Spanish. Reading material in English and Spanish available.
Windsor Terrace, 160 East 5 Street at Fort Hamilton Parkway (718-853-7265)

THE NEW YORK PUBLIC LIBRARY

This system encompasses the Bronx, Manhattan, and Staten Island. Although the flagship library is in the architecturally renowned central building at 42 Street and Fifth Avenue, the largest collection of children's books is not. The Central Children's Room is at the Donnell Library Center (20 West 53 Street, Manhattan: 212-621-0636). In addition to the circulating library, which includes children's records, tapes, and foreign-language books, the Central Children's Room has historical and reference materials. The Nathan Strauss Young Adult Library at Donnell has the system's largest collection of multimedia material for young adults.

To obtain a library card, children must be able to write their first and last names. They then take the application home to their parents, who fill out the information requested. On this registration slip, the parents can, if they wish, check off a box that limits the child's access to the "children's room only."

Books and records circulate for three weeks and can be returned to any branch library. During the summer, the "vacation loan" entitles children to borrow books for nearly three months. If you can't find a book at a branch library, you can request an interlibrary loan. You can also make a "reserve" request for a children's book.

Not all the branch libraries in the system have children's collections or provide services for children. The Central Children's Room and many of the branches, however, do have extensive programming. You can pick up the free monthly booklet *Events for Children* at any branch library. It lists films, story hours, picture book hours, and special events. In addition, call your local branch.

The New York Public Library has several special libraries and services that may interest you:

- **Early Childhood Resource and Information Center** (66 Leroy Street, New York, N.Y. 10014: 212-929-0815): Its Family Room contains books and records, but it's also a playroom for children—replete with toys, a carpeted block area, housekeeping and dramatic play space, rocking horses, and a sliding gym. Tuesday through Friday afternoons and all day Saturday, families come to use its facilities. The Resource Collection is a comprehensive parenting library, with books, magazines, and a huge clippings file. You can also attend weekly morning seminars (when the library is closed to children) on topics of interest to parents. For a program schedule, send a self-addressed, stamped legal-sized envelope. This step should also put you permanently on their mailing list. Call before visiting with children, since hours are restricted.
- **Library for the Blind and Physically Handicapped** (166 Avenue of the Americas, New York, N.Y. 10013: 212-925-1011 or 212-925-9699): Adults and children *living in New York City and on Long Island* who have difficulty using regular print materials because of a visual or physical handicap can use the library services offered free by mail. (There's no actual library where you can go to browse.) The library has Braille books and magazines, talking books, cassette books, and the cassette machines and record players needed to play the recorded books and magazines. Braille Service only for Long Island.
- **Media Center** at the Donnell Library Center: 16-mm. films and videotapes loaned free of charge. There's also a large selection of recordings.
- **Telephone Reference:** Answers to factual questions (212-340-0849).

The branches listed (with any special features noted) have children's books:

BRONX
Allerton, 2740 Barnes Avenue (212-881-4240)
Baychester, 2049 Asch Loop North (212-379-6700). Videotapes available.
Belmont Enrico Fermi Cultural Center, 610 East 186 Street and Hughes Avenue (212-933-6410). Children's books in Italian available.
Castle Hill, 947 Castle Hill Avenue (212-824-3838)
City Island, 320 City Island Avenue (212-885-1703)
Clason's Point, 1215 Morrison Avenue (212-842-1235)
Eastchester, 1385 East Gun Hill Road (212-653-3292)
Edenwald, 1255 East 233 Street (212-798-3355)

Fordham Library Center, 2556 Bainbridge Avenue (212-220-6573). Large collection of records, videotapes, Spanish-language books.
Francis Martin, 2150 University Avenue (212-295-5287)
Grand Concourse, 155 East 173 Street (212-583-6611)
High Bridge, 78 West 168 Street (212-293-7800)
Hunt's Point, 877 Southern Boulevard (212-617-0338). Children's books in Spanish available.
Jerome Park, 118 Eames Place (212-549-5200)
Kingsbridge, 280 West 231 Street (212-548-5656). Videotapes.
Melrose, 910 Morris Avenue (212-588-0110)
Morrisania, 610 East 169 Street (212-589-9268)
Mosholu, 285 East 205 Street (212-882-8239)
Mott Haven, 321 East 140 Street (212-665-4878)
Parkchester, 1985 Westchester Avenue (212-829-7830). Videotapes.
Pelham Bay, 3060 Middletown Road (212-792-6744). Videotapes.
Riverdale, 5540 Mosholu Avenue (212-549-1212). Small collection of Japanese books for children.
Sedgwick, 1553 University Avenue (212-294-1182)
Soundview, 660 Soundview Avenue (212-589-0880)
Spuyten Duyvil, 650 West 235 Street (212-796-1202). Videotapes available. Small collection of Japanese books for children.
Throg's Neck, 3025 Cross Bronx Expressway Extension (212-792-2612).
Tremont, 1866 Washington Avenue (212-299-5177)
Van Cortlandt, 3874 Sedgwick Avenue (212-543-5150)
Van Nest, 2147 Barnes Avenue (212-829-5864)
Wakefield, 4100 Lowerre Place (212-652-4663)
West Farms, 2085 Honeywell Avenue (212-367-5376)
Westchester Square, 2521 Glebe Avenue (212-863-0436)
Woodlawn Heights, 4355 Katonah Avenue (212-324-0791)
Woodstock, 761 East 160 Street (212-665-6255)

MANHATTAN

These branches have books for children:

Aguilar, 174 East 110 Street (212-534-2930). Children's books in Spanish available.
Bloomingdale, 150 West 100 Street (212-222-8030)

Chatham Square, 33 East Broadway (212-964-6598). Extensive collection of children's books in Chinese.

Columbus, 742 Tenth Avenue (212-586-5098)

Countee Cullen, 104 West 136 Street (212-281-0700). Extensive collection of children's books on the Black experience in the United States.

Donnell Library Center, Central Children's Room, 20 West 53 (212-621-0636). Large circulating library of children's books, records, tapes, audiocassettes, and foreign-language materials. Elsewhere in the center there is a young adult library and a film library, which lends films and videotapes.

Early Childhood Resource and Information Center, 66 Leroy Street (212-929-0815). A playroom along with the books. Large parenting book resource collection.

Epiphany, 228 East 23 Street (212-679-2645)

Fort Washington, 535 West 179 Street (212-927-3533)

George Bruce, 518 West 125 Street (212-662-9727)

Hamilton Fish Park, 415 East Houston (212-673-2290)

Hamilton Grange, 503 West 145 Street (212-926-2147)

Hudson Park, 66 Leroy Street (212-243-6876)

Inwood, 4790 Broadway (212-942-2445)

Jefferson Market, 425 Avenue of the Americas (212-243-4334). Large selection of videotapes available.

Kips Bay, 446 Third Avenue (212-683-2520)

Lincoln Center, Circulating Performing Arts Library, 111 Amsterdam Avenue (Children's Room: 212-870-1633). Focuses on the performing arts. An extensive collection of records and videotapes.

Macombs Bridge, 2650 Seventh Avenue (212-281-4900)

Muhlenberg, 209 West 23 Street (212-924-1585)

96th Street Library, 112 East 96th Street (212-289-0908)

115th Street Library, 203 West 115 Street (212-666-9393)

125th Street Library, 224 East 125 Street (212-534-5050)

Ottendorfer, 135 Second Avenue (212-674-0947)

Riverside, 190 Amsterdam Avenue (212-877-9186)

St. Agnes, 444 Amsterdam Avenue (212-877-4380)

Seward Park, 192 East Broadway (212-477-6770). Children's books in Chinese.

67th Street Library, 328 East 67 Street (212-734-1717). Videotapes available.

Tompkins Square, 331 East 10 Street (212-228-4747)

Washington Heights, 1000 St. Nicholas Avenue (212-923-6054)
Webster, 1465 York Avenue (212-288-5049)
Yorkville, 222 East 79 Street (212-744-5824)

STATEN ISLAND

Dongan Hills, 1617 Richmond Road (718-351-1444)
Great Kills, 56 Giffords Lane (718-984-6670)
Huguenot Park, 830 Huguenot Avenue (718-984-4636)
New Dorp, 309 New Dorp Lane (718-351-2977). Videotapes available.
Port Richmond, 75 Bennett Street (718-442-0158)
St. George, 450 St. Marks Place (718-442-8560). Large collection of records. The library at 10 Hyatt Street has been undergoing renovation.
South Beach, 100 Sand Lane (718-442-7420)
Stapleton, 132 Canal Street (718-727-0427)
Todt Hill-Westerleigh, 2550 Victory Boulevard (718-494-1642). Extensive collection of children's videotapes.
Tottenville, 7430 Amboy Road (718-984-0945). Videotapes available.
West New Brighton, 976 Castleton Avenue (718-442-1416)

QUEENS BOROUGH PUBLIC LIBRARY

The Central Library of the Queens Borough Public Library is at 89-11 Merrick Boulevard in Jamaica. The Children's Division (718-990-0767) has the largest children's collection in the borough including foreign-language books in Korean, Chinese, Japanese, Haitian, and French. Weekly films are shown. There's also a Young Adult Division (718-990-0768) and a Film Division, which lends films and videocassettes.

To obtain a library card, children must be able to write their first and last names. A postcard is mailed home to verify the address. On this the parent indicates whether the child has access to the adult stacks.

Books circulate for twenty-eight days and can be returned to any branch library. If you can't find a book at a branch library, you can request an interlibrary loan. You can also make a "reserve" request for a children's book.

All the libraries have children's books. Most have children's librarians and some feature monthly children's programming, including films and picture book and story-telling times. There is no central schedule published, so call the local branch to find out what's offered.

The Queens Borough Public Library has several special libraries and programs that may interest you:

- **Langston Hughes Community Library and Cultural Center** (102–09 Northern Boulevard, Corona: 718-651-1100): Among the offerings: Black heritage books and reference materials, cultural arts activities, including workshops in literature, poetry, drama, dance, and other performing arts, information and referral services. The **Homework Assistance Program** (for students in third through seventh grades: 718-672-2710) provides on-site adult supervision and local high school tutors for children, as well as liaison with parents and local schools.
- **Telephone Reference:** Answers to factual questions (718-990-0714).

The branch libraries are:

Arverne, 312 Beach 54 Street (718-634-4784)
Astoria, 14-01 Astoria Boulevard, Long Island City (718-278-0601)
Auburndale-Clearview, 25-55 Francis Lewis Boulevard, Flushing (718-352-2027)
Baisley Park, 117-11 Sutphin Boulevard, Jamaica (718-529-1590)
Bayside, 214-20 Northern Boulevard (718-229-1834)
Bay Terrace, 18-36 Bell Boulevard, Bayside (718-423-7004)
Bellerose, 250-06 Hillside Avenue, Bellerose (718-343-0303)
Briarwood, 85-12 Main Street, Briarwood (718-658-1680)
Broadway, 40-20 Broadway, Long Island City (718-721-2462)
Cambria Heights, 220-20 Linden Boulevard, Cambria Heights (718-528-3535)
Corona, 38-23 104 Street, Corona (718-426-2844). Spanish-language books available.
Douglaston–Little Neck, 249-01 Northern Boulevard, Little Neck (718-229-0590)
East Elmhurst, 95-06 Astoria Boulevard, East Elmhurst (718-424-2619)
East Flushing, 196-36 Northern Boulevard, Flushing (718-357-6643)
Elmhurst, 86-01 Broadway, Elmhurst (718-271-1020)
Far Rockaway, 1637 Central Avenue, Far Rockaway (718-327-2549)
Flushing, 1 Library Plaza, Flushing (718-445-0800)
Forest Hills, 108-19 71 Avenue, Forest Hills (718-268-7934)
Fresh Meadows, 193-20 Horace Harding Expressway, Fresh Meadows (718-454-7272)
Glen Oaks, 256-04 Union Turnpike, Glen Oaks (718-347-8200)
Glendale, 78-60 73 Place, Glendale (718-821-4980)
Hillcrest, 187-05 Union Turnpike, Flushing (718-454-2786)

Hollis, 202-05 Hillside Avenue, Hollis (718-465-7355)
Howard Beach, 92-06 156 Avenue, Howard Beach (718-641-7086)
Jackson Heights, 35-51 81 Street, Jackson Heights (718-899-2500)
Langston Hughes Community Library and Cultural Center, 102-09 Northern Boulevard, Corona (718-651-1100). Wide range of programming.
Laurelton, 134-26 225 Street, Laurelton (718-528-2822)
Lefferts, 103-34 Lefferts Boulevard, Richmond Hill (718-843-5950)
Lefrak City, 98-25 Horace Harding Expressway, Corona (718-592-0266)
Maspeth, 69-70 Grand Avenue, Maspeth (718-639-5228)
McGoldrick, 155-06 Roosevelt Avenue, Flushing (718-353-0839)
Middle Village, 75-30 Metropolitan Avenue, Middle Village (718-326-1390)
Mitchell-Linden, 29-42 Union Street, Flushing (718-539-2330)
North Forest Park, 98-27 Metropolitan Avenue, Forest Hills (718-261-5512)
North Hills, 245-04 Horace Harding Expressway, Little Neck (718-225-3550)
Ozone Park, 92-24 Rockaway Boulevard, Ozone Park (718-845-3127)
Peninsula, 92-25 Rockaway Beach Boulevard, Rockaway Beach (718-634-0101). Videotapes available.
Pomonok, 158-21 Jewel Avenue, Flushing (718-591-4343)
Poppenhusen, 121-23 14 Avenue, College Point (718-359-1102)
Queens Village, 94-11 217 Street, Queens Village (718-776-6800)
Queensboro Hill, 60-05 Main Street, Flushing (718-359-8332). Videotapes available.
Queensbridge, 10-43 41 Avenue, Long Island City (718-729-0798)
Ravenswood, 35-32 21 Street, Long Island City (718-784-2112)
Rego Park, 91-41 63 Drive, Rego Park (718-459-5140)
Richmond Hill, 118-14 Hillside Avenue, Richmond Hill (718-849-7150)
Ridgewood, 20-12 Madison Street, Ridgewood (718-821-4770)
Rochdale Village, 169-09 137 Avenue, Jamaica (718-723-4440)
Rosedale, 144-20 243 Street, Rosedale (718-528-8490)
St. Albans, 191-05 Linden Boulevard, St. Albans (718-528-8196)
Seaside, 116-15 Rockaway Beach Boulevard, Rockaway Park (718-634-1876)
South Hollis, 204-01 Hollis Avenue, South Hollis (718-465-6779)
South Jamaica, 110-36 Guy R. Brewer Boulevard, Jamaica (718-739-4088)

South Ozone Park, 128-16 Rockaway Boulevard, South Ozone Park (718-529-1660)
Steinway, 21-45 31 Street, Long Island City (718-728-1965)
Sunnyside, 43-06 Greenpoint Avenue, Long Island City (718-784-3033). Videotapes available
Vleigh, 72-33 Vleigh Place, Flushing (718-261-6654)
Whitestone, 151-10 14 Road, Whitestone (718-767-8010)
Windsor Park, 79-50 Bell Boulevard, Oakland Gardens (718-468-8300)
Woodhaven, 85-41 Forest Parkway, Woodhaven (718-849-1010)
Woodside, 54-22 Skillman Avenue, Woodside (718-429-4700)

PRIVATE LIBRARIES

Several private libraries may also interest you. Some are limited to members; others are not.

- The **Buttenweiser Library** (92 Street Y, 1395 Lexington Avenue, New York, N.Y. 10128: 212-427-6000) has both a large parenting and children's book collection. One specialty: Judaica for children. If you're enrolled in any of the Y's programs, you're entitled to borrow books from the library; if not, you can also pay a $30 annual library membership fee. Books are loaned for two to four weeks; you can renew them.
- The **Children's Book Council** (67 Irving Place, New York, N.Y. 10003: 212-254-2666) library is noncirculating and houses books donated by publishers. You can see almost any children's book published during the past two years.
- The **French Institute/Alliance Française** library (22 East 60 Street, New York, N.Y. 10022: 212-355-6100) has a collection of French picture books and children's literature as well as cassettes and records for children. Periodic storytelling in French for children ages three to six. Membership in the French Institute/Alliance Française entitles you to library use.
- The **Goethe House** library (1014 Fifth Avenue, New York, N.Y. 10028: 212-744-8310) has a small collection of children's books and records in German. Books are loaned for three weeks and you can renew by telephone. You don't have to be a member to borrow books, nor is there a charge. However, you must show identification.
- The **New York Society Library** (53 East 79 Street, New York, N.Y. 10021: 212-288-6900) is a private subscription library with a special

children's room (books circulate for four weeks with a two-week renewal period).

Not all libraries today focus on books. The **Adriel & Evelyn Harris Toy Library for the Disabled** (United Cerebral Palsy of Westchester, Box 555, Purchase, N.Y. 10577: 914-937-3800), which is open to families in New York City and Westchester, lends physically adapted toys to multihandicapped children. A child can borrow, for example, a jack-in-the-box with a battery-run handle so that the child just presses a switch to operate the toy. A mobile library will travel to your home or to your child's school to bring the toys. Toys are loaned for up to a month (and renewable if you want) and there's no charge for the service. To sign up, call or write United Cerebral Palsy of Westchester. If you're interested in learning more about toy libraries, contact the U.S.A. Toy Library Association (1800 Pickwick Avenue, Glenview, Ill. 60025: 312-724-7700).

Museums

There's an array of museums, both large and small, to visit. Some—like the Staten Island Children's Museum—were designed with kids in mind; others, like the Museum of Modern Art, will interest children although they are not child-oriented. Not all museums, however, welcome children. The Frick Collection does not admit children under ten. If you show up with a youngster, they'll turn you away.

To list all the museums in New York City is beyond the scope of this book. For a quick orientation, if you're in Midtown, use the "New York Culture Guide" in the lobby of the IBM Gallery at Madison Avenue and 56 Street. This computer, equipped with a touch screen, surveys cultural attractions in the city.

The museums singled out on the following pages will appeal to young children. Most have been chosen because their displays are intrinsically interesting to youngsters. At the majority of them, you'll also discover an emphasis on creating programs that families can participate in—often on a drop-in basis. These museums (as well as many museums not described here—such as the Guggenheim Museum and the Whitney Museum of American Art) also have extensive programming for school or camp groups. If you want to learn more about the educational resources of New York City's museums, contact Museums Collaborative (15 Gramercy Park South, New York, N.Y. 10003: 212-674-0030) or individual museums. For subway and bus travel information, call the New York Transit Authority (718-330-1234). For car directions, call the museums.

Zoos and institutions that concentrate on environmental education are described in the following sections.

BRONX

North Wind Undersea Institute (610 City Island Avenue, Bronx: 212-885-0701; hrs.: Daily 9–5; admission: $3 for adults, $2 for children; no eating facilities)

A marine museum that focuses on whaling and diving. There's a small aquarium room. For further information: 212-885-0701.

BROOKLYN

Brooklyn Children's Museum (145 Brooklyn Avenue, Brooklyn; hrs.: Mon., Wed., Fri. 2–5, Thurs. 2–8, Sat., Sun., summers, and when school's closed 10–5; closed Tuesdays; voluntary contribution requested; no eating facilities on premises or nearby)

Participatory children's museum with after-school and weekend workshops. Daily workshops noted on a blackboard. For further information: 718-735-4432.

Brooklyn Museum (200 Eastern Parkway, Brooklyn; hrs.: Open daily 10–5, except Tuesdays; admission: suggested contribution of $3 adults; children under 12 free; strollers permitted)

In addition to the permanent and temporary exhibitions that children will enjoy visiting, a special hour-long program—"What's Up?"—introduces children in grades one to six to the museum's collections through looking, drawing, and creative dramatics; held Saturday and Sunday at 2. Special art classes for children. For further information: 718-638-5000.

New York City Transit Exhibit (Boerum Place and Schermerhorn Street, Brooklyn; hrs.: Mon.–Fri. 10–4; check for weekend hours; admission: 50 cents/children; $1/adults; strollers permitted, no eating facilities)

Chock full of old subway cars and transit memorabilia. For further information: 718-330-3060 or 718-330-3063.

MANHATTAN

American Museum of Natural History (Central Park West at 79 Street, Manhattan; hrs.: Mon., Tues., Thurs., Sun. 10–5:45, Wed., Fri., Sat.

10–9. On days when public schools are open, no one under eighteen is permitted in the museum before 2 P.M. unless accompanied by an adult; admission: suggested contribution; strollers permitted)

From the Hall of African Mammals to the Morgan Memorial Hall of Gems, there's something for almost any age child. The dinosaurs are a sure draw, as is the great whale. The Alexander M. White Natural Science Center (Tues.–Fri. 2–4:30, Sat., Sun. 1–4:30; closed Mondays; hours extended during the summer; closed September) introduces young people to the plants, animals, and rocks of New York City. The Discovery Room, with its "Discovery Boxes," gives children five and up a chance to handle materials (Sat. and Sun. 12–4:30; free tickets distributed at 11:45 at the Information Desk). The Leonhardt People Center has extensive weekend events highlighting the cultures of different countries of the world. Naturemax Theater's four-story-high IMAX film projection facility offers continuous film showings (charge: $3.25 for adults, $1.50 for children—in addition to museum admission; for schedule: 212-496-0900). Weekend workshops for elementary school children (call the Department of Education: 212-769-5304). Additional programming for museum members' children. Available for purchase in the gift shops: *American Museum of Natural History Learning and Activity Book.* For further information: 212-769-5100.

American Museum of Natural History—Hayden Planetarium (81 Street and Central Park West, Manhattan; hrs.: Open daily: Mon.–Fri. 12:30–4:45, Sat. 10–5:45, Sun. 12–5:45 from October through June); Sat., Sun., hours in July–Sept. 12–4:45. admission: $3.75 for adults, $2.00 for children)

Although there are exhibits, the centerpiece is the Sky Theater with daytime astronomy shows and weekend nighttime laser shows. Preschoolers can attend their own special show, "Wonderful Sky," featuring the Sesame Street characters (212-769-5919). Reservations are recommended. Weekend courses for children (and parents). For further information: 212-769-5920.

The Children's Museum of Manhattan (314 West 54 Street, between Eighth and Ninth Avenues, Manhattan; hrs.: Tues–Fri. 1–5, Sat., Sun. 11–5; admission weekdays: $1 for adults, $2 for children, weekends: $2 for adults, $3 for children; no eating facilities)

Participatory children's museum ("Please touch"), with exhibitions focused on three themes: nature, culture, and perception. Weekly weekend crafts, nature, or performance workshops and special holiday programs. For further information: 212-765-5904.

Con Edison Energy Museum (145 East 14 Street, Manhattan; hrs.: Tues.–Sat. 10–4; admission: no charge; strollers permitted but will be kept behind the information desk)

You might want to stop by if you're at Union Square for a glance at the history of electricity. You'll also see what's below a typical New York City street. For further information: 212-460-6244.

InfoQuest Center (in the A.T.&T Building at Madison Avenue and 56 Street, Manhattan; hrs.: Tues. 10–9, Wed.–Sun. 10–6; admission: free)

Interactive exhibits that detail the history (and future) of communications. The star attraction: the robot Gor-don. For further information: 212-605-5555.

Intrepid Air-Sea-Space Museum (Pier 86, 46 Street and Twelfth Avenue, Manhattan; hrs.: Wed.–Sun. 10–5; admission: $4.75 for adults, $2.50 for children; strollers permitted; eating facilities)

Walk the decks of this battle-scarred aircraft carrier and see an eclectic collection of military planes and exhibitions on flight. For further information: 212-245-2533.

The Jewish Museum (1109 Fifth Avenue, Manhattan; hrs.: Mon., Wed., Thurs. 12–5, Tues. 12–8, Sun. 11–6; admission: $4 for adults, $2 for children six and up; free on Tuesday evenings; no eating facilities; no strollers)

A look at Jewish archaeology, art, history, and culture. When there are special exhibitions, the museum often creates self-guided activity sheets for children. Special Sunday family programs (about once a month and often in conjunction with Jewish holidays) featuring, for example, Klezmer music at Purim. Tickets (small charge—in addition to admission) sometimes can be purchased in advance. For further information: 212-860-1888.

Metropolitan Museum of Art (Fifth Avenue at 82 Street, Manhattan; hrs.: Wed.–Sun. 9:30–5:15, Tues. 9:30–8:45; admission: contribution requested, $4.50 per adult suggested, free to children under twelve accompanied by an adult; several eating facilities; strollers permitted weekdays only in all galleries except Egyptian and special exhibition areas; backpacks available with refundable deposit)

"Arms and Armor," "The Costume Institute," and "The Egyptian Galleries" are just some of the areas sure to fascinate even the toddler. If you're planning on viewing particular galleries, however, call ahead since some are periodically closed. At the Great Hall Information Desk, you can pick up free gallery hunts created for children. Among them: *Musical Instruments* and *Egyptian Families.* There's extensive free drop-in programming for school-aged children as well as studio classes and activities for members. Periodic special events programs. The best way to keep up is to call for schedules, 212-570-3932. For further information: 212-879-5500; recorded information: 212-535-7710.

Metropolitan Museum of Art: The Cloisters (Fort Tryon Park, Manhattan; hrs.: March–October: Tues.–Sun. 9:30–5:15, November–February: 9:30–4:45; admission: contribution suggested; no eating facilities)

Grounds and building are interesting to walk around. One Saturday a month there's usually an afternoon family program at noon and 2 P.M. For further information, 212-923-3700.

The Museum of Broadcasting (1 East 53 Street, Manhattan; hrs.: Tues. 12–8, Wed.–Sat. 12–5: admission: suggested contribution, $3.00 for adults, $1.50 for children under thirteen, $2.00 for students; no eating facilities; strollers permitted)

This museum collects radio and television programs. The "exhibitions" are daily showings of programs centered around themes that change periodically. Two examples: "Discovery: James Dean, The Television Work" and "The Museum of Broadcasting Celebrates Mobil Masterpiece Theatre: 15 Years of Excellence." You can also make an hour-long appointment to view any of the museum's recorded programs at a private console that can accommodate two people. Sometimes you can just stop by and watch immediately, but on weekends and holidays, plan on reserving in advance. For further information: 212-752-4690.

Museum of the City of New York (Fifth Avenue at 103 Street, Manhattan; hrs.: Tues.–Sat. 10–5, Sun. and holidays 1–5; free admission; no eating facilities; strollers permitted)

A toy collection, including dollhouses, fire-fighting exhibits, and much more. Special weekend programs, and selected days during Christmas and Easter week, include storytelling, films, and puppet shows for children three and up. At the "Please Touch" demonstrations in a re-created seventeenth-century Dutch room furnished with antiques, the children try on period clothing and can write with a real quill pen. Call for a schedule. For further information: 212-534-1672.

Museum of Holography (11 Mercer Street, Manhattan: hrs.: Tues.–Sun. 12–6; admission: $3.00 for adults, $1.75 for children)

If you're in SoHo, there are four galleries of holograms children may enjoy. For further information: 212-925-0526.

Museum of Modern Art (11 West 53 Street, Manhattan; hrs.: Mon., Tues., Fri., Sat., Sun. 11–6; Thurs. 11–9; admission: $5 for adults, children under sixteen free when accompanied by an adult, Thurs. 5–9 pay what you wish; strollers permitted; eating facilities)

Although the museum's programming is not geared toward children, even the youngest will enjoy many of the galleries and the sculpture garden. There are periodic parent/child workshops designed to help parents of children aged four to ten develop an understanding of art. Available in the Museum Shop: *How to Show Grown-ups the Museum.* For further information: 212-708-9480.

South Street Seaport Museum (207 Front Street, Manhattan; hrs. during the winter—December–March—Tues.–Fri. 11–4, weekends 11–5; rest of the year: Tues.–Fri. 10–5, weekends 10–6; admission for ships, tours, films, special programs: $4 for adults, $2 for children under twelve; strollers permitted)

At the Visitors' Center (207 Water Street) or the Pier 16–Pilothouse, pick up a guide and map as well as the "South Street Museum Broadside," which lists daily events. Children can clamber aboard the four-masted bark the *Peking* and the *Ambrose* lightship. At certain times, you can also explore the square rigger *Wavertree* (by tour only; call ahead for schedule). In the warmer months, you can sail on the nineteenth-century schooner the *Pioneer* or the sidewheeler *Andrew Fletcher* (call ahead for details and additional costs). Changing weekly and daily special events such as storytelling or pony rides in nineteenth-century carts. Fun to see is the movie *The Seaport Experience* at the Trans-Lux Seaport Theatre (210 Front Street; $4.25 for adults, $2.75 for children; shows are every hour daily, on the hour, from 11 A.M.; 212-608-7888).

Right there also are the vast Fulton Market and Pier 17 shopping complexes. Nearby too is the Fulton Fish Market. For further information: 212-669-9424.

The Studio Museum in Harlem (144 West 125 Street, Manhattan; hrs.: Wed.–Fri. 10–5, Sat., Sun. 1–6; admission: $1.50 for adults, free for students and children under twelve; no strollers; no eating facilities)

A museum of African-American art. Weekend and holiday workshops for children. For further information: 212-864-4500.

QUEENS

Jamaica Arts Center (161-04 Jamaica Avenue, Jamaica, Queens; hrs.: Mon.–Fri. 9–5, Sat. 10–5; admission: free; strollers permitted; no eating facilities but restaurants in neighborhood)

You'll find exhibitions of community artists and traveling exhibitions from the Gallery Association of New York State, as well as continuously changing performing arts programs. Weekend and after-school workshops in theater, dance, music, and the visual arts for students from ages five up. Weekend family workshops and performing arts programs for children. Some after-school and weekend workshops require that you register in advance; occasional special events. Special free after-school ArtReach program taught at selected community centers. For further information: 718-658-7400.

New York Hall of Science (Flushing Meadows Park, 48 Avenue and 111 Street; hrs.: Wed.–Sun. 10–5; admission: suggested contribution of $2.50 for adults, $1.50 for children, free on Wednesdays; no strollers but backpacks are provided; eating facilities)

A participatory science museum, newly reopened in 1986, with plenty to interest children. Workshops for children. For further information: 718-699-0675.

Queens Museum (New York City Building, Flushing Meadows Park, Queens; hrs.: Tues.–Fri. 10–5, Sat., Sun. 12–5; admission: contribution requested; no eating facilities; no strollers, next door is the World's Fair Ice Skating Rink)

Not to be missed: the *Panorama of the City of New York,* a 9,000-square-foot, detail-perfect model of the city's five boroughs. Free "Drop In Workshops" for children every Sunday afternoon during the school year. Frequent Sunday special events for families include magic shows, storytelling, theater, puppetry, dance. For further information: 718-592-5555.

STATEN ISLAND

Richmondtown Restoration (Staten Island Historical Society, 441 Clarke Avenue; hrs.: Wed.–Fri. 10–5, Sat., Sun. 1–5, Monday holidays 1–5; admission: $2 for adults, $1 for children, $5 for a family group; strollers permitted; eating facilities)

A historic village with costumed interpreters. Visitors can see the interiors of eleven buildings and demonstrations of early American trades and crafts, including leatherworking, redware pottery, tinsmithing, and open-hearth cooking. Little Folks Programs and Crafts participation activities in the summers. For further information: 718-351-1617.

Staten Island Children's Museum (1000 Richmond Terrace, Snug Harbor; hrs.: vary by the season, call for details; admission: $2 suggested contribution, children under three are free; no eating facilities)

Hands-on exhibits that make up an entire environment, workshops, and performance theater (musicals, puppets, films). Although exhibits change, "Building Buildings," which looks at architecture, was scheduled to run through the summer of 1988. The museum sits in Snug Harbor, which continues to be under restoration. On weekends and after school, there are workshops and performances. For further information: 718-273-2060.

Staten Island Institute of Arts and Sciences/Staten Island Museum (75 Stuyvesant Place, St. George, Staten Island; hrs.: Tues.–Sat. 10–5, Sun. 1–5; admission: voluntary contribution; strollers permitted; no eating facilities)

This small museum probably has its greatest appeal in its after-school and weekend programming for children (advance registration often required). For further information: 718-727-1135.

▽ ▽ ▽ ▽ ▽ ▽ ▽ ▽ ▽ ▽ ▽

Some Special Summer Programs

If you're looking for a summer enrichment activity, several museums have designed special programs to fill some of those vacation days. Keep in mind that programs are subject to change yearly.

♦ Alley Pond Environmental Center's "Summer Nature Workshops": Several four-day-long, four-hour workshops for children ages five to sixteen.

- Bronx Zoo's Animal Kingdom Zoo Camp: Week-long sessions (hrs: 10–4) that give children, ages eight to twelve, the chance to have daily personal contact with animals and acquire an in-depth knowledge of the zoo. The same program repeats weekly from June through August. There's a shorter week-long program (10:30–2:30), "Animals Around the World," for children ages five to seven. Teens can sign up for a special month-long animal care summer internship.

- Children's Museum of Manhattan's Museum Day Camp: Seven one-week sessions (9–4) for children ages five to twelve. The programs, which change weekly, are centered around themes such as "Carnival Week," "Science Week," "Media Production Week," and "Civilizations of Long Ago Week." It's possible sometimes to participate just for a day.

- High Rock Park Conservation Center's Summer Day Camp: Children, ages seven to twelve, can attend four-day sessions (several hours a day) during July and August. The program focuses on exploring the colors, textures, and shapes that make up the patterns of nature.

- Jamaica Arts Center's Summer Arts Camp: During the month of July, there's a three-day camp (9–3) for children ages five to nine and a four-day camp (9–4) for children ages ten to fourteen.

- New York Aquarium's Summer Aquatic Adventures: Three-hour thematic workshops, held weekly, for children ages six to nine, focusing on such subjects as "All About Sharks" and "Introducing Invertebrates."

- Richmondtown's Apprentice Program: Children ages eleven to fourteen come daily for two-week sessions (Wed.–Fri. 10–4, Sat., Sun. 1–5) to learn a trade such as pottery or harness making. They join the costumed interpreters of Richmondtown in presenting living history.

- Staten Island Institute of Arts and Sciences's Summer Junior Museum Curator: This program, designed for children seven to thirteen, runs 10–3. The children take field trips to other museums, and there are follow-up art and science projects at the institute.

- Staten Island Zoo Summer Safari: One-week-long morning sessions held during July and August for preschool through fifth grade. Three periods daily: art, recreation, and science.

△   △   △   △   △   △   △   △   △   △   △

Environmental Education

The visitor who never ventures beyond Manhattan will probably believe that the entire city is a mass of high-rises relieved only by the greenery of Central Park. But New York City kids know better. Among the jewels: not just Manhattan's Central Park, but the Bronx's Pelham Bay Park and Van Cortlandt Park, Brooklyn's Prospect Park, Queens' Flushing Meadows Park, and Staten Island's Clove Lakes Park. To find out what's happening in the city's parks, call the Parks Department's "Free Events Message": 212-360-1333. You can also write for a monthly copy of their *Calendar of Events* (Parks Information, 1234 Fifth Avenue, New York, N.Y. 10029).

City kids need to learn about both the urban and the natural landscape. **The Urban Park Rangers** in their Smokey the Bear hats patrol the parks, giving information and administering first aid when needed. But they also offer interpretative programs, including weekend guided walks and workshops for adults and children (advance registration required for the workshops). Children ages eight to fourteen can sign up to be Junior Rangers, participating in weekend or summer educational programs that meet periodically for two to three hours and feature outdoor crafts, nature studies, and park appreciation. The Rangers have also created special programs for schoolchildren, grades three to six, on themes such as "Plants and Trees," "Urban Animals," "Geology," and "Pond Life" that combine an in-park walking tour with an additional in-class visit by the Ranger. You don't have to be part of a school group to arrange a special tour. Any group, composed of a minimum of ten, can sign up. Programs are scheduled on a first come, first served basis and should be booked several weeks in advance. (Beware: School programs fill up in the fall.) For full details about the Rangers and their activities, call their offices (in Crotona Park in the Bronx, 212-589-0096; in Van Cortlandt Park in the Bronx, 212-548-7880; in Prospect Park in Brooklyn, 718-287-3400; in Central Park in Manhattan, 212-397-3091; in Flushing Meadows Park in Queens, 718-699-4204; in Clove Lakes Park in Staten Island, 718-442-1304).

Many of the city's parks and gardens also have their own educators who create programs—for schoolchildren, groups, and families.

Among the sites:

BRONX

The New York Botanical Garden (in Bronx Park; pedestrian entrance on Southern Boulevard, Bronx; hrs.: Tues.–Sun. 8–6; free admission to grounds, but $2.50 for adults and $1.25 for children for the Enid A. Haupt Conservatory building. Its hours are 10–4.)

Greenery to see both indoors in the Enid A. Haupt Conservatory and outdoors on the extensive grounds. Stop by "Greenworld Grocery" in the Conservatory, an exhibit that links foods we find on supermarket shelves to food plants from around the world. Spring and summer children's gardening program (advance registration and fee) features planning a garden layout, soil preparation, planting, tending, and harvesting. For further information: 212-220-8700.

Wave Hill Center for Environmental Studies (675 West 252 Street, Bronx; hrs: Labor Day–Memorial Day, daily 10:00–4:30; summers: Wed. 10–dusk, Sun. 10–7, Mon., Tues., Thurs.–Sat. 10:00–5:30; admission: Mon.–Fri. free; weekends: adults $2, children under twelve free; no food permitted on the premises)

A public garden on twenty-eight acres overlooking the Hudson River, with more than 350 varieties of trees and shrubs, formal gardens, greenhouses, and manor houses, the learning center is open on Saturdays and Sundays 12:00–4:30 P.M. On Sundays, there's a garden tour and you will often find special workshops and walks geared to children (a sampling: "Babies in Backpacks," "Autumn Leaf Collage," and "Spooky Faces"). Special events: spring maple sugaring and an annual folk day in the summer. For further information: 212-549-2055.

BROOKLYN

Brooklyn Botanic Garden (1000 Washington Avenue, Brooklyn; hrs.: April 1–September 30: Tues.–Fri. 8–6, Sat., Sun., holidays 10–6; October 1–March 31: Tues–Fri. 8:00–4:30, Sat., Sun., holidays 10:00-4:30; free admission; no eating facilities)

A beautiful place for a ramble. One particular spring delight: cherry blossoms. In the spring and summer, children ages nine through seventeen can grow vegetables and fruits in their own garden plots in the Children's Garden program (advance registration and fee). For further information: 718-622-4433.

MANHATTAN

Belvedere Castle (Central Park at 79 Street, south of the Great Lawn near the West Side; hrs: Tues–Thurs., Sat., Sun. 11–4, Fri. 1–4; free admission; strollers permitted; no eating facilities)

Central Park's learning center and a station for the National Weather Service. Activities and games in the Discovery Chamber. Free family workshops for children ages five to eleven, Saturdays at 1:00 (reservations required). For further information: 212-772-0210.

The Dairy (64 Street, east of the Carousel and just north of Wollman Rink in Central Park; hrs.: Tues–Thurs., Sat., Sun. 11–5, Fri. 1–5 (during Eastern Standard time, closes at 4 P.M.); admission: free; strollers permitted)

This is Central Park's Visitor Information Center, where you can pick up a map and a calendar of events. At 65 Street, in midpark, you'll find the Carousel (open year-round, 10:30–4:30, weather permitting, $.50 per ride).

For a tape-recorded message of Central Park's events: 212-397-3156.

QUEENS

Alley Pond Environmental Center (228-06 Northern Boulevard, Douglaston, Queens; hrs.: Tues–Sat. 9–5, Sun., September–June only, 11–4; free admission; strollers permitted in the center; woodchip trails make strollers inconvenient; picnic tables)

Animals, hiking trails, and hands-on exhibits are in this park. Weekend and weekday nature workshops for children four and up (advance registration required). Wetland family walks, Sundays (October–May) at 1 P.M. Occasional special events. For further information: 718-229-4000.

Queens Botanical Garden (43-50 Main Street, Flushing, Queens; hrs.: 9–5; free admission; no eating or picnic facilities)

Outdoor park with extensive rosebush plantings and a bee garden. Weekend family activities. Spring and summer children's garden program (advance registration and fee). For further information: 718-886-3800.

Queens County Farm Museum (73-50 Little Neck Parkway, Floral Park, Queens; hrs.: weekends only during school year; summers, Fri., Sat. 11–4, Sun. 1–4; admission: free, except when there are special events; no eating facilities but concessionaires are on the premises when there are programs; picnicking permitted)

Forty-seven-acre working farm, with animals, apple orchards, and pumpkin patches, that is now operated by the New York City Parks Department as an agricultural museum. Craft and nature courses; frequent weekend events. Highlights: July's Native American Indian pow-wow, which draws tribes from across the United States, and the Queens Country Agricultural Fair, usually the third weekend in September. For further information: 718-347-3276.

STATEN ISLAND

Clay Pit Ponds State Park (83 Nielsen Avenue, Staten Island; hrs.: headquarters are open Mon.–Fri. 9–1, Sat., Sun., and holidays 9–5; trails open dawn to dusk; admission: free; picnic area; strollers are permitted but may be difficult to use on trails)

This wetlands gets its name from the clay pits that were once mined in the area. You'll come across traces of the mining. Weekend programming for children; seasonal festivals with a nature theme. For further information: 718-967-1976.

High Rock Park Conservation Center (200 Nevada Avenue, Staten Island; hrs.: daily, usually 9–5; free admission; no eating on the grounds; strollers permitted but they'll be hard to manipulate on the trails)

A wonderful woodlands with a small Visitor's Center. In addition to woodchip trails, there's an observation area overlooking the marsh that can accommodate a stroller or wheelchair. After-school and weekend workshops for children require advance registration. Naturalist leads seasonal walks on Saturdays and Sundays. For further information: 718-987-6233.

Zoos and Aquariums

BRONX

Bronx Zoo (Bronx River Parkway at Fordham Road, Bronx; hrs.: from March to October, Mon.–Sat. 10–5, Sun. and holidays 10:00–5:30; from November–February, 10:00–4:30; admission: Tues., Wed., Thurs. donation; otherwise, from November to March: $1.75 for adults, $1.00 for children under twelve; from April to October: $3.75 for adults; $1.50 for children under twelve; strollers permitted and rentals also available; eating facilities).

Whether it's Indian elephants, polar bears, Siberian tigers, or the rhinoceros hornbill that you want to see, they're all at this zoo. Plan on spending an hour in the Children's Zoo (admission: $1.00 for adults,

$.75 for children; open April through October; last ticket sold an hour before closing), where children can climb a spider's web, try on a turtle shell, or crawl through a prairie dog tunnel. The Children's Zoo looks at animal homes, animal locomotion, animal defenses, and animal senses. Other attractions (some with additional fees): "Wild Asia" (opens in May for the summer), "World of Birds," "World of Darkness," and "Jungle-World." Camel and elephant rides, as well as the Skyfari aerial tramway and Safari tour train, open April through October. Occasional special events. The Education Department (212-220-6854) can tell you about workshops for children that require advance registration.

On weekends, particularly in the summer, the zoo can get very crowded, so come early in the day. Later in the day you may wait up to a half-hour to get inside "Wild Asia" or the Children's Zoo. For further information: 212-367-1010.

BROOKLYN

New York Aquarium (Surf Avenue and West 8 Street, just east of the Coney Island amusement area, Brooklyn; hrs.: 10–5; Memorial Day to Labor Day 10–6; admission: $3.75 for adults, $1.50 for children; strollers must be checked at the entrance; eating facilities)

You'll find beluga whales, sharks, bottlenose dolphins, and the giant Pacific octopus. In the summer, dolphins and sea lions perform daily in the Aquatheater, while in the colder months the beluga whales and sea lions are the stars. Other daily events: seal, penguin, walrus, and shark feedings and electric eel demonstrations. At the "Children's Cove," kids can handle starfish, horseshoe crabs, sponges, and sea urchins. Weekend and holiday workshops for children (advance registration and fee required). For further information: 718-266-8500.

Prospect Park Zoo and Children's Farm (Empire Boulevard and Flatbush avenues, Brooklyn; admission: free; hrs: daily 11–4; cafeteria open during the summer months).

If you're nearby, you might want to drop in. The children's farm with domestic farm animals is usually open April through Labor Day weekend. For further information: 718-965-6560.

MANHATTAN

Central Park Zoo (64 Street and Fifth Avenue, Manhattan)

The main zoo has been under reconstruction for several years. The small children's zoo (open daily 10–5, $.10 admission) might be enjoyed by a preschooler. For further information: 212-408-0271.

QUEENS

Queens Zoo and Children's Farm (Flushing Meadows Park, at 111 Street between 46 and 55 avenues, Queens; hrs.: daily 10:00–3:45; admission: free; eating facilities)

Small zoo with North American animals in a natural habitat setting. Domed aviary (closed at 3 P.M. and in bad weather). Children's farm has domestic animals. For further information: 718-699-7239.

STATEN ISLAND

Staten Island Zoo (614 Broadway, Staten Island; hrs.: 10:00–4:45; admission $1 for adults, children under three free, Wednesdays free; eating facilities; strollers permitted)

A gem of a small zoo with a world-renowned reptile collection that includes every known North American rattlesnake. There's also a children's zoo, a nursery of newborn animals, and a small aquarium with more than six hundred fish on view. Periodic art exhibits, after-school workshops, and weekend programs. Among the special events: "The June Zoo Olympics." For further information, including travel directions: 718-422-3100.

▽ ▽ ▽ ▽ ▽ ▽ ▽ ▽ ▽ ▽ ▽

NOT FOR TOURISTS ONLY

Don't wait for out-of-town friends to come to town:

- **Empire State Building** (350 Fifth Avenue, Manhattan; hrs.: 9:30 A.M.–midnight; admission: $3 for adults, $1.75 for children)

  You've got panoramic views of metropolitan New York from the observation areas on the 86 and 102 floors. Save this trip, however, for a day when the skies are clear and visibility is the greatest. For further information: 212-736-3100.

- **Lincoln Center Guided Tours** (Lincoln Center, Manhattan; starts at the concourse level, below the theaters; hrs.: 10–5; admission: $6.25 for adults, $3.50 for children; recommended for children who are at least elementary school aged; reservations not necessary but you can call ahead to find out the schedule)

This one-hour, behind-the-scenes walking tour takes you to the various performing arts buildings that make up the complex. On some mornings, you may catch a glimpse of a rehearsal going on in one of the theaters. An older child might also enjoy the separate hour and a half backstage tour of the Metropolitan Opera House that visits rehearsal facilities, the dressing rooms, and the shops where artisans create the Met's wonderful scenery and costumes. Tours are at 3:45 on weekdays and at 10:30 on Saturdays, cost $6 for adults and $3 for full-time students, and reservations are a must (for further information, contact Backstage Tours, Education at the Met: 212-582-3512). For further information: 212-877-1800.

♦ **NBC Studio Tours** (Rockefeller Center, Manhattan; hrs.: Mon.–Sat. 9:30–4:30; admission: $5.50; children under six not permitted)

A one-hour behind the scenes look at the world of NBC. For further information: 212-664-4000.

♦ **"The New York Experience"** (in the McGraw-Hill Building, 1229 Avenue of the Americas, Manhattan; hrs.: every hour, on the hour, Mon.–Thurs. 11–7, Fri., Sat. 11–8, Sun. 12–8; admission: $4.75 for adults, $2.90 for children under twelve)

A multiscreen extravaganza, introducing you to New York, New York. For further information: 212-869-0345.

♦ **Statue of Liberty** (Liberty Island; to get there you must take the ferry at Lower Manhattan's Battery Park; boat hours vary by the season. The boat ride costs $3.25 for adults and $1.50 for children under twelve, while there is no admission charge for the statue)

While Miss Liberty's the centerpiece, you can visit exhibits about the history of the statue and immigration. For further information: 212-363-3200 (or for the ferry: 212-269-5755).

♦ **United Nations** (visitors' entrance on First Avenue at 46 Street, Manhattan; guided tours 9:15–4:15 daily; admission: $4.50 for adults, $2.50 for students; $2.00 for students below ninth grade; children under five not permitted)

Older kids interested in world affairs will be fascinated with this behind-the-scenes look. Sometimes it's possible to sit in on a session. Don't forget to visit the gift shops. For further information: 212-754-7713.

♦ **World Trade Center Observation Deck** (2 World Trade Center; hrs.: 9:30–9:30 daily; admission: $2.95 for adults, $1.50 for children ages six through twelve: children under six free)

What a glorious view! As with the Empire State Building, however, save this trip for a day when the Twin Towers are not enshrouded in clouds. For further information: 212-466-7377).

△   △   △   △   △   △   △   △   △   △   △

Performing Arts

While the weekly pickings at movie houses can be slim, the number of live performances designed especially for young children is sizable. Year-round you'll find music, children's theater, puppetry, and dance. For starters, particularly on weekends, count on family entertainment at the three children's museums and several other museums. Often there's a special program at a library. But your choices just begin there.

To keep track of many of the possibilities, check listings in *New York* magazine, the Friday editions of *The New York Times* (the "Weekend" section's "Events for Children") and the *Daily News, PARENTGUIDE NEWS,* and local community papers (*The WestSider,* for example, conscientiously reports children's programs). Often you'll find that a school or Y has brought in a performing arts group as a fund-raiser. If you want to know what's playing, you can contact the information service N.Y.C./On Stage (800-782-4369 for out-of-state; 212-587-1111 in New York).

You can also request that your name be added to the free mailing lists of local performance halls, such as Manhattan's Lincoln Center and Town Hall or the Brooklyn Academy of Music. B.A.M., for example, has extensive weekday children's programming for groups but no regular children's weekend programs. However, since it's a hot spot for dance, theater, and music, you might discover that there are programs that appeal to you as family entertainment. Manhattan's Symphony Space rents its facilities to children's theater companies such as the Paper Bag Players. Catch the Paper Bag Players there or at several other locations around the city during the year. The Colden Center for the Performing Arts at Queens College and the Borough of Manhattan Community College Triplex have had their own "Children's Theater Series." You'll want to be notified about both specialized and general productions.

In comparison to the costs of adult entertainment, children's programs are relatively inexpensive. Tickets frequently range between $3 and $5 per child. Some performances for children can be pricey: A ticket to the

New York City Ballet's annual presentation of *The Nutcracker* costs as much as $42. However, free—and low-cost tickets—for school groups abound for some activities.

If you're interested in taking older children to Broadway or Off-Broadway productions but can't afford the prices, you can find "twofers" for some shows at schools, restaurants, hotels, and other public places. You can also try the TKTS booths (located in Manhattan at Duffy Square—47 Street and Broadway—and in Lower Manhattan—2 World Trade Center; in downtown Brooklyn at Borough Hall Park—Court and Montague streets). On the *day of performance,* these booths offer half-price tickets (with a small service charge) to selected shows (the participating theaters decide what's offered). The Lower Manhattan and Brooklyn TKTS booths also offer half-price tickets on the day *before* the performance for matinees and Sundays. The choices, however, may be limited. For tape-recorded messages giving the exact hours of sale, call 212-354-5800 for the Manhattan TKTS and 718-625-5015 for Brooklyn TKTS. If you want to attend opera, music, and dance performances, half-price tickets are sold at the Bryant Park TKTS booth (42 Street and Sixth Avenue in Manhattan; 212-382-2323). Tickets for Monday performances are sold on Sunday.

Teachers, clergymen, union members, senior citizens, and high school, college, or graduate students can also apply to the Theatre Development Fund (1501 Broadway, New York, N.Y. 10036: 212-221-0013) to be put on their mailing list. This not-for-profit corporation offers low-cost tickets to people who cannot regularly afford to pay the full price. Several times a year, T.D.F. sends its membership information about shows for which they can purchase tickets at reduced prices (about $9 each) for selected dates and productions. Members can also participate in the theater voucher program.

Listed are just some of the programs—and places—that make New York City a children's entertainment paradise:

BROOKLYN

"Family Community Concerts" of the Brooklyn Philharmonic at the Brooklyn Academy of Music (30 Lafayette Avenue)

Designed for elementary school-aged children and held three times a year (in the winter and spring) on Saturdays at 2 P.M. Ask to be put on their mailing list (the program announcement goes out in January). For further information: 718-636-4120.

"Family Time" at the Brooklyn Center for the Performing Arts of Brooklyn College (P.O. Box 163 Vanderveer Station)

A variety of theatrical experiences, held at Whitman Hall on the college campus, between September and May. For further information (and to be put on their mailing list): 718-780-5291.

Children's Theater Festival at Kingsborough Community College (2001 Oriental Boulevard)

The weekend shows during the school year are intended for a pre-kindergarten through fifth-grade audience. For further information: 718-934-5596.

MANHATTAN

Children's Series at the Third Music School Settlement (233 East 11 Street)

Monthly programs held Sunday afternoons at 1 and 3 P.M. during the school year. This is a subscription series and reservations are recommended. For further information: 212-777-3240.

"Family Matinee" of the New York City Ballet, New York State Theater at Lincoln Center

A Sunday matinee winter season nonsubscription performance designed to introduce audiences from "eight to eighty" to the universal concepts of ballet. The format is lecture/demonstration (for example: "The Art of Ballet" looked at different pas de deux). Programs change yearly. Tickets (from $7 to $42 in 1986) available at the box office when the season is announced (around October). For further information: 212-870-5570.

"Happy Concerts for Young People" of the Little Orchestra Society (c/o Orpheon Inc., 1860 Broadway)

A series of five performances, targeted for five- to twelve-year-olds, at Lincoln Center's Avery Fisher Hall (Broadway at 65 Street) on Saturdays from December through April. Subscription series (ranging from $36 to $76 in 1986–87) or individual tickets ($9 to $19) available. This group has also created **"The Lolli-Pops Concerts" of the Little Orchestra Society,** programs for three- to five-year-olds held at Lincoln Center's Bruno Walter Auditorium in the Library and Museum of the Performing Arts. Subscription $60. For further information: 212-704-2100.

Little People's Theater Company (Courtyard Playhouse, 39 Grove Street)

Take-offs on favorite fairy tales, with audience participation, performed on weekends at 1:30 and 3:00 P.M. Among their repertory: "Humpty Dumpty Falls in Love" and "Hansel and Gretel and the Mean Witch." Children as young as three will enjoy the shows. Closed July and August. For further information: 212-765-9540.

Michael Taubenslaj Productions (Jan Hus Theater, 351 East 74 Street)

Repertory of musical comedy using children's stories on Sundays at 1:00 and 2:30 P.M. during the school year. For further information: 212-772-9180.

92 Street Y (1395 Lexington Avenue)

Among their offerings: "The Magic of Music," classical music designed for children ages nine and up and "Family Entertainment Programs for VYP's" geared to youngsters aged three to six. Get on their mailing list, since programs sell out very fast. For further information: 212-996-1100.

Off Center Theater (436 West 18 Street)

Year-round, on Tuesdays, Wednesdays, and Thursdays at 10:30 A.M., there are usually performances of fairy tales or historical dramas about little-known patriots (for example, the Black cowboy Deadwood Dick). Call in advance to be sure that they are having a performance.

Summers there are free daytime performances in Harlem's Mount Morris Park and in other locations in the five boroughs. Call for a schedule. For further information: 212-929-8299.

On Stage, Children! (Hartley House Theater, 413 West 46 Street)

Family theater whose plays reflect contemporary social, moral, and political concerns done by an interracial, multiethnic company. Among their past offerings: "Jennifer and Her Bag Lady" and "The Alice-in-Wonderland Game." Performances from mid-September to mid-May on Saturdays and holidays at 1:00 and 3:30 P.M. For further information: 212-666-1717.

Paper Bag Players (50 Riverside Drive)

This theater company doesn't have a regular home and performs in the metropolitan area usually from January through March. The players are nationally recognized for the material they create for children ages four to nine. Using props and costumes made of boxes, the skits are about life today—going to school, taking a bath, going to bed—and emphasize audience participation. Weekend programs for families. To keep track of their schedule and performance locations, get on their mailing list.

NOTE: Ticket prices for shows vary by the location. For further information: 212-362-0431.

"Saturday Children's Theater Series" at the Borough of Manhattan Community College Performing Arts Center, Inc. (199 Chambers Street)

A variety of dance, puppetry, fairy tale, and musical programs offered during the school year. For further information: 212-618-1980.

Theatreworks/USA (at the Promenade Theatre on Broadway at 76 Street)

Musicals for elementary and intermediate school-aged children performed on weekends and during the Christmas holidays. The range is extensive: from "When the Cookie Crumbles, You Can Still Pick Up the Pieces," which looked at divorce, to their own version of the fairy tale "The Emperor's New Clothes." For further information: 212-595-7500.

Thirteenth Street Repertory Company (50 West 13 Street)

This company features original scripts based on children's stories such as *Rumpelstiltskin*. Performances on Saturdays and Sundays at 1:00 and 3:00 P.M. year-round. Special weekday shows for groups can be arranged. For further information: 212-675-6677.

"Young People's Concerts" of the New York Philharmonic (Lincoln Center, Avery Fisher Hall)

Subscription series of four concerts, Saturdays at 2 P.M., designed to introduce eight- to twelve-year-olds (not recommended for preschoolers) to the splendor of great symphonic music. There's a very high renewal rate for this series, so your best bet is to call the Audience Services of Avery Fisher Hall in the spring and ask to be put on the priority mailing list. Subscriptions for the 1986–87 season ranged from $16 to $40. Preconcert materials prepared by the Department of Educational Activities mailed to subscribers. For further information: 212-580-8700.

QUEENS

Children's Theater at Colden Center of Queens College (Kissena Boulevard and the Long Island Expressway, Flushing)

At least four theatrical performances, suitable for three- to eight-year-olds, during the school year on Saturdays or holidays. For further information: 718-793-8080.

PUPPETRY

For most children, the first performing arts program they're likely to see is a puppet show. You can count on finding several from which to choose. Among the places to look:

- **In Central Park:** At the Heckscher Puppet House (at 62 Street in Central Park; enter at 59 Street and Seventh Avenue; 212-397-3089) you'll find shows Monday through Friday at 10:30 A.M. and noon year-round. The same show plays for about a year. Tickets are $2 for adults and children and reservations are required. The puppet season at the Swedish Cottage Marionette Theater (at 79 Street in Central Park; enter at Central Park West and 81 Street; 212-988-9093) extends from November through May. The hour-long shows, changed about once a year, are open to the public on Saturdays at noon and 3:00 P.M. School groups with reservations attend Tuesdays through Friday at 10:30 A.M. and noon. Tickets cost $2 for adults or children.
- **In Museums:** The Museum of the City of New York has weekly Saturday shows at 1:30 P.M. from November through April. Tickets are $3. The Brooklyn Children's Museum, the Staten Island Children's Museum, and the Children's Museum of New York don't have weekly performances, but you're likely to find puppeteers appearing often.
- **In Public Places:** At the Market in the Citicorp Center (53 Street and Lexington Avenue in Manhattan), you'll sometimes find puppet shows (for a schedule of their current events, call 212-559-2330). At the World Trade Center, during the Christmas season, there are daily puppet shows, puppet-making demonstrations, and puppet displays.
- **At Special Puppet Theaters:** At Puppet Playhouse (555 East 90 Street, Manhattan: 212-879-3316), you're treated to productions by various puppeteers from September to June every Friday, Saturday, and Sunday at 11 A.M. and 1 P.M. Telephone reservations recommended. At Puppetworks (Old First Church, Seventh Avenue and Carroll Street, Brooklyn: 718-834-1828) there are full-length puppet shows, such as "Hansel and Gretel," lasting about an hour, during the school year every Sunday at 2 P.M.
- **In Stores:** Macy's at Herald Square operates a Puppet Theater, with shows several times daily, from the day after Thanksgiving through Christmas Eve. To find out about Macy's other special events programming for children, see their advertisements in *The New York Times* the last Friday of each month. The children's programming at Barnes and Noble Sales Annex (Fifth Avenue at 18 Street: 212-206-8800) used to be free puppet

shows in the second-floor children's book area, the first Sunday of the month at 11 A.M. and 1 P.M. Nowadays, it's more than likely that you'll see an acting troupe sans puppets.

If you want to hire your own puppeteer for an event, contact the Puppetry Guild of Greater New York (P.O. Box 244, New York, N.Y. 10116). Some years they publish a membership directory and a puppetry calendar. Some puppeteers also advertise in the Yellow Pages under the heading "Puppets and Marionettes" and in magazines such as *PARENTGUIDE NEWS* or *New York*.

△ △ △ △ △ △ △ △ △ △ △

Performing Arts Especially for Groups

Many cultural activities for children are designed for groups, particularly school groups, rather than for individuals and their families. Most museums and the larger performing arts organizations have education departments that develop workshops, tours, and learning materials. Some charge for providing these services; others do not.

If your child is attending a public school, be aware that *many* performing arts organizations have developed programs, underwritten by city and foundation funds, that are run through cultural institutions in cooperation with the Board of Education and local community school districts. The Lincoln Center Institute (140 West 65 Street, New York, N.Y. 10023: 212-877-1800) works in partnership with several community school districts to provide teachers and students the chance to experience a broad spectrum of performing and visual arts. The National Dance Institute offers free dance classes each year in certain public schools. The culmination of their year has been a dance event at Madison Square Garden with the children participating. Carnegie Hall produces six free children's concerts a year for public school children, grades three through eight, held in November. The Board of Education notifies schools and community school districts in the fall. The New York City Ballet's "Ballet for Young People" annually sends invitations to the district superintendent of the thirty-two community school districts, asking each to send seventy-five fourth- and fifth-grade students (usually two or three classes). The students' teachers are required to attend an orientation session; the students see an hour-long full-blown special performance in the New York State Theater.

The Joyce Theater, as part of the Board of Education's "Arts in General Education" network, permits parents, students, and teachers to attend dress rehearsals of visiting performing groups. Arts in General Education (718-935-4011) rests on the assumption that the arts are basic to learning, communication, self-expression, and self-confidence. The arts, therefore, should be an integral part of every child's education—beginning in kindergarten. Some forty elementary, junior, and senior high schools are network schools and have made this commitment to "all the arts to all the children."

Many of the performing arts organizations also offer lecture demonstrations, small intimate workshops, or performances (sometimes for no charge) at the schools. Funding for in-school activities may come from the school's or district's budget. Or perhaps a parents association decides to raise the funds to contract with an organization's education department for its services.

If you want your school to take advantage of the wide range of free and low-cost programs offered, you may need to get some wheels turning. Start by asking your school's principal and your community school district. If your child is in high school, check with the High School Division at the Board of Education. You can also contact the Education Office of New York City's Department of Cultural Affairs. The Department of Cultural Affairs provides funding to many New York City institutions and educational programming is one of their concerns.

The list that follows is just a sampling of some of the programs for groups. You can't order tickets for most of these performances yourself (exceptions are noted below), but *you can make sure* that your child's teacher knows about these opportunities. All the organizations say that they send flyers announcing their programs to school principals and often to the school's music teacher (long gone in many New York City public schools). Many organizations don't object to putting regular classroom teachers, or even interested parents, on their mailing lists. A few programs are borough-restricted, but many are not. Most of the free programs fill up fast, so teachers should book as soon as they receive the announcements. Spread the word.

Brooklyn Philharmonic (718-636-4120)
Free schooltime concerts given in the winter at the Brooklyn Academy of Music. Teachers can request a schedule.

Adventures in Music (administered by the Junior League of the City of New York's Music Committee: 212-288-6220)

Free tickets and free program notes for the "Happy Concerts for Young Children" of the Little Orchestra Society. Teachers and heads of services organizations can contact the chairman of the music committee to find out whether their group qualifies.

Invitation to the Dance (St. Luke's Chamber Ensemble, 225 Lafayette Street, Manhattan: 212-226-1115)

Free dance performances, by major companies such as the Ballet Hispanico of New York, held at selected performance halls on specific days during school hours. Recommended for grades three and up. Contact St. Luke's to get a program description and dates. There's also a free one-day Saturday workshop for teachers.

Meet-the-Artist Program at Lincoln Center (212-877-1800, Extension 547)

Students tour the center and then observe programs such as "Storytime at the Opera" or "Musical Travelog." In these programs, children get the chance to meet performing artists, hear them talk about their craft, and see a performance of their work. Tickets are $8.75 per student. "The Celebration Series" is given in conjunction with the National Dance Institute ($6 per ticket for groups; $8 for individuals).

Meet-the-Artist can also custom tailor programs for any group (minimum twenty-five, maximum two hundred; the charge varies based upon the size of the group).

Paper Bag Players (212-362-0431)

Special shows for public school children at minimal cost that sell out very quickly. Best bet: Put yourself on their advance mailing list.

Queens Symphony Orchestra's Music BAG (Queens Symphony Orchestra, 99-11 Queens Boulevard, Rego Park, Queens: 718-275-5000)

An hour-long free musical program for Queens youngsters, grades four to six, held in the spring during the school day at Flushing's Electrical Industry Auditorium. Public school teachers should contact their district's music coordinator. Private school teachers should call the Queens Symphony Orchestra directly.

Shadow Box Theater (325 West End Avenue, Manhattan: 212-724-0677)

A theater group that uses live music, shadow puppetry, and hand puppetry in free daily performances for public school children. This company has no permanent home, but usually can be found at schools around the city. Check with them about how you can see their shows.

The New York Shakespeare Festival Players (c/o the New York Shakespeare Festival: 212-598-7100)

Free performances for New York City public school junior and senior high school students, their teachers, and their parents at the Belasco Theater.

Staten Island Children's Theater (667 Castleton Avenue, Staten Island: 718-442-2225 or 718-981-7288).

This group brings several children's theater productions (for preschool to fifth grade) to the Williamson Theater of the College of Staten Island each year. Performances are held during the weekday to accommodate classes and tickets are low-priced ($3 to $5). Parents with preschoolers are welcome to bring their children without a group.

"Symphonic Revelations" and "Dance Revelations" of the Colden Center for the Performing Arts (718-544-2996)

Free school day performances to introduce school-aged children to the orchestra and to dance. Mailings sent to all school districts and schools in Queens.

Theatreworks/USA (212-595-7500)

Under the auspices of Theatreworks/USA, a variety of groups performs at Town Hall for school groups. Tickets are $3 per seat, with one free ticket for each fifteen ordered for 10:30 A.M. weekday performances. In the 1986–87 season, Theatreworks/USA also offered its own repertory to school groups at the Colden Center for the Performing Arts and at other sites in the metropolitan area. You can get a comprehensive schedule that outlines their programs.

The Children's Free Opera of New York (St. Luke's Chamber Ensemble, Inc.: 212-226-1115)

Free one-act operas, with complete sets and full costuming, sung in English at major performance halls on specific dates during school hours. Recommended for grades three and up; educational materials sent to teachers in advance. Contact St. Luke's to learn how to order tickets.

"The Performing Arts Program for Young People" at the **Brooklyn Academy of Music** (718-636-4130)

An extensive series of school day programming, showcasing performers from around the United States, for preschool through high school children at 10:30 A.M. and at 12:30 P.M. from October through June. Tickets have been priced at $2.50 each and one free ticket is provided for every ten ordered. *You can also purchase single tickets by mail or at the door ($3.00).*

WARNING: The majority of the tickets (particularly for programs suitable for younger children) are snapped up at the beginning of the school year. Check with the Education Department ahead of time, so that you're not disappointed.

The Traveling Playhouse (of the **Theatre for Young Audiences of Westchester, Inc.,** 104 Northampton Drive, White Plains, N.Y. 10603: 914-946-5289)

On weekdays during the school year, this company, which performs classic children's stories such as "Jack and the Beanstalk" and "The Golden Goose," appears in uptown Manhattan at the 92 Street Y on Lexington Avenue. Tickets are low-priced. It's also possible to arrange for the players to visit your child's school.

"Young People's Concerts" of the New York Philharmonic (212-580-8700)

The same four concerts that are seen by individual subscribers are offered on a weekday morning to junior high school students. Tickets ($10 per student for the series) are normally sold through the school's music department.

The **Theater Development Fund** also offers tickets at reduced rates to nonprofit groups (including schools) on short notice (usually less than three weeks) for Broadway and Off-Broadway productions (for current offerings, which change daily, call 212-221-0019; the maximum price is usually around $9; the minimum number a group can order is ten). To participate in T.D.F.'s program, your group must first have an application on file. Write to T.D.F., using your organization's stationery. After you submit your application, you'll receive confirmation of acceptance and details about how the program works. NOTE: T.D.F. always deals with one person who takes on the responsibility for ordering tickets by telephone, paying for them immediately (sometimes by mail and sometimes by hand-delivering a check to T.D.F.), and later, for receiving the tickets (which may have to be picked up).

T.D.F. also operates the Costume Collection, which loans more than 48,000 costumes and accessories, including costumes for many popular operas donated by the Metropolitan Opera. Your not-for-profit organization (school, church, performing arts group) can rent these for minimal cost (fee based on a sliding scale). You're expected to pick out your own costumes. For further information: 212-221-0885.

Annual Spectacles

What would New York be without these perennial favorites?

Free Shakespeare Summer Festival

Shakespeare—and something else—at the Delacorte Theater in Central Park near 81 Street during June, July, and August. Occasionally, the summer fare will move on to Broadway, so this is your chance to see next year's "hot" show for free. Tickets, distributed on the Great Lawn, are on a first-come, first-served basis at 6:15 P.M. on the day of the performance, but it's wise to line up in advance. If a show gets a rave review or stars a well-known actor, the line may form as early as 3:00 P.M. For a schedule and further information, call the New York Shakespeare Festival, 425 Lafayette Street, New York, N.Y. 10003: 212-598-7100.

Ice Capades

Colorful costumes, exotic lighting, ensemble skating, soaring jumps and spins, graceful pair skating, ice dancing, and even clowns who do tricks on two blades turn the ice into a glittering spectacle. Although adults will savor the virtuoso skating, there are always kiddie productions (in 1987, "The World of Teddy Ruxpin") and novelty acts, such as the stunt skater who jumps through a flaming hoop, to appeal to the kid in everyone. Count on finding the show at Madison Square Garden in January. They'll also perform at the Nassau Coliseum and the Meadowlands Arena, but the dates are not predictable.

Lincoln Center Out-of-Doors Festival on the plaza at West 65 Street and Broadway

For four weeks in August (continuing through Labor Day) there are free performances of dance, music, theater, mime, and children's theater by a multitude of ethnic groups from all over the United States. The programming runs from morning to evening. For a schedule of events (usually available in July), call 212-877-1800.

Macy's Thanksgiving Day Parade
While the parade is traditionally televised, the hardy line the streets to enjoy the floats and balloons of cartoon characters that stream down Central Park West to Macy's. The gala gets underway at 9 A.M. at 77 Street near the Natural History museum. Let the kids stay up late Thanksgiving Eve to see the balloon inflation at 77 Street. Work begins at 9 P.M., but aficionados report that the best viewing comes closer to midnight.

The Nutcracker performed by the New York City Ballet
From November to January the New York State Theater is "the" place for visions of sugar plum fairies, handsome princes, and tin soldiers. Although other companies also put on *The Nutcracker* at Christmas, George Balanchine's production has become the New York classic. Tickets go on sale at the box office (212-870-5570) the first Monday in November. However, mail orders are accepted as early as September 1. By the time box office sales begin, there aren't many tickets left, so plan this family event *well in advance.*

Ringling Bros. and Barnum and Bailey Circus
Springtime brings "The Greatest Show on Earth" to Madison Square Garden . . . a three-ring circus with elephants, lions, tigers, tumblers, acrobats, clowns, and trapeze artists. Each year the circus produces a new edition of the show. There are special discounted performances for children. The circus also appears at the Meadowlands Arena and Nassau Coliseum, but the dates vary by the year.

The Big Apple Circus
This intimate circus, where no one sits farther than thirty-five feet from the one ring, travels with its own heated tent. When the elephants march by or the high-wire trapeze artists soar overhead, you're right there. It's far less overwhelming and confusing for some young children than the three-ring extravaganza. The tent's pitched for eight weeks at Lincoln Center's Damrosch Park from November through January. From April through September, they usually tour through the five boroughs (performing at Prospect Park, Cunningham Park, Van Cortlandt Park, and Miller Field) and other spots in the northeastern United States. Order tickets in advance 212-391-0760 for Lincoln Center; you can probably get them at the door at the other sites.

Sesame Street Live!

A musical production, featuring adult-sized Sesame Street characters including Big Bird, Ernie, Bert, The Count, and Prairie Dawn. There's a new show every year. In the past: "Save Our Street," "Sesame Street Country," and "Missing Bird Mystery." Any Sesame Street addict, be he two or seven, will delight at what's served up. Count on seeing the show at Madison Square Garden from mid-December to the beginning of January. Appearances at the Meadowlands Arena and the Nassau Coliseum vary annually.

"Summer Parks Concerts" by the New York Philharmonic

Free summertime evening concerts held in major parks in the five boroughs as well as suburban communities. The finale is usually fireworks. Call the Philharmonic's public relations office for the schedule.

"The Magnificent Christmas Spectacular" at Radio City Music Hall

The precision high kicks of the Rockettes, dazzling special effects, opulent costumes, and the theatrical wonder of "The Living Nativity," complete with kings, shepherds, donkeys, camels, and sheep, are served up in this holiday confection. The show runs from mid-November to early January. Tickets are usually available at the end of September.

index

Admission procedures: for independent schools, 76, 90, 92–93, 94; for nursery schools, 74; for public schools, 84, 86; tests, preparation for, 86–87
Adoption: by agency, 26–28, 29; costs, 28, 29; home study, 26, 27; independent, 26, 27, 28, 29–30; information services, 34; intercountry, 26, 29, 30; leave, 11; options, 25–30; questions to ask, 29–30; support groups, 27, 34
Adoption: A Guide to Adopting in the New York Area (New York Junior League), 27
Adoption Resource Book, The (Gilman), 27
Adoptive parents, programs for, 31, 32; support group, 27, 34
Advisory services: for childbirth, 3–5; for schools, 74–75, 85, 86, 90, 91, 96. *See also* Support groups
Advocates for Children of New York, 96, 97
Affordable Baby, The (Bundy), 8
Afterschool, 60–61
After-school child care, 59–61; resource directories for, 60–61; Y's and community centers, 61–64

Agencies: adoption, 26–28, 29; intercountry adoption, 29, 30; voluntary day care, 53
Agency for Child Development (A.C.D.), 52–53, 54, 55, 57, 75
Alley Pond Environmental Center, 156, 190, 194
Alternative schools, 82, 84; high school, 86
Ambulance, calling, 109, 120–21
American Museum of Natural History, 156–57, 184–85
American Society for Psychoprophylaxis. *See* ASPO/Lamaze
Aquariums, 157, 191, 196, 197
Arthritis, juvenile, clinics for, 126
Arts programs: offered by public schools, 82, 206; in preschool, 73. *See also* Dance; Music; Performing arts; Theater
ASPO/Lamaze, 3, 22, 24
Asthma, programs and resources, 124
Au pairs, 45
Automobiles, car seats in, 137–38

Babies: clothing, buying, 160–66; daycare centers and programs for, 57; exercise classes, 153; infant mas-

Babies (*cont.*)
sage, 153; swim programs, 148; theater policies about, 159–60. *See also* Newborns
Babies Hospital at Presbyterian, 114, 115. *See also* Presbyterian Hospital
Baby equipment and furniture: buying, 160–66; for parents of twins, 37
"Baby + Life" course, 122
Baby-sitters, 67–70; college students hired as, 68–70; in co-ops, 68; registry for, 42, 43
Bank Street College of Education, 32–33, 69, 167; Fatherhood Project, 35
Baptist Medical Center, 110, 111
Barnard College Baby-sitting Service, 68, 69
Baseball, organized programs, 143–44
Basketball, organized programs, 144
Bathrooms: on playgrounds, 135; at public beaches, 151; restaurant facilities, 160; in subways, 137
Beaches, for swimming, 151–52
Bellevue Hospital Center, 16–17, 114, 115
Benjamin Cardozo High School, 81
Beth Israel Medical Center, 16–17, 69, 114, 115
Bing, Elisabeth, Center for Parents, 24, 32, 153
Birth attendant: locating, 5–6; questions to ask, 8–9
Birth centers, 2, 5. *See also* Childbearing Center
Birthday parties, 154–59; at home, 158–59; puppeteer, hiring, 155, 205
Birthday Parties for Children (Marzollo), 158
Birthing rooms, 2, 5, 10
Blind children, library for, 176
Board of Education, 72, 81–82, 85, 95, 97, 134, 137, 152, 205, 206; Division of Special Education, 96; fingerprinting, 140; home instruction program, 107
Boehm, Helen, 162
Books, selecting for children, 167
Bookstores, 166–67
Booth Memorial Medical Center, 8, 20–21, 116, 117

Bradley, Robert, 24
Breast-feeding, 10; support group, 11
Brezavar, Sarah, 132
Bronx, Borough of: beach, 151; community school districts, *map,* 83; environmental education program, 192–93; museum, 184; Parks Department, 73, 141; public libraries, 176–77; recreation centers, 142; swimming pools, 149; Y's and community centers, 62. *See also* Bronx hospitals
Bronx High School of Science, 81, 86
Bronx hospitals: childbirth policies, *chart,* 12–15; emergency rooms, *chart,* 110; pediatric care, *chart,* 110–11
Bronx-Lebanon Hospital Center, 12–13, 110, 111
Bronx Municipal Hospital, 12–13, 110, 111
Bronx Zoo, 195–96
Brookdale Hospital Medical Center, 14–15, 112, 113
Brooklyn, Borough of: beaches, 151; botanical garden, 193; community school districts, *map,* 83; ice skating rinks, 145–46; museums, 184; Parks Department, 73, 141; performing arts programs, 200–201; public libraries, 171–75; recreation centers, 142; stores for children, 161, 162–63, 168; swimming pools, 149–50; Y's and community centers, 62–63; zoos, 196. *See also* Brooklyn hospitals
Brooklyn Children's Museum, 158, 184
Brooklyn Hospital Center, 14–15, 112, 113
Brooklyn hospitals: childbirth policies, *chart,* 14–17; emergency rooms, *chart,* 110, 112, 114; pediatric care, *chart,* 111, 113, 115
Brooklyn Museum, 166–67, 184
Brooklyn Technical High School, 86
Bundy, Darcie, 8
Bunk beds, 133
Bus transportation, 136–37; school pass, 137

Camps: baseball, 143; basketball, 144; exhibition of, 66; gymnastics, 145; ice

hockey, 145; museum programs, 191; Parks Department, 65, 141; riding, 145; soccer, 147; summer, 64–66; tennis, 152
Caregiver, inside home, 40, 43–52; *au pairs,* 45; employment agencies for, 44, 46–48; foreign, 44–45; interview, 48–49, 50
Catholic schools, 88–89; admissions exam, 89; gifted and talented programs, 88
Central Board of Education, 85
Central Park, 204; ice skating, 145, 146; playgrounds, 134–35; Zoo, 196–97
Cerebral palsy, resources and information, 125
Cesarean birth, 3, 6, 8, 9, 10; fathers at, 9; hospital policies about, *chart,* 12–23
Child abuse: emergency assistance for victims, 34–35; reporting, 34
Childbearing Center, 2, 4
Childbirth: advice and information, 3–5; birth attendant and, 5–6, 8–9; cesarean 3, 6, 8, 9, 10; costs, 8; educators, 3, 11, 22–25; hospital, choosing, 5, 6–8, 9–10; hospital policies toward, 3, 6, 7, 10, *chart,* 12–23; hospital preparatory classes, *chart,* 12–23; options, 1–10; preparatory classes, 3, 11, 22–25, 31
Child care: after school, 59–61; arrangements, 39–43; baby-sitters, 68–69; costs, 40–41, 43, 44, 47, 51–52, 53, 57; emergency information for, 70; enrichment programs at Y's and community centers, 61–64; on holidays, 67; for infants and toddlers, 57–58; information and resource services, 40, 48, 56, 58; locating for children with special needs, 96; mother's helper, 50; public day-care centers, 52–53, 57; questions to ask, 41; referral services, 42–43; in summer, 64–67; tax credit, 52
Child care, inside home, 40, 43–52
Child care, outside home: day-care centers, 40, 52–53, 56–59; family day care, 40, 42–43, 52, 53–56, 58–59
Child Care, Inc., 40, 42, 48, 53, 56, 57, 58, 60, 66, 68, 75

Child Care Information Services, telephone consultation, 42, 56
Child Health Stations, 99
Child Life programs, in New York City hospitals, *chart,* 110–19
Children's Aid Society, 100, 127–28, 144
Children's clothing, buying, 160–166
Children's furniture, 132; bunk beds, 133; safety of, 162; stores, 160–66
Children's Museum of Manhattan, 154, 157, 185–86, 191
Children's rooms, designing, 131–32
Childwise Catalog, The (Gillis and Fise), 162
CHIPS' Warm Line, 33
Chorionic villi sampling (CVS), 25
Chromosomal abnormalities, detecting, 25
Churches, parenting programs in, 32
City Hospital Center at Elmhurst, 20–21, 116, 117
City University of New York, job referral services, 69–70
Clinics: dental, 127–28; pediatric, 99
Cloisters, The, 187
Clothes, buying. *See* Children's clothes
Colao, Flora, 139
Colitis, referrals for treatment, 126
Colleges: baby-sitting services, 68–70; baseball camps, 143; dental clinics, 128; dramatic performances, 156; job referral services, 68–70; parenting classes, 32–33; sports programs, 141; swim lessons, 148
Community board, 134, 136, 143, 147; pools, 147; sports activities, 140–41
Community centers: activities at, 60, 61–64; parenting programs, 31–32; summer programs, 65; swimming pools, 147
Community school districts, 81–82, 97, 152, 205, 206; fingerprinting program, 140; *map,* 83; preschool programs, 73
Con Edison Energy Museum, 186
Coney Island Hospital, 14–15, 112, 113
Cooper, Louis Z., 102, 103, 104, 105
Co-operatives, baby-sitting, 68; playgrounds built by, 135
Corey, Margaret, 76, 93

INDEX | 215

Corman, Avery, vii
Counseling: about education needs, 91, 93; locating, 128–29
CPR, classes in, 122
Crib rental, 166
Crime prevention programs, 139
Crohn's disease, referrals for treatment, 126
Cystic fibrosis, treatment centers, 125

Daily News, ix, 199
Dance programs, 199–200, 201–203, 205–10
Day camps, 65, 66; directories, 66; for handicapped, 65, 66. *See also* Camps
Day-care centers, 40, 52–53, 56–59; evaluating, 58–59; fees, 57; for infants and toddlers, 57–58; licensing, 57
Death, counseling for children, 35
DeMartini, Doreen, 82
Dental care, 127–28
Dentists, for children, 127, 128
Designing apartments, with children in mind, 131–32
Designing Rooms for Children (Gilliatt), 132
Diabetes, where to go for help, 126
Directory of Child Care for Infants and Toddlers, 57
Directory of Downtown Schools, 74–75
Directory of Nonpublic Schools and Administrators, 90
Directory of the Public Schools, 86
Disability benefits, pregnancy and, 11; for child care providers, 51
Doctors. *See* Physicians
Dodson, Marguerite, 172
Dolls, repairing, 168
Down syndrome: information and resources, 125; testing for, 25
Dramatics, preschool programs in, 73 *See also* Performing Arts; Theater
Drugs, generic, 126–27
Drug stores, all-night, 127
Dyslexia, educational resources for, 96

Early Childhood Direction Centers, 95, 123–24
Early Childhood Education Commission, 72
Education: evaluating schools, 76–80, 82, 84–85; for the handicapped, 94–96; policies about four-year-olds, 72. *See also* Catholic schools; Elementary schools; High schools; Intermediate schools; Preschools; Private schools; Public schools
Educational Records Bureau, 90, 91, 92, 93, 94
Elementary schools: admission to public, 84; evaluating, 76–80, 82, 84–85; gifted and talented programs, 87–88; independent, 74; public, 81–82, 84–85; visiting, 85. *See also* Independent schools; Catholic schools; Jewish schools; Public schools
Emergencies: calling ambulance, 109, 120–121; child abuse, 34–35; contacting pediatrician, 108; dental care, 127; first aid classes, 122; going to hospital emergency room, 108–109; poisoning, 121–122; teaching children to cope with, 138–39
Emergency information, for child care providers, 70
Emergency Medical Service (dialing 911), 109, 120
Emergency rooms, 108–109; in New York City hospitals, *chart,* 110–119
Employers: and maternity leave, 11; parents as, 45–46, 51–52
Employment agencies: for baby-sitters, 67–68; at colleges and universities, 68–70; hiring caregiver through, 44, 46–48; for mother's helper, 50; prepared list, 48
Enrichment activities, 60–61; for gifted and talented, 88; in museums, 183–84, 190–91; in the performing arts, 205–10; in the public schools, 82; at Y's and community centers, 61–64. *See also* Arts; Dance; Music; Performing arts; Theater
Entertainers, hiring for birthday parties, 154–55, 205
Entrance exams: to independent schools, 92, 94; for science high schools, 86–87; tutorials for, 86

Environmental education programs, 192–95
Epilepsy, association for, 125
Equipment: car seats, 137–38; playground, safety of, 136; shopping for, 160–66
Exercise class, for babies and toddlers, 153
Eyes, poisonous substances in, 122

Family day care, 40, 42–43, 52, 53–56, 58–59; evaluating, 58–59; fees, 53, 54, 55; information packet, 56; referral services, 42–43, 54–55
Family physicians: contacting in emergency, 108; hospital affiliation of, 102–103; interviewing and evaluating, 103, 104; questions to ask doctor, 104; questions to ask other parents, 105; referral services, 4–5, 104; selecting, 102–105
Family Resource Center, 42–43, 55, 68
Fatherhood USA, 35
Fathers, 6, 35; attendance at cesarean birth, 9, *chart,* 12–23; support groups for new, 31, 33; visitation rights to new babies, *chart,* 12–23
Faulhaber, Linda, 75
Federal law: and school records, 97; special education and, 94
Financial aid: for handicapped children, 96; to independent schools, 94
Fingerprinting, of children, 140
Fiorello H. LaGuardia High School of Music and the Arts, 86
First aid classes, 122
Fise, Mary Ellen, 162
Fishman, Joshua, 89
Fletcher, Quentin E., 66
Floating Hospital, 100
Flushing Hospital and Medical Center, 20–21, 118, 119
Foreign adoptions, 26, 29, 30
Fresh Air Fund, 65–66
Frick Collection, 159, 183
Furniture, buying. *See* Children's furniture

Generic drugs, 126–27
Genetic counseling, 8, 25

Gifted and talented programs, 87–88
Gilliatt, Mary, 132
Gillis, Jack, 162
Gilman, Lois, 27
Ginsberg, Susan, 30, 31, 60
Gold, Marji, 106, 108, 109
Goldman, Jane, 140
Greater New York Hospital Association, survey of hospitals and doctors, 99
GRF Tutoring Service, 86
Grief, counseling services for, 35
Growing Without Schooling, 97
Guggenheim Museum, 159, 183
Gymnastics programs, 144–45; for babies and toddlers, 153

Handicapped children: day camps for, 65, 66; in Head Start, 73, 96; library for, 176; playground designed for, 135; referral services, 95, 96; resources, 123–24; special programs for, 94–96; sports programs, 141, 152; toy library, 183
Hansen, Eileen, 108, 120, 121
Harlem Hospital Center, 16–17, 114, 115
Head Start. *See* Project Head Start
Health care: classes for parents, 31; Emergency Medical Service, 109, 120, 121; information and special resources, 123–26; in New York City, 99–102; Poison Control Center, 121–22; preventive, 99, 100; private sector, 100. *See also* Emergencies; Hospitals; Illness; Immunizations; Medical Services; Physicians
Health and Hospitals Corporation, 99
Health insurance, 100–101
Health Insurance Plan (H.I.P.), 5, 101, 102, 109
Health Maintenance Organization (H.M.O.), 5, 8, 101, 109
Hearing loss, services for children with, 125
Hechinger, Grace, 139
Heckscher playground, 134–35
Hemophilia, treatment centers, 126
Hertz, David, 76, 77, 93
High-risk maternity and newborn care, 9

INDEX | 217

High schools, Catholic, 88, 89
High schools, public, 85; admission procedures, 86; entrance exams, 86–87; school fairs, 86; specialty, 86; zoned, 85–86. *See also* Independent schools
Holidays, programs and child care during, 67
Hollingworth Preschool, 88
Home instruction, 97, 107
Homework assistance programs, 97–98, 180; hotlines, 97–98, 173
Horseback riding, 145
Hosansky, Tamar, 139
Hospitals: breast-feeding policies of, 10–11; childbirth education classes given by, 11, 22–23, 31; childbirth policies of, 3, 6, 7, 10, *chart,* 12–23; Child Life programs, 107, 108, *chart,* 110–19; choosing in emergency, 102–103, 120; classes for new mothers, 31; community, 99; emergency rooms, 108–109, *chart,* 110–19; day-surgery in, 105–106; evaluating and selecting for childbirth, 5, 6–8, 9–10; expenses, 8; nursery care for newborns, 9; obstetrical survey of, *chart,* 12–23; pediatric care, 102–103, 105–108, 109, *chart,* 110–19; physicians' affiliations with, 5, 6, 102–103; policies, *charts,* 12–23, 110–19; questions to ask, 9–10, 107–108; rooming-in, by parents of sick child, 106, *chart,* 110–19; sibling visitation of new baby, 6, *chart,* 12–23; specialty care referral centers, 120; support for parents of hospitalized child, 35, 108; visitation rights of new fathers, 6, *chart,* 12–23
Hotlines: about child rearing, 33; emergency dental care, 127; homework assistance, 97–98, 173; mental health, 128; missing children, 36; pregnancy advisory service, 4; runaways, 36; Sex Crimes Report Line, 34; Tel-Med, 123; victims of crime, 139
Housing codes, 132
Howland, Mary Ann, 121

How to Raise a Street-Smart Child (Hechinger), 139
Hunter College Campus Schools, 87

Ice hockey, 145
Ice skating, 145; rinks, 145–46
Illness: housing for families of critically ill children, 106–107; support group for parents of hospitalized children, 35, 108
Immunizations: by Children's Aid Society, 100; clinics sponsored by Department of Health, 99; insurance coverage of, 100, 101; required for school, 84
Independent adoption, arranging, 26, 27, 28, 29–30
Independent School Fair, 91, 92
Independent schools: admissions and applications, 76, 90, 92–93, 94; after-school care, 60; for children with special needs, 95, 96; directory, 74; elementary, 74; fair, 91, 92; financial aid, 94; gifted and talented programs, 88; holiday activities, 67; listing of schools, 90, 91; nondenominational, 89–94; summer programs, 65; swimming pools located in, 147; tuition and fees, 90–91
Independent Schools Admissions Association of Greater New York (ISAAGNY), 74, 90, 91, 93, 94
Infants. *See* Babies; Newborns
InfoQuest Center, 186
Injuries, playground, 136
Insurance, health, 100–101
Intercountry adoptions, arranging, 26, 29, 30
Interfaith Medical Center, 14–15, 112, 113, 124
Intermediate schools: admission to public, 84; "alternative," 82, 84; New York City public, 81–82, 84–85; registration, 84; visiting, 85
Internal Revenue Service, 51
Interracial families, resources and support groups for, 36
Intrepid Air-Sea-Space Museum, 186
I.P.A. (Individual Practice Association), 101

218 | INDEX

Ipecac, syrup of, 122
ISAAGNY, 74, 90, 91, 93, 94

Jack D. Weiler Hospital, 12–13, 110, 111
Jamaica Arts Center, 189
Jamaica Hospital, 20–21, 118, 119
Jewish affiliations: camps, 66; preschool programs, 74; private schools, 89; Tay-Sachs, testing for, 25; YM-YWHAs, 61–62
Jewish Museum, 186
Jewish schools, 89
Johnson, Howard, 77, 93
Joint Disease, North General Hospital, 114, 115
Junior League of the City of New York, 27
Juvenile arthritis, clinics, 126

Kennedy, Laetitia, 140
Kidnapping, prevention of, 138–40
A Kid's New York (Lawrence), 61
Kindergarten: age requirement, 84; registration, 84
Kingsbrook Jewish Medical Center, 112, 113
Kings County Hospital Center, 14–15, 112, 113
Koota, Ivan, 33, 102, 108, 109
Kramer vs. Kramer (Corman), vii, viii

Labor and delivery, options for childbirth, 1–10. *See also* Childbirth; Hospitals
LaGuardia Hospital, 6, 20–21, 118, 119
La Leche League, 11
Lamaze, Fernand, 24. *See also* ASPO/Lamaze
Lawrence, Peter, 61
Learning disabilities, special programs for, 94, 95
Lenox Hill Hospital, 18–19, 31, 114, 115, 123
Libraries: applying for card, 171, 172, 175, 179; private, 182–83; public, 171–82; toy, 183; for visually impaired, 176
Lifesaving techniques, courses in, 122
Lincoln Medical and Mental Health Center, 12–13, 110, 111, 124
Little League, 143

Little People's Theater Company, 156, 202
Living with Your New Baby (Rubin), 102
Long Island College Hospital, 14–15, 112, 113
Long Island Jewish Medical Center, 7, 20–21, 118–19. *See also* Schneider Children's Hospital
Lothian, Judy, 3, 9
Lutheran Medical Center, 14–15, 112, 113

Magic shows, for birthday parties, 156
Maimonides Medical Center, 16–17, 112, 113
Manhattan, Borough of: children's stores, 161, 163–65, 168–69; community school districts, *map*, 83; environmental education programs, 193–94; ice skating rinks, 146; museums, 184–89; Parks Department, 73, 141; performing arts programs, 201–203; playgrounds, 134–35; private libraries, 182–83; public libraries, 175–76, 177–79; recreation centers, 142; school directories, 74–75; sports clubs, 141; swimming pools, 150; Y's and community centers, 63–64. *See also* Manhattan hospitals
Manhattan Directory of Private Nursery Schools (Faulhaber), 75
Manhattan hospitals: childbirth policies, *chart*, 16–21; emergency rooms, *chart*, 114, 116; pediatric care, *chart*, 115, 117
Manhattan, inc., ix
Mark Twain Junior High School, 81
Mary Immaculate Hospital, 118, 119
Marzollo, Jean, 158–59
Maternity Center Association, 4, 24
Maternity leave, 11
Maternity services, 7–8. *See also* Childbirth; Labor and delivery
Medicaid, 100
Medical services: childbirth advisory services, 3–5; dental care, 127–28; Emergency Medical Service (911), 109, 120, 121; hospitals in New York City, emergency rooms and pe-

Medical services (*cont.*)
    diatric care in, *chart,* 110–19; mental health, 128–29; pharmacies, 127. *See also* Health care; Hospitals; Physicians
Medical Societies, 4–5, 104
Mental health, finding help, 128–29
Methodist Hospital, 8, 16–17, 112, 113
Metropolitan Hospital Center, 18–19, 116, 117
Metropolitan Museum, 166, 186–87
Mets, tickets for youth groups, 144
Midwives, 4, 5, 9; hospital affiliations and, 5, *chart,* 12–23; referral services for, 3–4
Miller, Anne, 6, 10
Minimum wage, for caregivers, 51
Missing children, hotlines, 3
Mitchell, Anne, 40, 43, 50, 59
Money magazine, 81
Montefiore Medical Center, 110, 111
Montessori preschool programs, 74
Mothers, new: classes for, 31, 32; support groups, 32, 33
Mother's helper, hiring, 66–67
Mount Sinai Medical Center, 7, 8, 18–19, 25, 31, 107, 116, 117, 124
Movement, preschool classes in, 73. *See also* Dance programs; Gymnastics
Movies, policies toward children, 159
Multiple births, help for parents of, 37
Museum of Broadcasting, 157, 187
Museum of the City of New York, 157, 187–88
Museum of Holography, 188
Museum of Modern Art, 183, 188
Museums, 183–90; birthday parties at, 154, 156–58; holiday activities, 67; puppet shows, 204; policies, 159, 184–90; summer "camp" programs, 65
Music: live performances, 200–203, 205–10; preschool programs, 73; in public schools, 82

Neonatal nurseries, 9
Newborns: breast-feeding, in hospitals, 10–11; care of, 9; sibling preparation classes, 24–25; visits by father and siblings, hospital policies about, 6, *chart,* 12–23
Newsletters, for parents, 33–34, 97
New York Aquarium, 157, 191, 196
New York City: childbirth statistics, 2; community school districts, 81–82, map, 83; Department of Health, 9, 75, 100; medical services, 99–102; public health system, 99–100; public libraries, 171–82; public schools, 80–87. *See also* Health Care; Hospitals; Medical Services; *school systems*
New York City Department of Parks and Recreation, 71; *Calendar of Events,* 192; day camps, 65, 141; free events recording, 143, 145; playgrounds, 134–35; preschool programs, 73; recreation centers, 142–43; sports programs, 141–43, 144, 145, 146, 147, 148, 151, 152; swimming pools, 147, 148–51; Volunteer Program, 134
New York Hall of Science, 157, 189
New York Hospital–Cornell Medical Center, 7, 18–19, 25, 108, 116, 117, 124, 135
New York Independent Schools Directory, 74, 90, 91
New York Infirmary–Beekman Downtown, 18–19, 116, 117
New York Knicks, tickets for youth groups, 144
New York magazine, viii, ix, 92, 131, 154–55, 199
New York State: Employment Service, 44; Labor Department Alien Certification Office, 45; listing of nonpublic schools, 90; tax credit for child care expenses, 52
New York State laws: about adoption, 28; breast-feeding and, 10; generic drugs, 126–27; hiring caregivers from abroad, legality of, 45; about home instruction, 97; immunization requirements, 84; maternity leave, 11; school attendance, 84; on seat belts, 137
New York Times, ix, 7, 8, 84, 134, 143, 199

New York Transit Authority Travel Information Bureau, 151, 184
New York Transit Exhibit, 184
New York University Medical Center, 7, 20–21, 107, 108, 116, 117
New York Urban Athlete, The (Goldman and Kennedy), 140
92 Street Y, 31, 36, 54, 122, 182, 202
North Central Bronx Hospital, 12–13, 110, 111
North Wind Undersea Institute, 184
Nurse–midwives. *See* Midwives
Nurseries, for newborns, in New York City hospitals, *chart,* 12–23
Nursery school: directories, 74–75; evaluating and selecting, 75–76; Montessori curriculum, 74; private, 73–74. *See also* Preschool
Nursing mothers. *See* Breast-feeding
Nursing students, as baby-sitters, 68, 69

Obstetricians: childbirth advisory and referral services, 3–5; choosing, 5–6, 8–9; fees, 8; group practice, 9; hospital affiliations of, 5, 6
Obstetric policies, of New York City hospitals, *chart,* 12–23
Our Lady of Mercy Medical Center, 14–15, 110, 111

PARENTGUIDE NEWS, 8, 34, 199
Parenting Center, The, 31–32
Parents: adoptive, support group for, 27, 34; of children with special needs, 124; of critically ill children, 108; death of, counseling for child, 35; genetic counseling for, 25; of hospitalized child, 35; in interracial families, 36; of missing children, 36; new, support groups for, 31, 32, 33; newsletters for, 33–34, 97; parenting programs for, 30–33; responsibilities as employers, 45–46, 51–52; rooming-in with hospitalized child, 110–19; of SIDS babies, 35; of twins and triplets, 37; visiting policies in hospitals, *chart,* 110–19. *See also* Childbirth; Programs for parents; Support groups
Parents for Parents, 35, 108, 115

Parents League of New York, Inc., 60, 66, 68, 74, 91, 93; birthday file, 155; membership information, 74; parent workshops, 139; School Fair, 91, 92
Parents' Resources, 33, 68, 134
Parent-teacher association, in public school, 85
"Parkbench" program, 31–32
Parks Department. *See* New York City Department of Parks and Recreation
Park Ranger program, 31–32
Parties, children's, 154–59
Paternity leave, 11
Pediatricians: contacting in emergency, 108; hospital affiliation of, 102–103; hospital residency programs of, *chart,* 110, 112, 114, 116, 118; interviewing and evaluating, 103, 104; parenting programs offered by, 33; questions to ask doctor, 104; questions to ask other parents, 105; referral services, 4–5, 104; selecting, 102–105
Pediatric Clinics, 99
Pediatric Treatment Centers, 99
Pedodontist, locating, 127, 128
Peninsula Hospital, 118, 119
Performing arts: annual events, 210–12; programs, 199–203; programs for groups, 205–10; puppet shows, 204–205. *See also* Dance; Music; Theater
Permits, for sports facilities, 143
Personal safety programs, 139–40
Pharmacies, all-night, 127
Physicians: choosing, 5–6, 8–9; hospital affiliations of, 5, 6, 102–103; locating, 4–6, 8–9; Medical Societies, 4–5, 104; referral services, 3–5, 104. *See also* Dentists; Family physicians; Obstetricians; Pediatricians
Planetarium, 185
Planned Parenthood of New York City, 4, 36
Playground for All Children, 135
Playgrounds, 134–36; safety on, 135–36
Poison Control Center, 121
Poisoning: emergency, 121–22; prevention, 122
Pollack, Isobel, 101, 109

INDEX | 221

Pregnancy: high-risk, hospital facilities for, 9; maternity leave policies, 11. *See also* Birth attendant; Childbirth
Prekindergarten, 73, 76
Prenatal testing, for genetic disorders, 25
Presbyterian Hospital, 7, 18–19, 25, 31
Preschools: for children with special needs, 96; directories, 74–75; evaluating and selecting, 75–76; private programs, 73–74; public programs, 73; recommended for four-year-olds, 72
Prescriptions: filling, 126–27; generic drugs, 126–27
Private schools. *See* Independent schools
Programs for parents: in churches and synagogues, 32; on college campuses, 32–33; hospital-based, 30–31; at parenting and family centers, 32; at pediatrician's office, 33; through support groups, 33, 34–37; at Y's and community centers, 31–32
Project Head Start, 57, 73, 96
Psychiatrists, locating, 128–29
Public schools: after-school care, 60; for children with special needs, 94–96; community school districts, 81–82, 97, 152, 205, 206; evaluating programs offered by, 82, 84–85; gifted and talented programs, 87–88; high schools, 85–87; *map* (community school districts), 83; parent-teacher associations, 85; performing arts programs, 205–10; profiles of schools, 85; ranking and test scores, 81, 85; records, obtaining copy of student's, 96–97; registration, 84; school board, 84; special education programs, 94–96; statistics, 80–81; transfers, 82; visiting, 85; zoning, 82
Public Transportation system, 136–37
Puppeteers, locating, 155, 205
Puppet shows, 187, 203, 204–205, 208

Queens, Borough of: beaches, 151–52; children's stores, 161, 165–66, 169; community school districts, *map*, 83; environmental education programs, 194–95; ice skating rink, 146; museums, 189; Parks Department, 73, 142; playground, 135; public libraries, 179–82; recreation centers, 142; swimming pools, 150–51; theater for children, 203; Y's and community centers, 64. *See also* Queens hospitals
Queens Hospital Center, 22–23, 118, 119
Queens hospitals: childbirth survey, *chart*, 20–23; emergency rooms, *chart*, 116, 118; pediatric care, *chart*, 117, 119
Queens Museum, 189
Queens Zoo and Children's Farm, 197
Questionnaire, for prospective caregivers, 48–49

R.E.A.C.H. (Recreation, Education, Athletics and Creative Arts for the Handicapped), 65, 141
Recreation. *See* New York City Department of Parks and Recreation; Sports activities and programs; *and names of individual sports*
Recreational centers, 65, 141–43
References, of caregiver, checking, 49
Referral services: for baby-sitters and child care, 42–43; for children with special needs, 96, 123–26; physicians', 3–5, 6
Registration, for public school, 84
Resource and information centers, 176, 182; medical information, 123; for parents with special concerns, 34–37, 123–26
Resources for Children with Special Needs, 66, 96, 124
Restaurants, policies toward children, 160
Richmondtown Restoration, 190, 191
Riding, horseback, 145
Rights: of handicapped child, 94; of parents of children in school, 96–97
Right Toys, The (Boehm), 162
Ronald McDonald House, 106
Rooming-in, 10; with new baby, hospital policies, 12–23; with sick child in hospital, 110–19
Rothman, Barbara Katz, 25

222 | INDEX

Rubin, Gloria, 102
Running, organized programs, 146–47

Safe Haven program, 139–40
Safety: of bunk beds, 133; of children's furniture and toys, 162; playground, 135–36; programs and workshops, 139; Safe Haven program, 139–40; street, 138–40; swimming programs, 148
St. John's Episcopal Hospital, 22–23, 118, 119
St. John's Queens Hospital, 22–23, 118, 119
St. Luke's–Roosevelt Hospital Center, 18–19, 116, 117
St. Mary's Hospital, 16–17, 112, 113
St. Vincent's Hospital, 6, 10, 20–21, 116, 117
St. Vincent's Medical Center of Richmond, 22–23, 118, 119
Salaries, for caregiver, 44, 46, 47, 51–52
Schneider Children's Hospital, 106–107, 118, 119
School fairs, 91, 92
School Profiles, 85
Schools: bus transportation to, 137; for children with special needs, 95, 96; directories and information services, 74–75, 85, 86, 90, 91, 96; evaluating, 76–80, 82, 84–85; home instruction, 97; vacations, child care during, 67. *See also* Catholic schools; Elementary schools; High schools; Independent schools; Intermediate schools; Jewish schools; Preschools; Public schools
Science: programs in public schools, 82, 84; specialty high schools, 86; summer programs, 190–91. *See also* Environmental education programs; Museums
Seat belts: laws about, 137; loaner programs, 138
September High School Fair, 86
Sex Crimes Report Line, 34
Sex education, classes in, 36
Siblings: preparatory classes, 24–25; visits to hospitalized children, 110–119; visits to new baby, 6, 12–23

Sickle cell anemia, 25, 126
SIDS, family counseling, 35
Simkin, Diana, 104
Single parents, groups and resources, 36–37
Skhool for Parents, 31, 115, 123
Skin, poisonous substances on, 122
Sleep disorders, treatment for, 126
Soccer, organized programs, 147
Social Security, for caregivers, 44, 51
Socolar, Sandy, 40, 42, 49, 58
Sommers, Elizabeth, 6, 103
South Street Seaport Museum, 188–89
Space, creative uses of, 131–32
Special education, 94–96. *See also* Handicapped children
Special Services for Children, 27
Spence-Chapin Services to Families and Children, 26
Spina bifida, treatment for, 126
Sporn, Stephanie, 22, 23
Sports activities and programs, 65, 67, 140–41; pools, 147, 148–51; sponsored by Parks Department, 141–43, 144, 145, 146, 147, 148, 151, 152. *See also individual sports*
Stanley H. Kaplan Educational Center, 86
Staten Island, Borough of: beaches, 152; community school districts, *map,* 83; elementary schools, 81; environmental education programs, 195; ice skating rinks, 146; museums, 157, 183, 190, 191; Parks Department, 73, 142; public libraries, 179; recreation centers, 143; swimming pools, 151; transit system, 136; Y and community center, 64. *See also* Staten Island hospitals
Staten Island Children's Museum, 157, 183, 190
Staten Island Hospital, 22–23, 118, 119
Staten Island hospitals: childbirth survey, *chart,* 22–23; emergency rooms, *chart,* 118; pediatric care, *chart,* 119
Staten Island Institute of Arts and Sciences/Staten Island Museum, 157, 190, 191
Staten Island Zoo, 197
Stepfamilies, support groups, 37
Stone, Richard K., 103, 122

Stores for children: books, 166–67; clothing and furniture, 160–66; toys, 167–69
Street smarts, teaching, 138–40
Strollers, at museums, 159
Students: as baby-sitters, 68; locating through job referral services, 68–69
Studio Museum in Harlem, The, 189
Stuyvesant High School, 86
Subways, 136–37; school pass, 137
Summer activities and programs, 64–67; camps, 64–66; mother's helper, hiring, 66–67; in museums, 190–91; in zoos, 191. *See also* Camps
Sunset Children's Furniture, 132
Sunset Ideas for Children's Rooms and Play Yards, 132
SUNY Health Science Center, 16–17, 114, 115
Support groups: for adoptive parents, 27, 34; on breast-feeding, 11; of interracial families, 36; for new moms, 32, 33; for parents of children with special needs, 33, 34–37, 96, 124; for parents of critically ill or hospitalized children, 35, 108; for single parents, 36–37; spina bifida, 126; for stepfamilies, 37
Surgery, day, 105–106
Swimming: city beaches, 151–52; instruction, 148; pools, 147, 148–51
Synagogues, parenting programs at, 32

Taxes: federal income, tax credit for child care expenses, 52; Social Security for caregivers, 44, 51; unemployment, 51
Tay-Sachs disease, 25
Teachers College Writing Project, 84
Tel-Med, 123
Tennis, organized programs in, 152–53
Tentative Pregnancy, The (Rothman), 25
Testing: for admission to independent schools, 92, 94; prenatal, 25; scores, parents' right to see, 96
Thalassemia, genetic counseling for, 25
Theater: parties, 156; performances, 199–203, 205–10; policies toward children, 159–60
Therapy: for adoptive families, 34; for child who has suffered death or grief, 35
Toddlers: activities for, 73–74; day-care centers and programs for, 57–58; exercise classes, 153; swim programs, 148
T.O.E.S.L. (Teaching of English as a Second Language), 82
Tours, 197–99
Toys: for handicapped children, 183; selecting, 162; stores, 167–69
Track and field programs, 146–47
Twins, support groups for parents of, 37

United States Immigration and Naturalization Service, 45; and foreign adoptions, 29

Victory Memorial Hospital, 16–17
Visual impairment, resources for children suffering from, 124–25

Wainwright, Patsy, 91, 93
Wall units, 132–33
Washington Market park, 135
Water baby classes, 148
Well-baby checkups, 100, 102
Whitney Museum, 159, 183
Window guards, 132
Wolfe, Linda, viii, 131
Woodhull Medical and Mental Health Center, 16–17, 114, 115
Worker's Compensation, 51
Wyckoff Heights Hospital, 114, 115

Yankees, tickets for youth groups, 144
Yarmolinski, Harriet, 55
Your Children Should Know (Colao and Hosansky), 139
Youth Games, 141
Youth groups: arranging for free performing arts programs, 205–10; baseball and basketball tickets for, 144
Y's: activities sponsored by, 60, 61–64; parenting programs, 31–32; pools, 147; sports programs, 144, 145; summer programs, 65

Zoned schools, 82, 85; high schools, 85–86
Zoos, 195–97; holiday and summer programs in, 67, 191